Local Peacebuilding and National Peace

Local Peacebuilding and National Peace

Interaction Between Grassroots and Elite Processes

**EDITED BY
CHRISTOPHER R. MITCHELL
AND LANDON E. HANCOCK**

continuum

Continuum International Publishing Group

The Tower Building
11 York Road
London SE1 7NX

80 Maiden Lane
Suite 704
New York NY 10038

www.continuumbooks.com

Library of Congress Cataloging-in-Publication Data

ISBN : 978-1-4411-5788-1 (hardcover)
: 978-1-4411-6022-5 (paperback)

Typeset by Deanta Global Publishing Services, Chennai, India
Printed and bound in the United States of America

Contents

Contributors

Landon E. Hancock is assistant professor at Kent State University's Center for Applied Conflict Management and Department of Political Science. His work focuses on ethnic conflict and peacemaking. He has published articles in several journals including *Ethnopolitics* (2011), *Peace & Change* (2011), *Peace and Conflict Studies* (2011), *Conflict Resolution Quarterly* (2011), *Irish Political Studies* (2011), *Journal of Peace Education* (2010), and *International Studies Review* (2008). With Chris Mitchell he edited *Zones of Peace* in 2007 and continues to work on issues related to identity conflict, peace processes, postconflict reconstruction, and transitional justice.

Yves-Renée Jennings is a conflict resolution professional and scholar-practitioner with deep understanding of societal and structural issues that often contribute to social conflicts. Her research focuses on human development within the context of transformation of social and structural barriers that the ability of groups to fully realize their potential as social agents. She worked in the private sector in Haiti for over ten years and retired from the World Bank after a career of over twenty years. Yves-Renée is currently a PhD candidate at the George Mason University Institute for Conflict Analysis and Resolution and Chief Executive Officer of Partners for Sustainable Peace (PSP), a nonprofit organization she co-founded in 2009. She has recently contributed the chapter "Organizing the Disenfranchised: Haiti and the Dominican Republic" in *Women Waging War and Peace: International Perspectives of Women's Roles in Conflict and Post-Conflict Reconstruction*, Sandra I. Cheldelin and Maneshka Eliatamby, Eds. Continuum, 2011.

Irakli Zurab Kakabadze is one of the leading contemporary Georgian writers. He is author of five books, including *Candidate Jokola* and *Compassionata* as well as scores of short stories and poems. He received the Oxfam Novib/PEN Award in 2009. During 2001–2004 he was the editor in chief of *Peace Times* magazine. His lyrics for the song "Postindustrial Boys" became a hit in Europe after its 2004 release. Kakabadze has taught arts and conflict resolution for the last twelve years at the Georgian Institute for Public Affairs, Hobart and William Smith Colleges and Cornell University, where he is currently a scholar in residence.

Christopher Mitchell is emeritus professor of Conflict Analysis in the School for Conflict Analysis and Resolution at George Mason University, Virginia. Apart from numerous books and articles on conflict and its resolution, he has recently been engaged with his colleague Jannie Botes on a project to record on video the recollections of over forty founding 'Parents of the Field' of conflict and peace research, many of which can now be viewed on the GMU/S-CAR web site.

Andries Odendaal was a regional coordinator of the Western Cape Peace Committee during South Africa's transition to democratic rule in 1993–1994. Subsequently, as a program coordinator at the University of Cape Town's Centre for Conflict Resolution and, since 2005, as an independent consultant, he continued to pursue his interest in local peacebuilding in various contexts. He was a Jennings Randolph senior fellow at the US Institute of Peace (2009–2010) and is currently a research fellow at the University of Pretoria (Department of Political Science), while also serving on the Expert Roster of the Bureau for Crisis Prevention and Recovery of UNDP and the Mediation Roster of the UN DPA Mediation Support Unit. He is the author of the forthcoming "Structures for Building Peace at the Local Level" (Washington DC: USIP).

Mery Rodriguez is the director of the Conflict Resolution Postgraduate Program in the School of Political Science at the Pontificia Universidad Javeriana in Bogota, Colombia. She holds a PhD and a MS in Conflict Analysis and Resolution from George Mason University and a BS in Communications from the Pontificia Universidad Javeriana. She is a bilingual researcher, facilitator, and mediator who has designed and implemented various processes on multicultural stakeholder dialogs in diverse themes such as access to justice, gender perspectives, human rights, and local peace building. She is an expert on the Colombian conflict and its dynamics for peace at the local, regional, and national levels, particularly analyzing the impact of national public policy in local peace building initiatives. She also centers her practice in collaborative methodologies and the conflict transformation approach.

Catalina Rojas is an expert in gender, development, and conflict resolution. As director of Global Partnerships at Women Thrive Worldwide, she created a worldwide women's network and led training and consultation processes to increase the advocacy capacity of women's NGOs and CBOs in Central America and West Africa. She also directed the Global Survey and Women in Muslim Majority Countries research project, which included over 200 women's NGOs in 13 countries, gathering input on their views on development and foreign assistance. Prior to joining Women Thrive, Dr Rojas was a consultant on gender, conflict, and development issues with various international organizations including the IIS, OAS, USAID, and UNIFEM. Dr Rojas has a Ph.D. in Conflict Analysis and Resolution. Originally from Colombia, she has over 15 years of experience working with southern civil society organizations, including working in the peace movement in her home country.

Wallace Warfield had a distinguished career with the Community Relations Service, starting as a street worker with local gangs in New York and ending up as director of the Service before moving into academia. He joined Jim Laue's Conflict Clinic Inc. at George Mason University and from there moved on to the Institute for Conflict Analysis and Resolution. While at ICAR, he completed a Ph.D. supervised by Seymour Martin Lipsett and commenced work on a series of publications on the themes of race relations, community leadership and the ethics of social intervention during intractable conflicts. He retired from ICAR in the summer of 2010 and tragically died shortly afterwards, leaving much planned work incomplete and the field of conflict research much the poorer.

Preface

Zones of peace as innovative frames

The field of conflict resolution has grown tremendously since its beginnings. Its current trajectory is marked by a high degree of differentiation due to the necessity to incorporate and respond to advances in related areas of study. Concerns around power have been central to the conflict resolution project for decades but have taken a different tone with a postmodern critique. Relationships have been key in the conflict resolution discourse and have been significantly enriched in their understanding by the emergence of gender studies. Context has always been crucial to conflict resolution scholars but has now taken a new contour with the growth of shared environmental consciousness. The next phase of the conflict resolution field is indeed exciting and filled with promises. Works such as this volume edited by Mitchell and Hancock contribute significantly to the field because they advance a shared understanding of phenomena not only from a purely speculative vantage point but also based on empirical cases. It is part—in my opinion—of the rising "practice-to-theory" movement, a contribution to the shared understanding of the field of conflict resolution that views "practice" not only as a verification ground for theories developed elsewhere, but accepts the challenge of generalizing insights based on actual cases.

Conflict resolution can be considered as (a) a field of inquiry; (b) a community of practitioners and scholars; and (c) a body of knowledge and procedures aimed at addressing conflict constructively. All three dimensions stress the need for an inclusive community of practice and learning; a community of scholars as learners. The overarching message of this book is that scholars should and must develop the interpretive frameworks, research tools, and empirical research projects needed to uncover and understand the many aspects of plurality of actors' key contributions to conflict resolution.[1]

This book uses the analysis of Zones of Peace as an opportunity to reflect more widely on the work of the field of conflict resolution itself.[2] Reflections on the experiences of conflict resolution that have emerged through civil society indicate that "practice" is the starting point of a shared understanding that may be accurately and correctly interpreted through proper models.[3]

To contribute to this process of collective, shared, verified knowledge is the overall objective of this text.

It appears that the field of conflict resolution may be ready for an attempt to synthesize what has been defined, measured, understood, and discovered to date, and also to allow the contributions of several scholars and practitioners to create a more robust, shared understanding.[4] Significant in this regard is the recent publication of a series of "handbooks" that address this shared desire for synthesis, coherence, and redefinition of the field (Bercovitch et al. 2008; Deutsch et al. 2006; Mitchell and Banks 1996; Sandole 2008). Of course, however, efforts have already been made to apply theories to actual practice. Indeed, important streams of literature take their roots from this endeavor (Fisher 2005). My point is that practitioners in conflict resolution should continue to engage in this work and by using intentionally self-reflective practices, they will fully participate in a rigorous effort to properly "theorize" (Fisher 2005).

In order to learn and to keep learning, we must be open, transparent, and self-conscious about our own "frames." As Peter Coleman, one of my colleagues at Columbia University's International Center for Cooperation and Conflict Resolution, aptly put it, we are, in many ways, "the frames that we are using" (Coleman 2003). Frames are cognitive constructs. They are the "shortcuts that people use to help make sense of complex information" (Kaufman et al. 2003). We all use frames. We all need them to make sense of the world. We reduce complexity into understandable categories through frames. The authors of this volume, who have very aptly created the original understanding in *Zones of Peace* (2007), are now revisiting it with new insights. They have explored new ways of doing things and explored different alternatives. Once again, the contribution is twofold: their initial innovation has allowed scholars to develop and present ideas that have changed the general perception of what is possible, proper, and doable; while practitioners have been able to experiment with processes and activities that employ frames that are less constrained by official protocol.

The long-term advantage of sustaining a collective conversation on Zones of Peace, and on frames and other critical points more generally, is that it allows us to follow the evolution of the field of conflict resolution, as well as identify themes, patterns, and foci, and support new research efforts (Bush 1998; Choucri and North 1975; Fisher and Keashly 1991). As medicine did not develop in a vacuum of theory-building, but in the "dirty" work of the scientists who dissected the human body and the practice of physicians who shared and challenged their knowledge so that others could live better lives, so the field of conflict resolution is poised to engage in a long-term effort that will take seriously both practice and theory (Sandole 2007).[5] This means we must take stock of what is known, or at least of what is believed to be known, and challenge it. We must verify our assumptions and results, while also moving beyond them and addressing new challenges (Galtung 1989; Rittberger and Fischer 2008).

In short, conflict resolution as a field needs to eschew the temptation of becoming merely an ideology and venture more into the realm of an effective, knowledge-based, collective effort.[6] Practice will then be removed from the isolation of self-righteousness and self-congratulation, and from the traps of donor-driven intervention and negative management habits that are justified by good intentions.[7] Instead, practice will take on an orientation based on results and service, where organizations survive and prosper based on their value-creation (Goodhand 2006). Theory, too, will refrain from self-congratulatory, isolationist stands. Instead, it will engage all disciplines in their own terms and take the direction of a scientific effort that is driven by the desire to actually improve the human condition (Rothbart and Korostelina 2006).

This book is indeed an important contribution and I am delighted that so many authors are colleagues at or graduates of The School for Conflict Analysis of Resolution at George Mason University.[8] The first 30 years of this remarkable institution have been rich and fruitful; yet, with contributions like these, there are clear signs that the next decades will continue to be productive and promising.

Andrea Bartoli
Dean, School of Conflict Analysis & Resolution
George Mason University

Notes

1 In particular, I believe that Dean Pruitt's orientation towards a "theory of inter-mediation" is very valid and promising. He presented the suggestion during a course on peacebuilding that I taught in the spring semester of 2008 at ICAR.

2 Several authors have described the evolution of the field of conflict resolu-tion, among them of particular relevance to this argument is Louis Kriesberg in *The Handbook of Conflict Resolution* Berkovich and others (eds) SAGE.

3 The problem of defining the conflict resolution field, exploring its challenges and opportunities, and reflecting on its interface with other areas of academic inquiry, was the subject of a seminar organized by Nadim Rouhana at Point of View, ICAR's research center, in November 2008.

4 Shared understanding does not equate to homogeneity. The very possibility of a shared understanding must assume relevant questions and a method to address them constructively.

5 To frame the conversation as a collective effort, and to learn from it and verify that learning, seems to be fundamental. Conflict is a human experience and its resolution must be a collective enterprise.

6 In this context, it must be noted that the field developed primarily in institutions of higher learning in the United States and that fully inclusive, sustained, and rigorous strategies will be necessary ingredients of this strategy.

7 As noted by Mary Anderson is her seminal work *Do Not Harm*, the risk of NGOs equating positive motivation with good results is very serious and must be challenged through a vigilant process of self-evaluation and external reviews.

8 In December, 2010, George Mason University recognized the continuing growth and development of the Institute for Conflict Analysis & Resolution by changing it from an institute into a full-fledged school.

Works cited

Anderson, Mary B. 1999. *Do no harm: how aid can support peace–or war.* Boulder, Colo.: Lynne Rienner Publishers.

Bercovitch, Jacob, Victor Kremenyuk, and I. William Zartman, eds. 2008. *The Sage Handbook of Conflict Resolution.* Thousand Oaks: SAGE Publications.

Bush, Kenneth. 1998. A Measure of Peace: Peace and Conflict Impact Assessment (PCIA) of Development Projects in Conflict Zones: International Development Research Centre.

Choucri, Nazli, and Robert Carver North.1975. *Nations in conflict: national growth and international violence.* San Francisco, CA: W. H. Freeman.

Coleman, Peter T. 2003. Characteristics of protracted, intractable conflict: Towards the development of a meta-framework - I. *Peace and Conflict: Journal of Peace Psychology* 9 (1):1–37.

Deutsch, Morton, Peter T. Coleman, and Eric C. Marcus, eds. 2006. *The handbook of conflict resolution: theory and practice.* 2nd ed. San Francisco, CA: Jossey-Bass Publishers.

Fisher, Ronald J., ed. 2005. *Paving the way: contributions of interactive conflict resolution to peacemaking.* Lanham: Lexington Books.

Fisher, Ronald J., and Loraleigh Keashly.1991. The potential complementarity of mediation and consultation within a contingency model of third party intervention. *Journal of Peace Research* 28 (1):29–42.

Galtung, Johan. 1989. *Solving conflicts: a peace research perspective.* Honolulu, HI: University of Hawaii Press.

Goodhand, Jonathan. 2006. *Aiding peace?: The role of NGOs in armed conflict.* Boulder: Lynne Rienner Publishers.

Hancock, Landon E., and C. R. Mitchell, eds. 2007. *Zones of peace.* Bloomfield, CT: Kumarian Press.

Kaufman, Sanda, Michael Elliott and Deborah Shmueli. 2003. Frames, Framing and Reframing. In *Beyond Intractability*, edited by H. B. Guy Burgess: Beyond Intractability. Conflict Research Consortium, University of Colorado.

Mitchell, Christopher R., and Michael Banks. 1996. *Handbook of conflict resolution: the analytical problem solving approach*. New York: Pinter.

Rittberger, Volker, and Martina Fischer, eds. 2008. *Strategies for peace. Contributions of international organizations, states, and non-state actors.* Farmington Hills: Barbara Budrich Publishers.

Rothbart, Daniel, and Karina V. Korostelina. 2006. *Identity, morality, and threat: studies in violent conflict*. Lanham: Lexington Books.

Sandole, Dennis J. D. 2007. Conflict Research and Diagnostics: Conflict Analysis as a Necessary Condition of Conflict Resolution – The Essential Bridge Between Theory and Practice. In *Human Conflict: Structures, Processes, and Resolution*, edited by D. Druckman, S. I. Cheldelin and K. P. Clements. London: Pinter (A Cassell Imprint).

—. 2008. *Handbook of conflict analysis and resolution*. New York, NY: Routledge.

1

Introduction: Linking national-level peacemaking with grassroots peacebuilding

Christopher Mitchell

The search for peace, a multi-level undertaking

Recent decades have seen a great deal of scholarly and practical interest in the development of local, grassroots peacebuilding before, during and in the aftermath of violent civil strife—an interest which matched the longstanding focus on negotiations to end such conflicts undertaken at the national level. However, much less attention has been paid to the question of how these two levels of effort to bring peace—or at least an end to violence—might affect one another. It often seems to be assumed that two obviously "good" processes must complement one another and make a durable peace much more likely. Indeed, much thinking about local peace efforts in the 1980s and 1990s often seemed to assume that the establishment of local zones of peace or peace communities, of small humanitarian zones, of regional zones of tranquility and of informal, triadic negotiations between local leaders, insurgents and government security forces would help to start, re-start or accelerate peacemaking at the national level, perhaps through encouraging a general "culture of peace." One clear example of this hope was expressed in the preamble to a bill introduced into the Philippines House of Representatives in 2000 (The Peace Zones Policy Act) which stated that peace zones were primarily to protect civilians but "also to contribute to the more comprehensive peace process." One common metaphor was of some kind of expanding "leopard spot" process, whereby "patches of peace" gradually spread themselves throughout society, crowding out violence and those wishing to continue using it.[1]

Subsequent events and analysis seem to have shown that the relationship between local and national peace processes is more complicated than was first assumed. Practically speaking, experience has shown that, in some strife prone societies, local efforts to encourage national peace or to establish peace locally, have been encouraged and supported by national authorities and by insurgent leaders. In other cases, they have been regarded by these elites and authorities as interfering with "serious" national efforts to bring about peace (whether through coercion or negotiation) and, in some cases, as another form of challenge to the authority of government or aspiring governments. In some countries, local peacebuilders have been included in national-level negotiations between incumbents and insurgents, yet in others they have been deliberately excluded from having any voice at all in efforts to end a conflict through talks—and even from the "talks about talks" stage. The record of the range of possible relationships between local and national-level processes is a mixed one and it is difficult to come up with any patterns or even repetitions amid the welter of different details from case to case.

Academics and activists actually involved in local peacebuilding processes have themselves attempted to analyze those processes that they have been involved in and have thrown some light on what effects these have had, locally and nationally, and what obstacles they have had to overcome. In the Philippines, for example, which is the country which has possibly seen the most active involvement of civil society in both local peacebuilding and national peacemaking efforts, many have made a distinction between "horizontal" and "vertical" peacebuilding. Talking about the recent peace process in Mindanao, Father Roberto Layson, the Co-chairman of the MPC (the Mindanao Peoples Caucus), a regional NGO in Mindanao,[2] who had been intimately involved in the establishment of the pioneering "space for peace" in the village of Nalapaan,[3] persuasively argued that there were two levels or "arenas" where peace processes take place—the vertical and the horizontal. "The vertical aspect is the formal Peace Talks or negotiations between the GRP (Government of the Republic of the Philippines) and the MILF (Moro Islamic Liberation Front) and the horizontal is the peace process within and among communities at the grassroots level ..." (Layson 2003, 1).

Fr. Layson went on to comment that, while national-level peace agreements may create a conducive space, "they are not a guarantee that there will be instant peace in our communities." Therefore a lot of work would still need to be done "in the grassroots level" (Layson 2003, 1).

Given this as a starting point, it is not surprising that some attention has been focused on efforts (1) to undertake activities that create or extend non-violent relationships at the local level between mistrustful constituencies; and (2) to influence warring elites, incumbent and insurgent, at the national level to engage seriously in efforts to mitigate the effects of violence, to undertake confidence-building measures and to conduct meaningful negotiations to resolve the conflict. Again, taking the Philippines and the conflict on Mindanao as an example, local initiatives there have involved developing institutions that involve membership from all three communities (Moro, Catholic and Lumad) on the island;[4] holding dialogues and seminars on differing histories and different cultures on Mindanao; training peace workers, for example at annual meetings of the Mindanao Peace-building Institute; providing relief and refuge for IDPs; providing micro-credit facilities; analyzing the effects of partisan journalism on the conflict; establishing trilateral "spaces for peace," "sanctuaries for peace" or—via UNDP—"peace and development communities;" and lobbying for and the involvement of civil society organizations in official peace processes at the national level.[5]

As always, it is hard to trace through the precise impact of all these locally based initiatives to build cross-community bridges, create a "culture of peace," diminish local violence or lessen mistrust and hostility among local communities, particularly those who have felt the impact of local combat—although it seems clear that pressure from civil society groups on Mindanao at least contributed to President Arroyo's decision to put together an all Mindanaon peace panel to face the MILF peace negotiators. Similar lobbying led to Lumad representatives being included in the government's negotiating team. However, the point is that Philippine experience seems to bear out the widely held contention that there are many positive ways in which the two dimensions—or peacebuilding arenas—can be linked, as illustrated in Figure 1.1 below:

However, this approach to the links between arenas of the peace process, and the horizontal–vertical model of peacebuilding it implies, often seems to leave out of consideration one other relationship that is important—perhaps because that relationship seems so obvious as to require little direct comment. This is the undoubted influence on local peacebuilding processes exercised by relationships at the national level between incumbents and insurgents. It seems banal to point

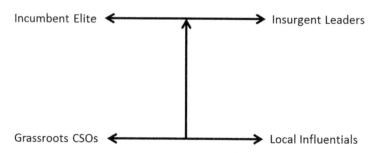

Figure 1.1 Dimensions of Peacebuilding.

out that it will make a huge difference to the effectiveness of local peace efforts whether the incumbents and insurgents are locked in intense conflict—the "all-out war" waged by President Estrada's Philippine government between 2000 and 2001—or are actively involved in the search for a negotiated peace under a continuing ceasefire—such as the "all out peace" campaign waged briefly by Estrada's successor, President Arroyo, from 2001 to breakdown in 2003. Again, what might be the "vertical" effects on local peacebuilding processes of a complete breakdown of elite-level negotiations on which many hopes had been built, such as occurred in February 2002 when—following the hijacking of a Colombian airliner by the FARC—a frustrated President Pastrana abruptly ended the faltering negotiating process with the guerrillas and resumed full scale military operations? Even peacemaking "success" at the national level is no guarantee that peace arrangements will work at local levels, particularly if elite-level negotiations have been held separately and at a distance from non-involved local people. The failure of the "Special Zone for Peace and Development" (SZOPAD) established on Mindanao by President Ramos' own directive as part of the 1996 settlement with the MNLF was largely because local support was taken for granted but proved largely absent in the months that followed. The governing "Southern Philippines Council for Peace and Development" set up to lead development in the 14 provinces of SZOPAD turned out to have no resources, no police powers and no real voice at the national level. Just as importantly, it proved also increasingly lacking in local credibility as time went on. As many observers of this and other peace processes have argued (see in this respect the chapter on Northern Ireland by Landon Hancock in this volume) there is always a need for careful coordination of efforts at both elite and grassroots social levels, as both levels interact in complex ways, as illustrated in Figure 1.2:

The point to be made here is that acknowledging the existence of such a relationship between arenas adds still further to the task of disentangling the complexities of possible inter-actions between national peacemaking and local peacebuilding. Developing some usable analytical framework - even to start the task - appears a monumental challenge.

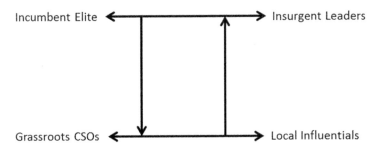

Figure 1.2   Expanded Dimensions of Peacebuliding.

The influence of differing political environments

One likely starting point for explaining the huge variation in inter-actions between national peacemakers and local peacebuilders might well be sought in the "stage" of the conflict in which both sets of protagonists find themselves operating.[6] If local intermediaries are attempting to negotiate local-level agreements about, for example, non-violent zones, prisoner release, times of local truce, the de-mining of a locality or the inviolability of a particular development project, it will surely make a major difference to them and their combatant contacts if the incumbents and insurgents are killing each other in (relatively) large numbers, are in the midst of a fragile ceasefire or are engaged in promising talks about a final end to coercion and violence.

Hancock and Iyer (2007, 29–31) have proposed a useful typology of stages in a protracted, intra-state conflict in which local peacebuilding initiatives (in this case local zones of peace) might well take place. The framework makes a distinction between initiatives which take place (1) while violent combat continues; (2) during a peace process—that is, while negotiations are taking place or, an agreement having been reached, while strategies to implement the terms of the agreement are being put in place; and (3) in the long term, during the post-conflict period. This is a useful framework, and what follows in Table 1.1 is partly based in the Hancock–Iyer distinction between the stages of all-out combat with no negotiations in sight and (2) the existence of some kind of elite-level peace process—although it does seem useful to divide this second stage into two sub-processes; during actual negotiations and during the implementation of any agreement that might be reached.[7]

However, the changing circumstances brought about by the relationship between incumbents and insurgents represent only one set of factors likely to affect the relationship between local peacebuilding and national peacemaking. Others can include the nature of the local peacebuilding activities themselves

Table 1.1 National and local strategies

		National-Level strategies		
		Violence	Negotiating	Implementing
Local-level strategies	Violence	Civil war	?	Civil unrest
	Peacebuilding	?	Multi-level peace process	Reconstruction & reconciliation

and the differing reactions—levels of approval and disapproval—that might well be exhibited by the adversaries, incumbent and insurgent. Compare, for example the widely different attitudes of the two sides to any local peace promoting efforts that involve making it far, far easier for local youngsters to abandon life with insurgents or paramilitary groups and to return home in order to resume some kind of civilian life.[8] Again, the same government side might display very different reactions to localized declaration of neutrality from communities in strategically important communications centers compared with those from remote and isolated communities on the geographical periphery on a widespread struggle.

There is a great deal of research currently needed into the different ways in which combatant strategies affect the circumstances in which local initiatives take place, and how changes in those strategies can either make it easier or harder to continue to pursue those strategies. Then again, local communities are not simply reactors to national policies nor—as has been implied thus far—are they always pacific groups constantly seeking an end to violence in which they are caught up. There are enough examples of local people being encouraged to take up arms—initially, at least, in "self-defense"—and through the formation of such organizations as the Tadtad in the Philippines or the Civilian Defense Patrols in Guatemala, widening the scope of the violence.[9]

Furthermore, one has to take account of the large number of situations of protracted conflicts where a conflict system involves multiple, interlocking conflicts taking place at different levels, and where peacemaking at a national level is by no means a guarantee that peace will break out locally. Indeed, it may be that peace made at the national level may actually provide an opportunity for local adversaries to wage local war with even greater intensity.[10] At least theoretically, we have to consider the possibility that local and national strategies might be out of synchronization in a variety of ways—or at least following scenarios based in fundamental opposites:

One possible research strategy—touched upon but not used directly in one of the chapters in this book—is to examine what happens when a new leadership comes to political power in a country torn by civil strife and completely reverses the strategies of its predecessor, leaving local leaders and organizations having to cope with a political environment which is quite different from the one in which they were operating before.[11] Empirically speaking, many such cases seem to involve a new set of political incumbents coming to power and switching official strategy from coercion and violence towards some, if not most, of the insurgents to one of calling for a ceasefire while offering—and later opening—peace talks. In other cases, new leaders abandon apparently futile peace talks and take up arms once again in an attempt to win the conflict by destroying the insurgents as a viable organization. Especially in these latter cases, the change of strategy at the national level seems likely to have a major impact on local-level peacebuilding and may leave local initiatives "high and dry" in some fashion.

The effects of such changes in national leadership can be observed in many countries struggling to find a solution to a protracted and intractable conflict—or to several such. Two cases can be mentioned as examples: one—Colombia—in Latin America; and one in the Asia-Pacific region—the Philippines. In both countries, changes in top leadership on the government side of the struggle have led to drastic reversals in national peacemaking policies that local leaders and institutions have had to cope with.

Colombia

- **1998–2002.** President Andreas Pastrana. Negotiations with both major insurgent groups (ELN and FARC). Ended in Spring 2002.

- **2002–2006.** President Alvaro Uribe. Strategy of armed "democratic security" against FARC and ELN, together with efforts to disarm and reintegrate pro-government paramilitaries (AUC).

- **2006–2010.** President Alvaro Uribe. Democratic Security II. Extradition of some paramilitary leaders to the USA on drug charges.

- **2010–2014.** President Juan Manuel Santos. At his inauguration in August 2010, Santos promised to "keep up pressure on the drug-running insurgents." FARC responded with a fall offensive against military and civilian targets (Bronstein 2010).

Philippines

- **1986–1992.** President Corazon Aquino. Negotiations both with the National Democratic Front (NDF) and the MNLF in Mindanao, but both break down.

- **1992–1998.** President Fidel Ramos pursues a "comprehensive peace program" that results in peace agreements with dissidents in the AFP (1994) and with the MNLF (1996), plus a ceasefire agreement with the MILF (1997) and an agreement on human rights with the NDF (1998).

- **1998–2003.** President Joseph Estrada. Although promising to continue Ramos's policies in search of a negotiated peace, Estrada announced a policy of "all-out war" against the MILF in 2001. He was ejected from office in 2003 well before his term was due to end and was replaced by his Vice President (Gloria Arroyo Macapagal).

- **2003–2010.** President Gloria Arroyo Macapagal, Replaced Estrada's strategy with one of "all-out peace" and achieved a ceasefire in 2003 but, amid on-again/off-again talks, local violence continued and the government abandonment of the Memorandum of Agreement on Ancestral Domain left the national-level peace process in limbo.

- **2010–2016.** President Benigno Aquino III. Began to pursue a policy of "peace through dialog." Talks opened in February 2011 with local governmental consultations taking place through May 2011.

The lists outlined above provide only a sketch of the highly different backgrounds against which local peacebuilders in Colombia and the Philippines had to work over the last two decades. Conditions in both countries were at various times, either conducive to local horizontal peacebuilding efforts and to vertical attempts to influence national-level processes. At others they were wholly antithetical to such efforts. In both countries, of course, such efforts continued, but as some of the work that follows this Introduction shows, with very mixed results. Local peacebuilding in the best of circumstances appears under-resourced and fragile, and as we have shown elsewhere, sometimes even positive and practical government support can prove detrimental to sustainability (Mitchell and Hancock 2007, 194–7).

In spite of the anecdotal data presented above, given the present state of our *systematic* knowledge about the links—or lack of them—between the two levels of peacemaking and peacebuilding activities, it seems foolish even to start a process of classification and comparison, except perhaps as a launching pad for debate. However, on a priori grounds, it does seem just possible—and maybe useful—to start by suggesting that there might be a continuum of possible reactions that incumbents and insurgents might take up vis-à-vis local communities' efforts to maintain at least some form of negative peace "in their own back yard" and perhaps to influence efforts at national-level peacemaking, even while the combatants get on with their own efforts to win the struggle. Possible reactions as outlined in Table 1.2 might, therefore,

Table 1.2 Incumbent/insurgent reactions

Incumbent reaction	Insurgent reaction
Sanctioning	
Forbidding/Banning	
Undermining	
Verbal Disapproval	
Toleration	
Verbal Support	
Sponsoring/Funding	
Taking Over/Founding	

be seen as forming a continuum from positive to negative responses, from embracing local initiatives to condemning or undermining them.

Naturally, what governments like, guerrillas are likely to dislike—and vice versa—which does raise an interesting question as to whether there are any kinds of local initiative that might have benefits to both sides at any point in a struggle, and thus be tolerated—at least—by both at the same time. Perhaps the agreement, negotiated at grassroots level by Unionist and Nationalist guerrilla leaders—plus local civil society leaders—in Northern Ireland in the mid-1970s not to attack Post Offices in one another's neighborhoods was also tacitly approved in government circles in both Belfast and London. Thus, it could stand as a small example of local peacebuilding that at least did not interfere with national-level peacemaking efforts, although it was a long stretch between the mid-1970s and the signing of the final peace agreement in 1998.

Different approaches to local and national peace

Further research may enable the list of possible reactions by incumbents and insurgents—but especially by national governments—to be worked into a usable scale of (dis)approval for local peacebuilding initiatives. However, all that seems possible at the present stage of research is to provide illustrative examples of the kind of empirical national-level reactions from the combatant elites in strife torn polities. These can run the gamut from national leaders' efforts to create their own grassroots "peacebuilding" movements or institutions to utter condemnation of such efforts and sustained campaigns to undermine or destroy them. It may be that the best local peacebuilders can hope for is bilateral *toleration*, at least while the combat continues and there are no national efforts being made to bring the conflict to an agreed close. At least this acknowledges the danger that any reaction other than toleration at elite level may result in a perception among one set of leaders that the locals clearly favor their rivals. As Pedro Valenzuela points out in his study of peace communities in Colombia, it is more difficult to maintain a position of neutrality in protracted civil strife than it is in inter-state conflict, so toleration is often the best local leaders can hope for (Valenzuela 2009, 40–1).

"On a more positive note," many local peacebuilding initiatives have been supported—to a greater or lesser degree—by both sides even during periods of intense conflict and even when they take the form of efforts to withdraw whole communities or territories from the battle. *Verbal* expressions of *support* are never costly to make, as long as they do not compromise members of national elites, so that Colombian President Pastrana's message of congratulation to the *municipio* of Mogotes on the latter's attaining the national peace prize in 1999 was relatively easy to make, especially as it did not run counter to Pastrana's national search for a negotiated peace then under way. There are, of course, many more ways in which official support or approval can be expressed. The physical presence of the Provincial Governor, the mayor, representatives of the Armed Forces of the Philippines, the police *and* of representatives of both the MNLF and the MILF at the formal launching of the *barangay* at Panicupan in North Cotobato on Mindanao as a "space for peace" was importantly symbolic, especially as the attendees at the ceremony came from both sides on the conflict. Presence implies endorsement, and to a degree implies a level of joint cooperation with the local people involved in local peacebuilding efforts to ensure that the latter's goals can be met, at least at a local level.

Verbal or symbolic support is one thing, however, but concrete action in support of a local initiative can prove much more difficult for both incumbents and insurgents. Instructing combatant forces to respect the neutrality of local peace zones, for example, is a huge step towards *cooperation*, while continuing an embargo on violence, arms carrying and even access is often beyond the commanders of local combatant units once an armed struggle intensifies. Moreover, it is one thing to cooperate with local leaders and organizations on an ad hoc, case by case basis but quite another to cooperate with local peacebuilding efforts on a polity wide basis. Efforts by members of the Philippines House of Representatives in 2000 to pass a "Peace Zones Policy Act," which not only contained provisions for the formal recognition of a Filipino peace zone but also sanctioned members of the AFP for violations of provisions for maintaining such a zone were a step too far and died in the legislature, possibly as one result of President Estrada's strategy of "all-out war" against the MILF.[12]

Clearly, there are some forms of local peacebuilding activities that can win the approval and cooperation not merely of the government side but also—on many occasions—of the insurgents. Local efforts to organize relief and rehabilitation for IDPs will usually win cooperation from local combatants but also from their national-level leaderships. Should a ceasefire be achieved, local leaders and organizations can become part of a region or nationwide monitoring effort, such involvement having—in the eyes of national-level leaders—the great advantage of local knowledge and local contacts; thus the presence of local leaders and members of the MCP on teams monitoring the AFP/MILF ceasefire on Mindanao between 2001 and 2003.

At the implementation stage of any agreement there will need to be a high degree of cooperation between national-level officials (for example, OPAPP—the "Office of the Presidential Advisor for the Peace Process" in the Philippines) and local institutions and influentials. Unfortunately, as the history of the post-agreement era in such countries as El Salvador, Guatemala, and Nicaragua demonstrates, such post-agreement cooperation and coordination is frequently lacking, resulting a flawed, incomplete peace process (see Rojas 2006; Arnson 1999).

Examples from other cases, however, seem to indicate that, while cooperation between local peacebuilding initiatives, even those simply aimed horizontally, and national-level initiatives that take the next step involving *sponsoring* or funding can sometimes be fruitful, sometimes it can backfire. Some of the original, locally initiated peace zones in the Philippines were formally recognized by President Ramos's government during the 1990s as part of Ramos' "Comprehensive Peace Policy." In seven cases, this strategy went beyond recognition through official approval and even beyond local/national cooperation. The government declared the zones to be Special Development Areas (SDAs) and hence eligible for direct government funding—actually amounting to some 5 to 7 million pesos. While the official recognition from the government proved to be valuable for the chosen zones, (although divisive for the overall peace zone movement) becoming an SDA proved to be a mixed blessing. Hardy surprisingly, the NPA saw government sponsorship as a means of winning over the local communities to its side in the armed struggle—in other words they viewed the SDAs as part of an overall counter-insurgency strategy. For some of the SDAs, moreover, the availability of such high levels of funding proved internally highly divisive, increasing the divisions with communities over who should control the spending of the funds, and what it should be spent on (Avruch and Jose 2007; Lee 2000; Santos Jr 2005).

At the extreme, there have been cases of national-level efforts to create local peacebuilding efforts "from the top"—and occasionally without any genuine participation from local leaders or institutions at all. One of the more notorious examples of such strategies was the attempt of the Estrada government to establish local "zones of peace" in areas of Mindanao wrested from the control of the MILF between 2001 and 2003. One effect of claiming that such "liberated" zones were similar to grassroots generated initiatives to establish neutral areas free from violence was the general corrupting of the title "peace zone." Hence, the next generation of really local efforts at peacebuilding began to adopt different titles—"sanctuaries of peace" or "spaces for peace"—so that they would be differentiated from government run and protected communities.

At first sight and on a priori grounds, it does seem more likely that national-level reactions from both incumbents and insurgents to local peacebuilding initiatives are likely to be negative rather than positive, especially from the government side. It is a rare government that can accept the idea of local initiatives limiting its sovereign rights to carry out the policies it chooses, especially those to do with national security, on its own territories. Frequent statements from members of Colombian President Uribe's government—and from Uribe himself—to the effect that only the national government has the right to carry out negotiations or other peacemaking activities with any of the illegal insurgents made the point quite clear. Governments do not really and truly like such independent actions by local people, even when they contribute to forwarding government policy and certainly not when they appear to undermine it. Much verbal criticism has been directed by officials at peace communities in Colombia and at local leaders who have attached themselves to national-level processes to negotiate limited local deals—about demining operations for example—around their communities.

Far worse, from the local communities' viewpoint, can be official statements implying that local peacebuilding initiatives are simply screens that conceal local support for one side or the other in the protracted struggle. Such a reaction can often be expected from insurgents and incumbents but it is particularly damaging when the charge of being "guerrilla sympathizers" is launched by government members and officials. Again, this has been a frequent feature of the reaction of the Uribe government to local peace initiatives in Colombia and has reinforced the perception among security forces that they are surrounded by a covertly hostile population who thus become targets for harassment and assault—if not by the army and police then by their paramilitary allies. This whole process is described in greater detail by Mitchell and Rojas in Chapter 3.

Apart from verbal criticism, most protracted and intractable intra-state conflicts demonstrate a whole variety of ways in which national elites can *undermine* local peacebuilding efforts of which they disapprove. One common strategy for the government side is to insist upon establishing an army post or a police station within a community committed to carrying on with its own peacebuilding strategy in the face of disapproval from the central government. Refusal to abide by the terms of a locally negotiated deal about entering an area, or carrying arms openly in that area, or refraining from the forced recruitment of local youth, or allowing free passage of goods to and from markets, are other common strategies open to both national government forces and to local insurgents, although the freedom of action open to local guerrilla commanders often appears greater than that available to subordinate military commanders who are usually under much firmer central control.

Efforts to undermine local peacebuilding initiatives—especially what in the Philippines have come to be known as horizontal initiatives—are usually preliminary to efforts to ban them and ultimately to sanction those who insist upon continuing with such efforts. On the insurgent side the sanctions can take the extreme form of death threats for those attempting to practice some form of neutrality or to interfere with the process of violent—and hopefully successful— resistance and revolution through disruptive intermediary activities. Many local peacebuilders have lost their lives in attempting to establish sanctuaries, negotiate local truces or ceasefires, protect local civilians, argue for the observance of human rights or simply get on with local development projects.[13]

On the other side, governments have a wider range of actions they can take in order to sanction local peacebuilding efforts of which they disapprove. Passing laws making it a criminal offence for their citizens merely to talk with members of "the other side" (as the Israeli government did for many years) and locking up any who insist on talking to the enemy about local initiatives has proved a common, if frequently ineffective, way of deterring local peacebuilders from taking initiatives they deem to be in the local interest. Fines, confiscation of property or exile are less extreme penalties that have been used to enforce rules about not having contacts with insurgents for any purposes whatsoever, usually on the grounds that, at least, such contacts would appear to confer a minimum of legitimacy on those contacted and on their aims and aspirations. As with positive responses to local initiatives, negative reactions can take many concrete forms as national-level leaders react to local-level peacebuilding and perceive it as helpful and supportive action or as unwarranted and possibly illegal interference.

Case studies and conclusions

Even from this superficial introduction, making some sense out of a record of historical relationships between peace processes at the national and the local levels seems to present a daunting task. However, the authors in this volume share a belief that it is also a much needed task and many of the chapters which follow begin by describing various historical examples of local peacebuilding efforts and also explore the reactions of governments and guerrillas to such efforts and thence to the impact of such local efforts on the likelihood of a successful national-level peacemaking process coming about and being successful.

Without anyone consciously using a framework involving different "stages" of a peace process, many of the chapters can be seen as falling into one or other of the stages outlined by Hancock and Iyer, which have been discussed—and to some degree modified—above. The chapter by Mitchell and Rojas, for example, examines a period in recent Colombian history in which national-level peacemaking processes were abandoned by the Colombian government and an all-out military campaign was waged against the insurgents of the FARC and the ELN, at the same time as that government was attempting to bring the paramilitary forces fighting against the guerrillas—and persecuting local communities—under some kind of control. In a similar setting of continued violence in Colombia, Mery Rodriguez describes how some of the local peace communities have adapted their strategies to the changing circumstances of "democratic security," but also how the central government in Bogota has attempted to limit their freedom of action by funneling resources through central government agencies.

By contrast, the chapter by Andries Odendaal examines efforts to contain local violence at a time when national leaders were negotiating a settlement to the long drawn out struggle over apartheid in South Africa and over the ANC's quest for majority rule in that country. Odendaal was himself heavily involved in the work of the provincial Peace Committees established to try to bring about an end to locally generated violence. He provides an interesting analysis of the manner in which national-level peacemaking can actually open up spaces for localized violence, and what might need to be done from both "top-down" and "bottom-up" perspectives to prevent the lack of local peace from wrecking negotiations and restarting the struggle at the national level.

Hancock's chapter looks at local peacebuilding processes that take place in the aftermath of a nationally negotiated settlement, which then has to be implemented by local people and institutions. He evaluates the effects of a top-down process which concentrates on reconciliation and community-building in "interface" communities in Northern Ireland, arguing that attempts to "build bridges" between Nationalist and Unionist communities in the province need to be linked to development processes—at least in the eyes of local people.

Two provocative contributions fall outside this "stages" framework. Wallace Warfield and Yves Renée Jennings speculate about the possible uses of local peace zones as means of preventing violent conflict in the first place. They argue that establishing such a peacebuilding initiative in sensitive areas, such as in border regions where frictions constantly arise, might well be a means of preventing escalation and designing solutions to problems before these become the source of mutual coercion and violence They give an example of one border site in the Caribbean where such an initiative might be successful. Lastly, in an ambitious reconsideration of the whole concept of "peace zones" and as part of an ongoing and needed challenge to the dominant "nation-state" paradigm inherited from the seventeenth century, Irakli Kakabadze raises the question of whether an idea developed locally for local peacebuilding amid intra-state wars could be applied internationally. Kakabadzi suggests that such "thinking outside the box" could offer a range of solutions to the rigidity in thinking imposed by the model of the sovereign territorial state in regions such as the Caucasus, where that model surely leads to more problems than it solves.

Finally, in a last chapter, the editors attempt to summarize what general lessons about interactions between local peacebuilding and national peacemaking might be drawn from the variety of cases and countries covered in the various contributions. Nothing conclusive should be anticipated but it might be hoped that the case studies and the lessons learned from diverse relationships between national and local levels will lead to a greater understanding of how local-level initiatives can contribute to helping national-level peacemaking and how national-level peacemaking can provide opportunities for local peacebuilding initiatives, rather than stifling them through a misguided search for uniformity and central control.

Notes

1 This legislation, sponsored by Representative Jaime Jacob, was read into the record of the Committee on Local Government on September 20, 2000 and, according to the Philippine House of Representatives Legislative Information System (LEGIS), it remains pending with this committee.

2 The Mindanao Peoples Caucus is an NGO founded in 2001 partly as a response to President Estrada's "all-out war" on the MILF It is based in Davao City and draws its membership from all three communities in central Mindanao—Moro, Christian and Lumad. Co-chaired by Father Bert Layson, together with his fellows from the Lumad and Moro communities, the MPC was originally organized to promote mutual understanding among the three peoples of Mindanao. Among other local activities it has lobbied Manila for the inclusion of indigenous representation on national peace institutions.

3 The Nalapaan "space for peace" was a *barangay* in Pikit containing members of all three Mindanaon peoples. It was started in 2000 when the peace talks had collapsed and the war resumed. A year later four more *barangays* became part of the space, the whole being supported by OXFAM and the Notre Dame University's Peace Center.

4 Many of the local NGOs on Mindanao have attempted to portray themselves as and to actually become "triadic," in that they involve members of the three communities—indigenous, Moro and settlers—on the island.

5 The Mindanao Peace-building Institute was initiated by the Catholic Relief Service in 2000 and since then has held annual workshops every year. MPI provides training in conflict management and transformation, peace education and the culture of peace. Participants come from other countries in the region (Indonesia, Vietnam, India, Pakistan, East Timor, Sri Lanka) as well as from Bulgaria and the former-Yugoslavia, and all regions of the Philippines.

6 I don't wish to imply by the term "stage" that I am assuming that conflicts go through s set of pre-determined and clearly differentiated sets of circumstances that follow one another in a typical pattern. However, clearly local peacebuilders are likely to confront different problems and different reactions from governments and insurgents if both are locked in a pattern of violent mutual coercion, or are negotiating though a fog of mutual suspicion and mistrust, or have reached some agreed settlement and now have to rely on local people to implement its provisions.

7 At some future time it might be helpful to distinguish more carefully between environments for local peacebuilding that take place (1) during violent combat; (2) during a preliminary ceasefire; (3) during ongoing negotiations at the national level; and either (4) during efforts to implement national-level agreements or (5) in the aftermath of a complete breakdown in negotiations. Lastly, what local peacebuilding initiatives might be needed—and successful—during the aftermath of a protracted, violent conflict which might include efforts to implement truth and reconciliation processes as well as more conventional efforts at reconstruction and reinsertion of combatants.

8 National government reactions to such a local program of "reinsertion" of former fighters can also vary a great deal, depending on how strongly people in the government feel about the need to punish former guerrillas as opposed to rewarding their defection.

9 The Tadtad were a Filipino militia who were especially—and lethally—active around the town of Tulunan in North Cotobato during the Marcos regime. The name "Tadtad" comes from the local verb meaning to chop into little pieces (Avruch and Jose 2007, 58). Civilian Defense Patrols (PACs) involved over a million local Guatemalans at one stage in that civil war and were responsible for some of the worst of the over 400 massacres carried out in that country in an effort to keep local communities—mainly indigenous—under control (Proyecto Interdiocesano Recuperación de la Memoria Histórica (Guatemala), Catholic Institute for International Relations, and Latin America Bureau 1999, 31). Other armed groups were created by the state or used surreptitiously by state forces in Colombia (the CONVIVR program), in Peru (see Langdon and Rodriguez 2007) and Loyalist paramilitaries in Northern Ireland.

10 Brosché (2008) has made an excellent argument with respect to the linked, multiple conflicts in Darfur in the Sudan that at least four conflicts are interlocked there. Hence, it seems unlikely that finding a solution to the conflict between central Sudanese and local Darfurian elites would have much positive effect on the conflicts between local Darfurian rivals over political leadership, power and resources or between and among rival pastoral and sedentary communities over land, grazing, and water.

11 Given that insurgent organizations are unlikely to be involved in regular changes of leadership which parallel national elections in many countries—even those involved in civil wars—the problems for local peacebuilding posed by change of insurgent leadership leading to major changes in national-level insurgent strategies seem likely to present less of a problem to local peacemaking institutions than those posed by any form of democratic process pursued by rival political incumbents and aspiring incumbents.

12 See note 1 above.

13 One indication of this can be found in the number of community members of Colombia's peace community in San José de Apartadó who have been killed since the Peace Community was inaugurated in 1997. Another is the number of local clergy killed in Colombia during the period 1994–2007. Catholic Doors, an organization that keeps track of "Catholic Victims of Violence" worldwide, estimates that 30 of the over 500 clergy killed during that period were killed in Colombia. This total does not include the 118 parishioners killed in 2002 by a misdirected FARC mortar round while sheltering during an attack in the church in Boyaca in the department of Choco. See http://www.Catholicdoors.com/news/martyrs.htm.

Works cited

Arnson, Cynthia, ed., 1999. *Comparative peace processes in Latin America.* Washington, DC, Stanford, CA: Woodrow Wilson Center Press, Stanford University Press.

Avruch, Kevin, and Roberto S. Jose. 2007. "Peace Zones in the Philippines." In *Zones of peace*, edited by L. E. Hancock and C. R. Mitchell. Bloomfield, CT: Kumarian Press.

Bronstein, Hugh. 2010. "Colombian rebel attacks intensify, dozens killed." *Reuters, Africa*, Sept 10.

Brosché, Johan. 2008. "Darfur – Dimensions and Dilemmas of a Complex Situation: UCDP Paper #2." Uppsala, Sweden: Uppsala University, Department of Peace and Conflict Research.

Hancock, Landon E., and Pushpa Iyer. 2007. "The nature, structure and variety of 'peace zones'." In *Zones of peace*, edited by L. E. Hancock and C. R. Mitchell. Bloomfield, CT: Kumarian Press.

Langdon, Jennifer, and Mery Rodriguez. 2007. "The Rondas Campesinas of Peru." In *Zones of peace*, edited by L. E. Hancock and C. R. Mitchell. Bloomfield, CT: Kumarian Press.

Layson, Fr. Roberto. 2003. *Reflections on public participation in peace processes in Mindanao.* Notre Dame, IN: Catholic Peacebuilding Network.

Lee, Zosimo E. 2000. "Peace Zones as Special Development Areas: A Preliminary Assessment." In *Building peace: essays on psychology and the culture of peace*, edited by A. B. I. Bernardo and C. D. Ortigas. Manila, Philippines: De La Salle University Press, Inc.

Mitchell, Christopher R., and Landon E. Hancock. 2007. "Local Zones of Peace and a Theory of Sanctuary." In *Zones of peace*, edited by L. E. Hancock and C. R. Mitchell. Bloomfield, CT: Kumarian Press.

Proyecto Interdiocesano Recuperación de la Memoria Histórica (Guatemala), Catholic Institute for International Relations, and Latin America Bureau. 1999. *Guatemala, never again!* Maryknoll, NY, London: Orbis Books, CIIR, Latin America Bureau.

Rojas, Catalina. 2006. "Adjusting to peace: The political economy of post-war reconstruction land, privatization and fiscal reform in post-war El Salvador and Guatemala." Ph.D., George Mason University, Virginia, USA.

Santos Jr., Soliman. 2005. *Peace zones in the Philippines: concept, policy & instruments*. Quezon City: Gaston Z. Ortigas Peace Institute & the Asia Foundation.

Valenzuela, Pedro. 2009. "Neutrality in internal armed conflicts: experiences at the grassroots level in Colombia." Originally presented as the author's thesis (doctoral), Uppsala University, Uppsala, Sweden.

2

A ZoPs approach to conflict prevention

Wallace Warfield and Yves-Renée Jennings

Introduction

Many scholars and practitioners have argued that since the early 1990s, our world has witnessed new kinds of conflicts where contentious and devastating violence has emerged within states among antagonists at the communal level rather than between states at the international level (Ackermann 2003; Marshall et al. 2005; Ramsbotham et al. 2011). Unfortunately, the costs of these intra-state communal conflicts have been significant in terms of loss of life, destruction of infrastructure, disruption of the economy, and the overall lack of human security (Lund 2000; van de Goor and Verstegen 2004). While smaller in number than conflicts in the past, these post-Cold War conflicts have resulted in higher levels of devastation, despair, disease, lawlessness, poverty, and destruction of the social fabric.

The international community, consisting of the UN, member states, NGOs, aid and relief organizations, and multilateral financial institutions, has provided significant resources and expended significant efforts toward violence mitigation once these conflicts have started, but aside from a few well-publicized cases, little effort has been expended on conflict prevention at the sub-state level. In general, efforts at violence mitigation and, at times, post-conflict reconstruction, have primarily focused on peacekeeping, peacemaking, and humanitarian assistance designed to address the structural and proximate causes of the conflicts and to address the deprivation of basic needs felt by affected populations. What has often been missing in many of these initiatives is a focus on providing affected communities with opportunities to build their own capacities for future conflict prevention

Within the context of this missing piece, this chapter argues for the need to assist communities to learn how to prevent the destructive impact of intrastate conflicts and reduce their human, psychological, and material costs. Such preventive efforts can occur by assisting communities to participate in development and human rights efforts geared at combating poverty, providing justice, and instituting the rule of law. These efforts can also take place through capacity-building efforts designed to address the root causes of simmering conflicts while dealing with issues related to structural violence, lawlessness, injustice, and inequality.

In this chapter, we propose a different approach to preventing intrastate or communal conflicts, one which uses a conceptual and theoretical framework based on the idea of a zone of peace (ZoP). From a conflict resolution perspective a ZoP is a social sanctuary which is viewed as a physical environment or social space where individuals are protected against personal violability based on agreed rules of public order (Hancock and Mitchell 2007). A ZoP offers a stable, yet dynamic, mechanism that allows communities the space to respond proactively to conflicts before they escalate into violence. In addition to acting as a mechanism for conflict prevention, a ZoPs approach to conflict prevention offers a framework within which communities can build capacity towards the goal of creating cultures of peace and addressing underlying issues of structural violence, a lack of development, and widespread poverty. Finally, we believe that a ZoPs approach to conflict prevention would encourage community members to acquire and hone skills that would allow them to positively contribute their voices to decision-making at multiple levels; constructively influencing and participating in the transformation of social systems and structures.

Zones of peace: Possibilities for prevention

Zones of peace have served as mechanisms for conflict mitigation and safe havens in regions as far flung as the Philippines, Colombia, and Bosnia. They have also served as peace implementation mechanisms as parts of official peace treaties in places like El Salvador, Aceh, and Zimbabwe/Rhodesia; as post-conflict peacebuilding and development zones in places like El Salvador; and a number of temporary or specialized zones have been created in places like Nicaragua, Sudan, and Sri Lanka.[1]

ZoPs have been established for peacemaking purposes based on rules developed by those living in war-torn or post-war areas; or based on rules created by the UN, humanitarian relief agencies or the parties to peace agreements when used as a part of a larger, comprehensive agreement (Hancock and Iyer 2007). Based on analyses of ZoPs in the Philippines, Colombia, and El Salvador, it has been argued that the most sustainable ZoPs are those that have been created based on the efforts of local communities as opposed to those spearheaded by external actors, who often have a limited knowledge of the local situation or fail to consult community members adequately about what can help them sustain a stable peace (Mitchell and Hancock 2007).

The emphasis on local ownership of the process is evident from the very beginning of El Salvador's local zone of peace, founded in 1998 as a response to endemic conditions of violence and poverty following the resolution of that country's 12-year civil war (cf. Hancock 2007; Chupp 2003). In their decision to start the Local Zone of Peace, "the Coordinadora's constituent communities committed themselves to ending the violence . . . and resolved to change the region's culture of violence to one of reconciliation, collaborative problem solving and non-violent conflict resolution."[2]

In pointing out the effectiveness of ZoPs in the Philippines and El Salvador as mechanisms to create conflict-free places where people became empowered to create and establish peace, Rupesinghe observes that one of the chief objectives that conflict prevention efforts should be concerned with is "empowerment"—that is by:

> Helping local populations to build the will and the mechanisms to hold governments and guerrillas accountable for their breaches of international and national humanitarian standards once conflict has escalated to violence, mobilizing people to pressure those who make war to engage in dialogue instead and protecting and building on the peace once it is achieved. (Rupesinghe 1995, 327)

Rupesinghe's thinking conforms to Woodhouse's assertion that peacebuilding from below can help strengthen local communities' resources and capacity; as was the case with many of the ZoPs in Colombia (Woodhouse 1999). In Colombia, communities organized themselves to deal non-violently with the escalation of rampant violence after the failure of the peace process between President Andrés Pastrana and the FARC (Revolutionary Armed Forces of Colombia) resulting in the escalation of violence in February of 2002. Rojas (2007) articulates that this effort resulted in the establishment of a plethora of peace zones because of the constructive outcomes and the positive experiences of the people as they strived to articulate their voice toward the peaceful resolution of the conflict.

This kind of grassroots orientation to ownership and direction is evident in most, if not all, of the successful ZoPs that have been studied to date. The question we pose for the use of ZoPs as conflict prevention mechanisms is what role, if any, could be played by those outside the local community, whether they represent larger civil society organs, elements of the state, or international organizations? Despite the willingness and, possibly, the organizational ability of many local communities to attempt to address the conditions which lead to violence in their local communities, often violence on a local level can be triggered by forces beyond local control. Additionally, as noted in an *International Alert and Saferworld 2000 G8 Summit* report, the proactive involvement of civil society in providing support to local communities is imperative because it can be "a powerful force in building constituencies and zones of peace in countries where violence is endemic and the state is unable to provide security and stability" (Project Ploughshares 2000).

As we approach this conundrum of meshing local and larger efforts in an attempt to more successfully prevent violence, we next turn to a review of prevention efforts, which, as we will see below, are largely devoid of the kinds of grassroots efforts that characterize successful ZoPs. Following this review, we will suggest a theoretical and practical approach for using the Zones of Peace framework as an approach for successfully implementing conflict prevention efforts.

Conflict prevention

In 2006 Kofi Annan, then Secretary-General of the United Nations, delivered a report to the General Assembly on the state of prevention efforts. In the report, Annan stressed the responsibility of the international community to assist states and localities to prevent violent conflict, arguing that:

> An unacceptable gap remains between rhetoric and reality in the area of conflict prevention. The time has come to ask some hard questions about why this gap has proved so difficult to bridge. What more can we do to bridge it?. . . Too often the international community spends vast sums of money to fight fires that, in hindsight, we might more easily have extinguished with timely preventive action before so many lives were lost or turned upside down. Over the last five years, we have spent over $18 billion on United Nations peacekeeping that was necessary partly because of inadequate preventive measures. A fraction of that investment in preventive action would surely have saved both lives and money. (UN General Assembly, 60th Session, and Agenda Item 12 2006, 4)

In the past two decades an extensive literature on conflict prevention has been developed, largely favoring different kinds of interventions in order to stop conflict before it begins or to mitigate its consequences in order to reduce human suffering and the economic and social costs of the conflicts themselves as well as those experienced by neighboring states and peacekeeping and peacemaking forces. The result of this scholarship and activism is a broad spectrum of works defining conflict prevention as well as determining, or proposing, methods for effective conflict prevention practice. Definitions and practices have been established by scholars like Lund (1998, 2000, 2002, 2004), Wallensteen (2001), Wallensteen and Bercovitch (1998), Wallensteen and Möller (2003), Munuera (1994), Boutros-Ghali (1996), the Carnegie Commission on Preventing Deadly Conflict (1997), Miall et al. (1999), and Carment and Schnabel (2003). We note, however, that Anderlini and Stanski's perspectives on conflict prevention appear to be the most comprehensive, especially with regard to the necessity for in-depth work:

> No matter how poor or oppressed a society is, or how provocative and manipulative political leaders may be, communal violence does not erupt suddenly. Inevitably, it is the manifestation of accumulated aggression and hostility. In order to prevent violence, it is necessary to address the hostile mistrust and belligerence before it reaches a point where each side believes that violence is their only recourse. The goal of prevention is to create a situation in which differences and conflicts can be addressed in a non-violent and constructive manner (International Alert and Initiative for Inclusive Security 2007, 2).

Anderlini and Stanski posit that in several instances, conflict prevention efforts have been deployed to areas that have already become violent, but where an escalation in violence is imminent. For instance, the United Nations' and the United States' intervention efforts to help stop genocide in the Darfur region; or the UN deployment of peacekeeping forces to Haiti and Liberia in 2004 to help monitor the negative or fragile peace in these countries and prevent the re-emergence of violence. During such prevention measures, various international and local interveners have typically engaged in either or in both of the main types of prevention efforts identified in the literature:

> Operational prevention (or direct prevention) – measures to address immediate crises (e.g. sending high-level diplomatic missions to mediate between parties, using economic tools such as sanctions, inducements, or collecting weapons and demobilising fighting units), and employing forceful measures such as deploying peacekeepers to a region; and structural prevention (or root causes prevention) – addressing root causes

such as poverty, political repression and uneven distribution of resources, which can, if left unattended, escalate into violence (International Alert and Initiative for Inclusive Security 2007, 2).

The bulk of work and research into prevention focuses on what is known as operational, or light, prevention efforts. These kinds of efforts include crisis interventions by official or unofficial actors who can pursue a whole range of strategies from negotiation, facilitation, mediation, back-channel communication, problem-solving workshops, inducements, sanctions or even just the use of negative publicity (Ramsbotham et al. 2011, 135). Additional prevention efforts have centered on the use of military forces (typically UN peacekeepers) to interposition themselves between two parties who have begun hostilities or are escalating towards them. To date the only successful use of such preventive intervention has been in the Former Yugoslav Republic of Macedonia and, though that case is seen as largely successful, the intervention did not manage to prevent the abortive conflict there in 2001 (Väyrynen 2003).

According to Ramsbotham et al. (2011) deep or structural prevention is largely concerned with four main areas; governance, development, reducing economic inequality and the reduction of human rights abuses. Programs focused in these areas, especially those focused on governance, have a tendency to pursue top-down or government oriented strategies designed to persuade governmental officials to pursue policies which are intended ameliorate the conditions that lead to conflict. The problem with this focus is the extent to which these programs as elements of structural prevention obscure their own destabilizing effects (Ramsbotham et al. 2011, 130). Overall, deep or structural prevention is analogous to what John Burton described as conflict *provention*, the "removal of the causal conditions" for conflict, though it falls short of his requirement that such removal also contribute to "the positive promotion of environments conducive to collaborative relationships" (Burton 1990, 18).

Achieving effective conflict prevention is quite difficult, as outlined by research and experience of scholars and practitioners like Sriram (2003), Talentino (2003), Väyrynen (2003), and Hampson and Malone (2002) who have brought to light numerous challenges that are often encountered when moving conflict prevention from theory to practice. Hampson and Malone highlight these realities based on their observation that:

> Recent events underscore the fact that current strategies for conflict prevention and reduction are woefully inadequate. There is a growing consensus among practitioners and scholars alike that international responses to conflict require greater coherence, coordination and

integration as well as upstream planning and action to transform societies and to promote coexistence and economic and social development. Yet at virtually all levels—from the local to the global—there is little capacity to meet these challenges. (Hampson and Malone 2002, 229)

As we can see here, apart from preventive intervention, many activities which have been described as part of the conflict resolution canon have become increasingly described as methods for conflict prevention (Lund 2004, 122). This convergence may be regarded as a natural consequence of the diffusion of conflict resolution theory and practice, but should not yet be taken as a sign that conflict prevention theorists, practitioners, and, above all, policymakers have fully embraced the necessity for action at multiple levels of analysis and practice rather than just at the elite level. The failure of conflict prevention to address local level conflicts and issues is due partly to a lack of will, but it is also due partly to a lack of a way (Lund 2004). The rest of this chapter will attempt to address the latter question, with the hope that our proposal to use a Zones-of-Peace approach to conflict prevention will provide a way that can, at least at a local level, generate the will to engage with prevention.

The ZoPs approach to conflict prevention

If ZoPs can be an effective mechanism for conflict mitigation or the prevention of re-emerging conflicts during actual violence or post-conflict periods, then why couldn't they be used as a method of conflict prevention in situations where possible or probable tensions exist? The combination of conflict prevention efforts and the zones of peace mechanism could greatly reduce the chance of the outbreak of violent conflicts at a local level and, if widely used, could save lives and avoid the devastating human, material, and psychological costs of such conflicts. These *Conflict Prevention Zones of Peace* (*CoPZoPs*) could be established in communities perceived to be at risk. Like other ZoPs, CoPZoPs would be established by community members themselves, albeit with technical assistance and possibly material support from conflict resolution practitioners. Like other ZoPs, CoPZoPs would also provide a social and educational place where community members could develop their own capacities to be constructive human rights advocates, mediators, facilitators, and community leaders with the abilities and competences necessary to assist community members to address effectively latent and emerging conflicts before they escalate into rampant violence.

A theoretical basis for peaceful prevention

To conceptualize the CoPZoP approach, we use a theoretical lens that proposes that all conflicts have *origins*, *processes*, and *outcomes* even when the conflict is latent or only manifested through intermittent tensions (Warfield 2006). Based on this perspective, a precipitating event is not the origin of a given conflict. The origin lies, rather, in the underlying causal issues, which are framed by needs-based worldviews, values or interests that are, more often than not, unarticulated but which can become the *sotto voce* narrative or behavioral script for how the conflict is expressed once a triggering event occurs. Processes, naturally, speak to how the conflict is engaged. In general terms, parties can oppose each other in various scenarios designed to produce winners and losers, or they can engage in a range of conflict-reducing behaviors in order to end the conflict consensually. Outcomes are the products of process, representing "a confluence" of origin and process, and playing out over the short and long-term (Warfield 2006, 481). These, then, are the elements of a latent conflict and the first level of analysis that a CoPZoP approach would need to engage with in order to identify, analyze, and design a targeted intervention in order to help a community to establish and maintain a safe environment effectively to prevent the outbreak of destructive conflict.

Applicability

The main tension that would need to be addressed in any application of the CoPZoP model would be that between the necessity for grassroots ownership and control and our understanding that some form of outside assistance would be required to successfully establish and possibly maintain the zone. This tension between grassroots efforts and top-down efforts lies at the heart of both the successes and failures of other ZoPs, but may be more of a problem for our CoPZoP due to the fact that some conflict prevention skills, such as early warning and analysis skills, are typically more specialized than the basic peacebuilding and development skills used in other ZoPs. Because of the special skills needed for successful conflict prevention efforts, we recognize that a delicate balance must be struck between outsiders and locals in order to ensure that local strengths and capacities are built up through a collaborative process involving the local community, local NGOs, local institutions, and international agencies—either official or unofficial— which would provide necessary assistance, training and, at times, guidance, to support the local community's efforts. The goal of this support is to help communities to become engaged in sustaining their own social and cultural development while training them to develop conflict prevention skills that will enable them to achieve positive and stable peace in their own locales.

In addition to conflict prevention skills, pertinent peacebuilding processes that promote economic development and growth are crucial to empowering the local population, building local leadership in different social sectors, and promoting gender equality. Such processes would also aim at providing education about a wide range of topics including civic responsibility, health issues—such as HIV/AIDs prevention—sustainable agricultural processes, business management and marketing skills and, where necessary and possible, technological and information management skills. One *sine qua non* condition for a successful CoPZoP would be skill-building and training in some of the core areas of structural conflict prevention, including good governance and the rule of law, compliance with human rights, respect for minorities, a functioning economy, and the resilience to cope with competitive pressures within a structural environment. The acquisition of these skill sets would also provide the community with the ability and opportunity to share their views and concerns constructively though dialogues and established forums collaborate with leaders at different levels and contribute to the type of social transformation that leads to sustainable peace.

To ensure that the creation of a CoPZoP results in a meaningful and holistic process of change, we recommend that a multi-track diplomacy system approach be adopted (Diamond and McDonald 1996). This multi-track intervention framework highlights the various stakeholders who can come together to support the effective realization of a social change process. The framework itself is based on twelve operating principles, which ensure that each intervention is approached with respect to its particularities. The most prominent of these principles focus on relationships, emphasizing long-term commitment and partnership. Within the context of multi-track interventions, relationships matter because they help develop interactions that allow concerned stakeholders to learn about each other and build the trust necessary to undertake this delicate and challenging work. Long-term commitment matters because it takes time to achieve any type of lasting social change that can benefit an entire society. Partnership is vital because it helps develop comprehensive interventions that recognize the important contribution of different partners which is imperative to the sustainability of such efforts (Diamond and McDonald 1996). This comprehensive system approach would allow community leaders and members, supporting stakeholders, and interveners to work together to come up with a needs assessment, a feasibility study, and to develop an implementation plan to lay the foundation for the effective realization and sustainability of the CoPZoP.

A second model that informs the practice of a CoPZoP is Lederach's (1997, 39) multi-level participation model with its elite/macro, mid-level/meso, and grassroots/micro levels. Lederach's vision includes the incorporation of representation at each of these levels which, when combined with representation from as many as Diamond and McDonald's nine tracks as possible provides the inclusive and multi-level approach necessary for a comprehensive understanding of the related causal factors creating conflict tensions.[3] In addition, these frameworks, illuminated by the focus on relationships, long-term commitments, and trust-building allow for a rich environment to generate the ideas, options, and consensually-agreed solutions necessary to transform threatened communities into constructive and sustainable CoPZoPs.

A model approach for a CoPZoP

An approach to put a CoPZoP into practice would require the early identification of rising tensions by scholar-practitioners, who would then carry out a needs analysis and a feasibility study while working with local community representatives. The goal of these stages would be to assess the latent conflict situation, identifying the existing potential causes of conflict sources and dynamics as well as potential triggers which could lead to violence.

As illustrated in Figure 2.1, beginning with the needs analysis, such scholar-practitioners would continue to work with other peacebuilding experts to

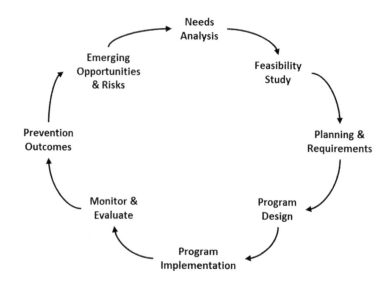

Figure 2.1 CoPZoP Framework.

help the community devise their CoPZoP, including planning requirements, program design, program implementation, monitoring, and evaluation of the implementation, conflict prevention outcomes, and any emerging opportunities and risks. This process would be dynamic and would take into account areas that become obsolete or need adjustments.

As a part of our preliminary proposal for the CoPZoP, we will illustrate the first two stages of our dynamic framework based on an analysis undertaken in the community of Dajabon, which lies in the Dominican Republic and near the border with Haiti, in 2005. That research was undertaken by Warfield and three Masters students from George Mason's Institute for Conflict Analysis and Resolution and was carried out to examine the then current state of Dominican and Haitian immigrant relations and cultural identities.[4] We recognize that the historical relationship between Haiti and the Dominican Republic is complex and fraught with tensions, but, for the sake of brevity, we will not delve into it extensively here. Instead, we will focus on Warfield's (2006) conception of all conflicts as having origins, processes, and outcomes as discussed above.

Dajabon is located in the north-western part of the Dominican Republic and has a population of approximately 25,600. Just across the border lies the Haitian city of Ouanaminthe, whose sizeable population of Dominicans intermingle with the Haitians there as well as interact daily with Dominicans in Dajabon. These interactions create interdependence between the two peoples and serve as both a possible source of tension and a potential site for the creation of a CoPZoP.

In this respect, border communities become natural settings to study the potential for peace zones and to explore the dialogic processes that might encourage this potential. From our work in Dajabon, we may be able to determine which conflict prevention processes could possibly be exported to other border locales experiencing similar forms of tension and conflict.

The needs analysis

The goal of the needs analysis is to establish whether or not there is sufficient justification to establish a CoPZoP. In order to do this the analysts will need to examine the origins and processes of the situation using established indicators to see if there are any early warning signs of latent conflicts. They then should evaluate these signs in order to set priorities for urgent action and determine whether, where, and how a CoPZoP might make use of the best available resources and have the greatest impact on addressing the most urgent risks of violence.

When looking at the Dajabon situation it is important to understand that history plays a major role in the formation of the Dominican/Haitian immigrant conflict and emphasizes the idea that origins derive from social constructions, which then contribute to the conceptualization of polarized identities expressed by both communities (Maringet al. 2005; Watkins and Mohr 2001). Identity polarization is arguable felt most strongly by Dominicans, many of whom consider themselves Spanish, despite having range of skin coloring that extends to the darker end of the spectrum. And even where there is some ambiguity about this ancestral claim, Dominicans often adamantly deny they are of African descent (Howard 2001).

Looking at underlying processes, we can determine that while neither country can be called a bastion of economic and political stability, the Dominican Republic has fared comparatively better than its neighbor. Since the early 1900s, poor Haitians have migrated to the Dominican Republic as seasonal workers and labored in sugar cane plantations (Martinez 1999). Some of these immigrants never returned to Haiti and with the spiraling poverty and instability in that country during the last few decades, they were joined by a significant number of undocumented immigrants who entered through the porous border in order to secure work during the Dominican Republic's economic recovery (Gavigan 1997). As a result of this influx the Dominican Republic has attempted to rid the country of undocumented Haitians whenever they create social problems or their numbers reach 'undesirable' levels (Roebling 2007).

In border cities such as Dajabon, both peoples often manage to coexist, although contentious dynamics can result from their acrimonious past and present cultural differences. In the past few years news regarding the treatment of Haitians in the Dominican Republic and, in particular, the drive for citizenship by Dominican-born children of Haitian descent, have led to an increase in tensions and dynamic interchanges (Minority Rights Group International 2005). Additionally, other negative propaganda have led to an increase in Haitian–Dominican tensions, especially in Dajabon and at the border near Ouanaminthe (Deparle 2007; Jimenez 2008).

Returning to our definition of a ZoP as a social space where individuals are protected against personal violability based on agreed rules of public order, we believe that the region surrounding Dajabon and Ouanaminthe could serve as test case for a Zone of Peace that could address rising tensions in the area as well as create a safe space for social, cultural, and economic development. Rising local and nationwide tensions indicate that there is a need for some form of intervention, and the high level of local interaction between the two groups, coupled with social, cultural, and economic needs, indicates that a

CoPZoP may be an effective form for conflict prevention, peacebuilding, and development to meet local needs.

Proposed feasibility study

Any feasibility study for the creation of a CoPZoP would need to determine whether a number of crucial factors were present, or how to create missing factors. In addition it would need to answer a number of specific questions about local resources, processes, and links to the national and international levels. To begin with, the study should determine whether or not viable leadership exists at various levels of society. This is absolutely necessary because of the grassroots orientation of peace zones and the requirement that any ZoP, especially a CoPZoP, would need to be fully integrated into and largely managed by locals. Examples from Bosnia, the Philippine, and Aceh show that comprehensive and longer-lasting peace zones only succeed with local control (Iyer and Mitchell 2007; Mitchell 2007).

The next stage of the feasibility study is to complete a conflict analysis assessment, taking into account aspects pertinent to the community and the country as a whole. This would include specific issues that could lead to violence and would be based on a comprehensive conflict mapping framework.[5] The analysis would provide a detailed perspective of trends affecting structural, sub-structural, and relational issues as well as other factors that could impact the creation of a CoPZoP in the short, medium, or long term. It would also provide information about areas that need to be strengthened through training, education, conflict resolution practices, peacebuilding activities, civic capacity-building, and other development-oriented efforts.

The main questions that a CoPZoP feasibility study would be required to answer include:

- What processes need to be put into place to assist with conflict prevention efforts over the short, medium, and long terms?

- What indicators would constitute a basis for sustainable peace among community members?

- Who are the community leaders and opinion-makers whose support and buy-in will be necessary for the success of a CoPZoP?

- Which stakeholders and organizations will need to collaborate with the community, and its leaders, in order to facilitate the conceptualization, creation, and implementation of the CoPZoP? How can these groups participate in a manner designed to increase the effectiveness and longevity of the CoPZoP?

- What roles do local and national governmental leaders need to play in order to effectively realize the CoPZoP and contribute to its successful implementation and sustainability?

- What kind of support and awareness are needed within the community in order to promote an environment of solidarity, engagement, and commitment while creating the conditions for all stakeholders and community members to support the effectiveness and sustainability of the CoPZoP?

- What kinds of skill-building activities will be required to help community members learn how to achieve and maintain peace?

- What actions need to be taken to ensure the peaceful coexistence within the CoPZoP while helping community members create and engage in peacebuilding activities that benefit the stability of the entire community?

- What kinds of assistance will the communities and their leaders need in order to create the conditions that ensure a peaceful environment within the CoPZoP?

The feasibility study would then be shared with relevant stakeholders and community members based on a participatory format that invites input, refinements, and adjustments to promote and ensure ownership by all community members. The study, once accepted by the community, would provide the basis for further discussions and actions to move the CoPZoP initiative forward.

Applying these concepts to the situation in Dajabon and Ouanaminthe, we find that some of the tasks required for a formal feasibility study have been completed but others still need to be done. Following the work done by Warfield's research team, initial contacts were opened by Jennings, who found great interest in the establishment of a ZoP in Dajabon. Discussions with a few stakeholders working with communities at the border between Dajabon and Ouanaminthe confirmed the perceived benefits that communities could draw from this initiative.

During that time Jennings proposed that an exploratory action research project would be initiated by members of ICAR in order to determine 1) what would constitute a strong basis for sustainable peace among the two peoples; 2) how would the CoPZoP help Haitians and Dominicans in Dajabon and Ouanaminthe build better relations; 3) who would take the lead in designing, developing, implementing, coordinating, and evaluating various aspects pertinent to the CoPZoP; 4) how would the two peoples ensure the CoPZoP's sustainability or undertake needed changes; 5) what issues, actors or forces could hinder the CoPZoP's creation and sustainability; and 6) how would the CoPZoP's members address and/or marginalize spoilers.

Moving forward, members of ICAR planned to develop these first steps into an action-research project proposal, which would then be shared—and hopefully discussed—with key local governmental officials in Dajabon, the religious community, local NGOs, and the community representatives of national and international NGOs as well as their Haitian counterparts in Ouanaminthe. If these discussions were to be successful, we expected that a formal feasibility study would be implemented as a part of the action research project and the first step towards realizing the CoPZoPs model would begin to be taken.

Unfortunately, steps for the proposed action-research projects with communities in the two border towns, Dajabon and Ouamaminthe, have encountered a number of unforeseen delays, chief among them the 2010 Haitan earthquake, which devastated that part of the island and resulted in the loss of many Haitan lives. Although unfortunate, this tragic natural disaster has also revealed, that indeed, Dominicans and Haitians have the potential to come together and collaborate. Therefore, as a next step, ICAR will seek to carry out an update of the previous needs assessment, taking into account the latest development in the relationships between the two peoples in Dajabon and Ouamaminthe.

Conclusion

Overall there are different scenarios which might take place in any community facing rising tensions and an awareness of the possibility of future conflict. The first of these would be that the community would take no action and continue with the status quo in the hopes that tensions do not rise to the level of outright violence. This is typically not recommended, particularly in areas that have already experienced violent conflict in one form or another, as has Haiti, because of the predilection for cultures of violence to take root where cultures of peace are not specifically planted.

A second plausible outcome, particularly when faced with latent or emergent conflicts, is for locals to call upon the central government to address the problem, in effect passing the buck upwards. As has been noted elsewhere, the difficulty with leaving decision-making in the hands of national elites is the danger that local interests, and especially local knowledge and contacts, will be sidelined as national elites continue to "reinvent the wheel" in a search not only for some solution that will work, but a solution that serves their political interests first and local needs second.

The third possible outcome is one that we recognize may be less plausible at this point in history but it is one that we believe holds the most promise for addressing both the operational and structural elements of conflict prevention and combining them with well-established forms of peacebuilding and development. This option is, of course, the adoption of our proposed Conflict Prevention Zone of Peace that will meet the communities' needs for positive peace and development while building their local capacities and ensuring that locals are able to take ownership of the process and reap the benefits in order to prevent the emergence of violent conflicts.

Before concluding, we need to return to a key elemental difference between our proposed CoPZoP and existing local ZoPs as discussed by Mitchell and Hancock (2007). This key difference is the general necessity for some sort of complementarity between local groups and national or international authorities. As previously described in *Zones of Peace* (2007) and discussed throughout this volume, one of the more delicate issues that any ZoP faces is the tension between the need for grassroots ownership and the perception, or reality, that such ownership might run afoul of national prerogatives or be seen as a threat to national sovereignty.

This tension between the bottom-up and top-down is even more important to address in the CoPZoP model because of the preventive aim of the zones. Unlike the local ZoPs model, the CoPZoP model envisions involvement by stakeholders at multiple levels, particularly at the national governmental level. In addition, many of the preventive practices, particularly the early warning and analysis practices, will need to be undertaken by internationals; at least until local members can be trained to undertake the tasks themselves. This involvement of 'outsiders' in the creation of the CoPZoP means that leadership functions, funding issues, and reporting responsibilities will need to be clearly delineated to ensure that neither resources are wasted, nor local ownership and control diluted to the extent that locals abandon the effort. Given the importance of local efforts in sustaining any zone of peace, we feel that these elements, and possibly others, need to be addressed during the conceptual stage and that inter-level processes and agreements need to be made during the creation of the CoPZoP.

In conclusion, while this theoretical and conceptual approach is in its infancy, and more research and application need to be undertaken before implementation, we feel that the blending of conflict prevention efforts and the local zones of peace model into a CoPZoP approach holds promise for addressing and preventing violence in tense areas like those of Dajabon and Ouanaminthe. We look forward to continuing this research and, hopefully, fulfilling the promise of peace made largely by, and for, regions like these.

Notes

1 For more detail, see Hancock in this volume and Hancock and Mitchell (2007).

2 "The Coordinadora Del Bajo Lempa is a grassroots movement in El Salvador representing approximately 35,000 low-income rural farmers and fishers. This democratic, representative organization works to provide long-term solutions to the problems that its members face." Retrieved, October 17, 2008, http://fssca.net/coordinadora/index.html.

3 Although not explained in depth here, the multi-track framework envisions working towards peace through one or more of nine possible tracks: government; professional conflict resolution; business; private citizen; research, training and education; activism; religious; funding; and public opinion/communication (Diamond and McDonald 1996, 4–5).

4 The three MS students, Clayton Maring, Elizabeth Neal and Danielle Picariello, conducted one week of field research under the guidance of Dr Warfield as a part of their practicum requirements at ICAR.

5 There are multiple possible frameworks one could use, including Sandole (2003), Dugan (1996), Himes (1980), and Mitchell (1981).

Works cited

Ackermann, Alice. 2003. "The Idea and Practice of Conflict Prevention." *Journal of Peace Research* 40 (3): 339.

Boutros-Ghali, Boutros. 1996. "Challenges of Preventive Diplomacy: The Role of the United Nations and its Secretary-General." In *Preventive diplomacy: stopping wars before they start*, edited by K. M. Cahill. New York: BasicBooks and the Center for International Health and Cooperation.

Burton, John. 1990. *Conflict: resolution and provention*. 4 vols. Vol. 1, *The Conflict Series*. New York: St. Martin's Press.

Carment, David, and Albrecht Schnabel. 2003. "Introduction – Conflict Prevention: A Concept in Search of a Policy." In *Conflict prevention: path to peace or grand illusion?*, edited by D. Carment and A. Schnabel. Tokyo, New York: United Nations University Press.

Carnegie Commission on Preventing Deadly Conflict. 1997. *Preventing deadly conflict: final report with executive summary*. Washington, DC: The Commission.

Chupp, Mark. 2003. "Creating a Culture of Peace in Postwar El Salvador." In *Positive approaches in peacebuilding: a resource for innovators*, edited by C. Sampson, M. Abu-Nimer and C. Liebler. Washington, DC: Pact Publications.

Deparle, Jason. 2007. "A global Trek to Poor Nations, From Poorer Ones." *International Herald Tribune*, Dec. 27.

Diamond, Louise, and John W. McDonald. 1996. *Multi-track diplomacy: a systems approach to peace*. 3rd edn, *Kumarian press books for a world that works*. West Hartford, CT: Kumarian Press.

Dugan, Máire. 1996. "A Nested Theory of Conflict." *Leadership Journal* 1 (July): 9–20.

Gavigan, Patrick. 1997. "Migration Emergencies and Human Rights in Haiti." In *Conference on regional responses to forced migration in Central America and the Caribbean*, edited by S. f. L. A. Organization of American States. Washington, DC.

Hampson, Fen Osler, and David Malone, eds. 2002. *From reaction to conflict prevention: opportunities for the UN system*. Boulder, CO: Lynne Rienner Publishers.

Hancock, Landon E. 2007. "El Salvador's Post-conflict Peace Zone." In *Zones of peace*, edited by L. E. Hancock and C. R. Mitchell. Bloomfield, CT: Kumarian Press.

Hancock, Landon E., and Pushpa Iyer. 2007. "The Nature, Structure and Variety of 'Peace Zones'." In *Zones of peace*, edited by L. E. Hancock and C. R. Mitchell. Bloomfield, CT: Kumarian Press.

Hancock, Landon E., and C. R. Mitchell, eds. 2007. *Zones of peace*. Bloomfield, CT: Kumarian Press.

Himes, Joseph S. 1980. *Conflict and conflict management*. Athens, GA: University of Georgia Press.

Howard, David. 2001. *Coloring the nation: race and ethnicity in the Dominican Republic*. Oxford, Boulder, CO: Signal Books, L. Rienner Publishers.

International Alert and Initiative for Inclusive Security. 2007. *Inclusive security, sustainable peace: a toolkit for advocacy and action*. London, Washington, DC: International Alert, Initiative for Inclusive Society

Iyer, Pushpa, and Christopher R. Mitchell. 2007. "The Collapse of Peace Zones in Aceh." In *Zones of peace*, edited by L. E. Hancock and C. R. Mitchell. Bloomfield, CT: Kumarian Press.

Jimenez, Manuel. 2008. "Dominican Army on Alert on Tense Haitian Border." *Reuters Foundation, Alert Net*, Feb 17.

Lederach, John Paul. 1997. *Building peace: sustainable reconciliation in divided societies*. Washington DC: United States Institute for Peace.

Lund, Michael. 1998. "Preventing Violent Conflict: Progress and Shortfall." In *Contributing to preventive action*, edited by P. Cross, Berlin: Conflict Prevention Network.

— 2000. "Preventing and Mitigating Violent Conflicts: A Revised Guide for Practitioners." In *Thesaurus and glossary of early warning and conflict prevention terms*, edited by A. P. Schmid and S. N. Anderlini. Rotterdam, London: Synthesis Foundation and Forum on Early Warning and Early Response.

— 2002. "Preventing Violent Intrastate Conflicts: Learning Lessons from Experience." In *Searching for peace in Europe and Eurasia: an overview of conflict prevention and peacebuilding activities*, edited by P. v. Tongeren, H. v. d. Veen and J. Verhoeven. Boulder, CO, London: Lynne Rienner Publishers, Forum on Early Warning and Early Response.

— 2004. "Operationalizing the Lessons from Recent Experience in Field-Level Conflict Prevention Strategies." In *Facing ethnic conflicts: toward a new realism*, edited by A. Wimmer. Lanham, MD: Rowman & Littlefield.

Maring, Clayton, Elizabeth Neal, and Danielle Picariello. 2005. "*Against each other's backs: a study of Dominicans, Haitians and race relations.*" Arlington, VA: Institute for Conflict Analysis and Resolution.

Marshall, Monty G., Ted Robert Gurr, and University of Maryland (College Park Md.). Center for International Development and Conflict Management. 2005. *Peace and conflict 2005: a global survey of armed conflicts, self-determination movements, and democracy.* College Park, Md.: Center for International Development & Conflict Management.

Martinez, Samuel. 1999. "From Hidden Hand to Heavy Hand: Sugar, the State, and Migrant Labor in Haiti and the Dominican Republic." *Latin American Research Review* 34 (1): 57.

Miall, Hugh, Oliver Ramsbotham, and Tom Woodhouse. 1999. *Contemporary conflict resolution: the prevention, management and transformation of deadly conflicts.* Cambridge, UK, Malden, MA: Polity Press, Blackwell.

Minority Rights Group International. 2011. *Directory of migrants: Haitians in the Dominican Republic* [Web Page] 2005 [cited June 26, 2011]. Available from http://www.minorityrights.org/2561/dominican-republic/haitians.html.

Mitchell, Christopher R. 1981. *The structure of international conflict.* New York: St. Martin's Press.

— 2007. "Comparing Sanctuary in the Former Yugoslavia and the Philippines." In *Zones of peace*, edited by L. E. Hancock and C. R. Mitchell. Bloomfield, CT: Kumarian Press.

Mitchell, Christopher R., and Landon E. Hancock. 2007. "Local Zones of Peace and a Theory of Sanctuary." In *Zones of peace*, edited by L. E. Hancock and C. R. Mitchell. Bloomfield, CT: Kumarian Press.

Munuera, Gabriel. 1994. "Preventing Armed Conflict in Europe: Lessons from Recent Experience." In *Challiot papers 15/16.* Alençon, France: Western European Union.

Project Ploughshares. 2000. *The G8 and conflict prevention: turning declarations into action* [Web Page]. Project Ploughshares 2000 [cited October 17, 2008]. Available from http://www.ploughshares.ca/content/g8-and-conflict-prevention-turning-declarations-action.

Ramsbotham, Oliver, Hugh Miall, and Tom Woodhouse. 2011. *Contemporary conflict resolution: the prevention, management and transformation of deadly conflicts.* 3rd edn. Cambridge, UK, Malden, MA: Polity.

Roebling, Elizabeth James. 2007. *Neighbours, but not friends.* Inter Press Service, June 20, 2007 [cited Sept 2, 2008].

Rojas, Catalina. 2007. "Islands in the Stream." In *Zones of peace*, edited by L. E. Hancock and C. R. Mitchell. Bloomfield, CT: Kumarian Press.

Rupesinghe, Kumar. 1995. "Non-governmental Organizations and the 'Agenda for Peace'." *Ecumenical Review* 47 (3): 324.

Sandole, Dennis. 2003. "Typology." In *Conflict: from analysis to intervention*, edited by S. Cheldelin, D. Druckman and L. A. Fast, London: New York: Continuum.

Sriram, Chandra Lekha. 2003. "Insights from Cases: Opportunities and Challenges for Preventive Action." In *From promise to practice: strengthening UN capacities for the prevention of violent conflict*, edited by C. L. Sriram and K. Wermester. Boulder, CO: Lynne Rienner Publishers.

Talentino, Andrea. 2003. "Evaluating Success and Failure: Conflict Prevention in Cambodia and Bosnia." In *Conflict prevention: path to peace or grand illusion?*, edited by D. Carment and A. Schnabel. Tokyo, New York: United Nations University Press.

UN General Assembly, 60th Session, and Agenda Item 12. 2006. "Progress report on the prevention of armed conflict: Report of the Secretary-General." Document A/60/891. New York: United Nations.

van de Goor, Luc, and Suzanne Verstegen. 2004. "'Mainstreaming' Conflict Prevention Policies of Third Party Actors: Building In-house Capacity for Preventive Action." In *Conflict prevention from rhetoric to reality: opportunities and innovations*, edited by D. Carment and A. Schnabel. Lanham, MD: Lexington Books.

Väyrynen, Tarja. 2003. "Challenges to Preventive Action: The Cases of Kosovo and Macedonia." In *Conflict prevention: path to peace or grand illusion?*, edited by D. Carment and A. Schnabel. Tokyo, New York: United Nations University Press.

Wallensteen, Peter. 2001. *Conflict prevention through development co-operation: an inventory of recent research findings – with implications for international development co-operation, Research report*. Uppsala, Sweden: Department of Peace and Conflict Research, Uppsala University.

Wallensteen, Peter, and Jacob Bercovitch, eds. 1998. *Preventing violent conflicts: past record and future challenges, Report no. 48*. Uppsala, Sweden: Department of Peace and Conflict Research, Uppsala University.

Wallensteen, Peter, and Frida Möller. 2003. *Conflict prevention: methodology for knowing the unknown, Uppsala peace research papers*. Uppsala, Sweden: Department of Peace and Conflict Research, Uppsala University.

Warfield, Wallace. 2006. "Managing Racial/Ethnic Conflict for Community Building." In *The SAGE handbook of conflict communication: integrating theory, research, and practice*, edited by J. G. Oetzel and S. Ting-Toomey. Thousand Oaks, San Francisco, CA: Sage Publications, Jossey-Bass/Pfeiffer.

Watkins, Jane Magruder, and Bernard J. Mohr. 2001. *Appreciative inquiry: change at the speed of imagination*, edited by B. J. Mohr. San Francisco, CA: Jossey-Bass/Pfeiffer.

Woodhouse, Tom. 1999. "Preventive medicine: can conflicts be prevented?" *British Medical Journal (International Edition)* 319: 396.

3

Against the stream: Colombian zones of peace under democratic security

Christopher Mitchell and Catalina Rojas[1]

Introduction

The 1990s were a decade of considerable activism for peacemaking and peacebuilding efforts in Colombia, although it might well be argued that the multi-level search for peace had its roots in the period 1987–9 as a reaction against the increased violence and particularly the number of kidnappings that characterized those years. Both at the formal governmental level and especially at the level of civil society there was an active seeking for peace through a variety of sustained activities. These grew in number during the decade and peaked in the last years of the 1990s. They all reflected a widespread feeling among many Colombians that the time had come to put an end, finally, to the struggle between the Colombian state and the guerrillas of FARC–EP and the ELN. If peace had been achieved earlier with the cadres of the M-19, with Quintin Lame and with at least some parts of the EPL, why could not a similar process be put in place to end the violence in the countryside and in peripheral regions of the country, and a durable peace finally constructed for the long suffering peoples of Colombia?

Civil society and peace movements

At the level of civil society, the whole period from 1988 to 1998 saw a huge mobilization of efforts at national, regional, and local levels—peace marches, peace forums, and the founding of pro-peace and pro-democracy organizations— all helping to push the country down the path towards a general peace. Early initiatives included the first countrywide *Semana por la Paz* in September 1988, thereafter established as an annual event. In 1991 more than 30 peace organizations combined to launch a pro-peace campaign under the title of "*Viva la Ciudadanía.*" While the early 1990s saw a great deal of grassroots activities starting up regionally and in the countryside, the best publicized pro-peace initiatives took place in the cities and particularly in Colombia's capital, Bogotá. The most obvious civil society mobilizations thus took place at the national level, such as the "Children's Movement for Peace" organized in 1996 by the Bogotá based NGO, REDEPAZ.[2] A year later REDEPAZ also organized the Citizens' Mandate for Peace as part of the election process, garnering over 10 million votes for peace cast as part of the October 1997 elections. Two tendencies reinforced civil society mobilization at this national level. The first was the tendency for events to lead on to permanent organizations, as when the November 1996 International Day Against Violence against Women led to the foundation of the *Ruta Pacífica de las Mujeres para la Paz*. The second was the tendency for a consolidation of smaller movements and institutions into larger networks and organizations, one result of which was the 1998 establishment of the umbrella organization *Asamblea Permanente de la Sociedad Civil para la Paz*, which brought together peace and human rights organizations, plus a variety of socio-economic "sectors," as well as regional groupings from across the country.

Not surprisingly, regional institutions pushing for peace tended to develop first and most strongly in those areas—Urabá, Magdalena Medio, Putumayo— which were most affected by violence and—in the early 1990s—by drug trafficking. Thus, 1991 saw campaigns for peace and negotiation or against terrorism start up in Urabá, around Cali and in the Valle de Cauca, as well as in the *departamentos* of the Atlantic coast. Medellín was also a center of growth for civil society peace initiatives, starting with the "Medellín in Peace" campaign in 1990 and the "Day of Active Neutrality" in July 1996, which brought together a large number of NGOs in Antioquia, including some representing indigenous peoples and IDPs as well as representatives of local peace communities and peace zones throughout the department.

This last group of local level, grassroots civil society institutions also began to flourish and develop during the 1990s and became one of the most dynamic and innovative forms of peacebuilding in Colombia, especially during the Pastrana years. The idea of local peace communities—local communities ranging from small *veredas* or *corregimientos* (hamlets) to complete *municipios*—taking the initiative in declaring themselves zones free from violence, neutral in the struggle between guerrillas, paramilitaries, and state security forces, off limits to recruitment and information gathering, and able themselves to carry out needed socio-political reforms—had taken roots in a few parts of Colombia in the 1980s, partly inspired by ideas gained through connections with similar peace communities in the Philippines.[3] The best known of these originated in 1987 in a remote *corregimiento* in the Department of Santander known as La India, which rapidly generated local support from the region surrounding the River Carare to become the *Asociación de Trabajadores Campesinos del Carare* (ATCC). The ATCC survived both verbal and physical attacks by all of the armed combatants in the region, including the assassination of its main leader, Josué Vargas, by local paramilitaries. The community was awarded both the Alternative Nobel Peace Prize and the Right Livelihood Award in 1990. Together with the peace communities of Mogotes (in Santander) and San José de Apartadó (in Urabá), both founded in 1997, and Samaniego (in Nariño), founded in 1998, ATCC demonstrated that local peacebuilding based on withdrawal and neutrality could be a possibility, even amid continuing high levels of violence.

The idea that peace might be built locally as well as nationally and regionally really began to take hold in the last years of the decade, with support from local Church organizations, such as the Jesuits' *Justicia y Paz*, and of civil society organizations such as CINEP and of some Colombian universities. In 1998, following its work on the Citizens Mandate for Peace, REDEPAZ launched its project intended to establish 100 "municipalities of peace" throughout the country, using European Union funding as a base and Mogotes (Santander) as a model. Largely through vigorous and dedicated efforts by REDEPAZ at the center and by other local and regional organizations—efforts which included visits, publicity, conferences, trainings, but above all encouraging local communities to develop organizations based on their own needs—this and related projects focused on local peacebuilding flourished during the last years of the 1990s and the first years of the 2000s. Against a parallel national background of tentative political negotiations, more than 100 local peace "*experiencias*" were established between 1998 and 2002, in spite of frequent efforts to undermine them by locally based combatants.

Political peacemaking in the 1990s

In the national political sphere, the successes in demobilizing and integrating back into society at least some of the insurgent groups, plus the successful reform of the Colombian constitution in 1991, gave rise to hopes that the decade might usher in a time of genuine and sustained peace. At least, there might be a start of negotiations that would end the long drawn out guerrilla struggle that continued to be fought out both in Colombia's major cities and more particularly in remote regions of the country where state authority—and even presence—was minimal. These hopes remained high even after the increase of guerrilla activity after 1991 and the declaration of the "integral war" against guerrillas and drug cartels by President Cesar Gaviria's administration (1990–4). However, they were inevitably dampened by the charges of corruption, the linkages with drug lords and the overall "governability crisis" that afflicted the subsequent administration of President Ernesto Samper—(1994–8). By the middle of the decade, it seemed that many of the opportunities arising from the adoption of the new 1991 Constitution had been missed, and the scandals that dogged Samper's administration prevented any serious efforts to seek the peace that had seemed tantalizingly on the horizon. The closely fought election in 1998 of the Conservative party's candidate, Andrés Pastrana, for the next four-year presidential term, seemed to present the promise of a real chance for peace. Pastrana had campaigned on a "peace platform" and had promised to use his best efforts to start a negotiated peace processes with the insurgent movements, even meeting with some of their leaders before he was due to take up his office formally.

Once in office, Pastrana indeed worked seriously and continuously to bring about a negotiated end to the long-drawn-out conflict, agreeing to FARC's demand for a large piece of safe territory as a *zona de distención* (demilitarized zone) within which negotiations could take place, restraining military—although not paramilitary—operations and meeting personally with the late FARC leader, Manuel Marulanda Vélez. At the same time he initiated preliminary talks in Havana with the ELN, but faced the frustrating consequence that the ELN too demanded a similar safe zone to the "FARC zone" which had been set up around San Vicente del Caguán.

Even more frustratingly, the negotiations with the FARC, which were never going to be easy, proved even more difficult, delayed, and unproductive than had been feared at their outset in 1999; especially as FARC units appeared unwilling or unable to exercise what could have been regarded by the government as acceptably reciprocal restraint. The final straw occurred in early 2002, when the FARC hijacked an airliner and kidnapped many of the important passengers thereon, an act which led Pastrana to call off the peace talks, declare an end to the *zona* and resume full scale military operations against the insurgents.

The failure of the Pastrana peace talks in early 2002 and the accompanying and widespread disillusion among advocates for a peacefully negotiated settlement had a major effect on the elections that year which brought to power a President determined to pursue a radically different approach to achieving peace. Alvaro Uribe made no secret of his disbelief in any kind of negotiations with insurgents, apart from those arising from a position of dominance. He announced—and proceeded to pursue—a strategy known as "Democratic Security" as a means of providing—among other things—a platform for successfully bringing the insurgent conflicts to an end in the long term. This strategy inevitably would have a major impact on the local peace communities, which had been formally discouraged but actually tolerated—or at least not specifically targeted—during the Pastrana years. Democratic Security was to create a completely different environment for local peacebuilding initiatives.

The nature of democratic security

President Uribe formally came into office in August 2002 and, perhaps prompted by the FARC's Inauguration Day mortar attack on the presidential palace which left 15 civilians dead, at once declared a "state of internal commotion" that would enable him to carry out the measures he deemed necessary to restore security and "law and order" throughout the country. Uribe's overall security policy was based partly on increasing the size and effectiveness of the Colombian military and police forces in order to restore (and, in many areas, to initiate for the first time) a strong state presence throughout Colombia; and also to batter the guerrillas into a condition whereby they would abandon the military struggle and sue for a peace, the terms of which would then be dictated by the government.[4]

The other major part of the Uribe policy was to involve civil society in the provision of local security through a series of measures additionally intended to involve local individuals and institutions in the prosecution of the conflict. They were all to be firmly and obviously on the side of the state and the national security forces. This aspect of the government's overall policy was given the name of "Democratic Security." The name implied not only that security would be *provided* for all Colombian citizens wherever they might be, but that the citizens themselves would be expected to *contribute* to their own security and safety by unambiguously assisting the state security forces.[5] This was officially described as "more actively engaging the civilian population" and aiming "to shift collaboration and support from illegal groups to legitimate forces," with the somewhat ominous implication that at least some of this civilian population were viewed—unambiguously—as being collaborators with these illegal groups.[6] This mindset—that you were either for or inevitably against the state—became fairly general, not merely among state agents but also within much of the civilian population.

Specifically, and focusing on civilian involvement, the strategy of Democratic Security involved establishing:

1   Military or police posts in every municipality throughout the country, especially in those regions where even a minimal state presence had previously been lacking;

2   A local force of armed "peasant soldiers"—eventually aiming at over 20,000 participants—who would take over many of the protective functions previously lacking in many parts of the country and thus freeing up regular military forces for active counter-insurgency operations[7];

3   A network of local "informants" who would be paid to supply information and intelligence about criminal, insurgent, and paramilitary activities. This was described as being an aspect of "the voluntary and patriotic cooperation of Colombian citizens in performing their constitutional duties and . . . in demonstrating the *solidarity* demanded by the modern social democratic state to help prevent crime and terrorism" (Colombia 2003, 57 emphasis added);

4   A strengthened judicial system and speeded up judicial processes so that the system could take action against "crimes of high social impact" (Colombia 2003, 57). If necessary, it was announced, "Articles in the Constitution will be amended without affecting civil rights and liberties . . . enabling the State to pursue individuals, such as terrorists and illegal drugs traffickers, who represent the greatest danger to society and democracy" (Colombia 2003, 35–6).

These measures were to be accompanied by a large increase of military expenditure, together with an expansion and reorganization of the Colombian military, preparatory to a series of major offensives against "illegal groups." These were to be aimed at reasserting state control over guerrilla dominated territory, and especially over the national road system.[8] In addition, the Uribe administration pledged itself to a major effort to demobilize illegal groups. In the event, this led to a process whereby the notoriously violent paramilitary forces, which had become repressive surrogates for the Colombian military in many regions and since 1997 had been loosely organized under the umbrella of the *Autodefensas Unidas de Colombia* (AUC), began what many have claimed was a seriously flawed process of disarmament, demobilization, and reintegration (DDR).[9]

Even in its theoretical stage, the espousal of Democratic Security raised some concerns about its possible impact throughout Colombia on human rights, civil liberties, and the rule of law. However, the overall mood in the country in 2002 was such that concerns about security and the restoration of law and order were paramount and Democratic Security appeared to promise a way of dealing with the security issues facing the country following the collapse of the Pastrana peace initiative. However, as the strategy was implemented, it became apparent that many of the initial concerns were justified. As early as 2003, one analyst was cautiously pointing to the strategy's (over)emphasis on the military aspects of the overall policy and to the fact that the strengthening of the government's coercive powers (detention of civilians for several days, searches without warrants, interception of communications) plus the deliberate weakening of governmental institutions protecting human rights (for example, the Ombudsman's office)—might—or might not—result in increased security, but only at the price of restricting human rights (Mason 2003, 398–402).

Moreover, as the implications of Democratic Security revealed themselves at a national level, it became more and more evident that its provisions were not simply being employed against illegal armed groups but also against Colombia's non-violent opposition and against any civil society individuals and organizations (labor leaders, human rights organizations, journalists, opposition political parties, peace organizations) that were deemed to be critical of the government and its policies. Attitudes of many members of the Uribe government—including the President himself—seemed increasingly to be, "If you are not wholly and wholeheartedly for us, then you are against us—and will be treated accordingly."

Publicly, the government's frequent response to any criticism took the form of denying that the country was facing an internal, "civil conflict" but that it was simply confronting a criminal or a terrorist threat. This reframing enabled the state to adopt extreme measures to deal with "criminals" within a brutal "law and order" framework. The argument became more frequent following the US government's panicked declaration of the "global war on terror" after the events of September 2001 and it conveniently did away with the need to be concerned about international humanitarian or human rights law as applicable within Colombia.

Against such a background, local communities that had attempted to withdraw from the violent struggle between the Colombian state and the leftist insurgents and somehow to declare themselves "neutral" found themselves facing even more problems than before. Several of the peace communities, especially in those parts of the country where the Colombian military and its paramilitary allies were fighting to reassert state control (or take over valuable local assets), found themselves facing even higher levels of violence than before. As the purely military part of the Democratic Security strategy unfolded—Plan Patriota in the south, for example—and the state attempted to re-establish control over areas it had previously left under the control of guerrilla units, more and more rural communities became embroiled in extreme levels of conflict, which placed even greater strains on their efforts to remain outside the struggle.

Moreover, in many parts of the country, the ambiguous effects of paramilitary "demobilization" had to be dealt with. Thus, in almost all regions of the country, the drive to establish the state presence in each *municipio* through setting up police posts and military bases—some of which inevitably became likely targets for guerrilla attacks—challenged local aspirations to stay out of the violence, as did the recruitment and training of local people to become "peasant soldiers." As a background to all this was the drumbeat of constant criticism and attacks from government spokespersons about the impossibility—and immorality—of remaining neutral in the struggle against illegal and violent narco-guerrillas or narco-terrorists—attacks that were an inevitable accompaniment of a strategy that sought to involve the whole of civil society on the government side of what was still—in spite of denials and efforts to reframe it—a civil war.[10]

Even worse was the growing tendency of government members and spokesmen to imply—or even assert openly—that the peace communities and their supporting organizations were simply fronts for the guerrillas and could thus be treated not simply as guerrilla sympathizers or supporters (bad enough) but as covert guerrillas whom the security forces could treat accordingly.

It is with this increasingly hostile background in mind that we turn to a brief description of the recent histories of four Colombian peace communities, most of which were the subject of previous analyses carried out as part of the Institute's "Local Zones of Peace" project.[11] Previous descriptions have dealt with the origins, establishment, and early achievements of the people of Mogotes, Samaniego, Tarso, and San José de Apartadó during the period between 1997 and 2002—roughly the Pastrana years. Those years could hardly be described as "easy" and the stories of these and other communities reveal the appalling difficulties that caused their members to contemplate establishing themselves as peace communities and the tasks they undertook to establish their new status as "outside" the violence yet able to institute their own visions of "positive peace" within their communities. However, the lengthening Uribe years and democratic security posed new problems for each, to which we now turn.

San Jose de Apartadó: Region of Urabá (Northwestern Colombia)

The peace community of San Jose de Apartadó was one of the first to be created. It was originally set up in March 1997 quite separately from the REDEPAZ initiative aimed at establishing one hundred municipalities of peace by the end of the decade, although its founding was greatly assisted by many local NGOs, particularly the Catholic *Justicia y Paz*.[12] The Colombian region around the Gulf of Urabá had, over the years, developed into one of the main areas of contention between the guerrillas of the FARC and the EPL, the security forces, and the paramilitaries of ACCU who moved into the region from the nearby department of Córdoba.[13] The guerrillas had initially entered the region—for them an important transit route between the Caribbean and Pacific coastal areas—in the early 1980s. In the absence of any significant presence of agencies of the Colombian state, the insurgents had established almost total control of the whole area to such a degree that the Colombian army only made occasional forays into the mountainous region around Apartadó, but never tried to maintain a permanent presence there. Politically, the local population strongly supported left wing organizations, initially the Colombian Communist Party and subsequently members of the *Unión Patriótica*. One of the long-term results of this history was that the local population developed a reputation—deserved or not—of being strong "guerrilla supporters." This image remains strongly held even today, especially among members of the Colombian army. It is also prevalent among the population of urban dwellers in the region, who remain remote from the rural armed conflict, supportive of the paramilitaries and sure that rural communities are full of guerrillas—or at least of FARC sympathizers.

Conflict and violence escalated in the first half of the 1990s, with paramilitaries from Córdoba (members of the ACCU founded by the Castaño brothers) moving into the region, together with associated efforts by the military, mainly represented by the army's 17th Brigade, to establish a state presence in the area, at least in the towns and along the roads. Inevitably, the local population became caught up in counter insurgency operations, and a familiar pattern of their being trapped between armed state, para-state, and insurgent combatants emerged. Violence escalated and all sides carried out massacres and counter-massacres of local people, although by the mid-1990s it was clearly the case that most killings around Apartadó were being carried out on behalf of the military, largely through their paramilitary surrogates.

The decision to establish a peace community around San José de Apartadó mainly resulted from two massacres that took place in and around the town towards the end of 1996. Both were carried out by the military and the paramilitaries and resulted in the murder of several community leaders on each occasion. This, together with the continual displacements that had taken place over the past years with both guerrillas and paras forcing people from their homes and fields, plus a virtually permanent presence of the paramilitaries on the road from Apartadó to San Jose, spurred local people to declare San José a peace community at a formal ceremony on March 23,

1997.[14] The ceremony took place in the presence of CINEP, *Justicia y Paz* and the Bishop of Apartado, Mgr. Isais Duarte. The Bishop had encouraged the whole process, and personally prevented an attempt by the then Governor of Antioquia, Alvaro Uribe, to try to incorporate the new community into his scheme for "neutral zones" in Antioquia—which were actually zones controlled by the security forces or their paramilitary allies.[15]

Response from the local combatants was immediate. At the end of March, security forces and paramilitaries invaded several hamlets, killed a number of *campesinos*, and expelled the inhabitants from their homes. A few days later, the FARC assassinated Ramiro Correa, one of the leaders of the new peace community and two others. In spite of this, a year later some people began to return to their homes in La Union, while Peace Brigades International (PBI) began a process of accompanying local people in order to provide some unarmed protection for community members.

In spite of such protection, which was increased in February 2002 when the Fellowship of Reconciliation also began a permanent presence in La Unión as a response to the 2000 massacre, this pattern of harassment, attacks on, and killings of peace community members continued during the Pastrana years. By 2000, over 50 members of the peace community had been assassinated, one of the worst massacres that year again occurring at La Union, when six members of that community were killed by paramilitaries. The overall number of killings had increased to 130 by the end of 2002, when the new President, Alvaro Uribe, began to implement his strategy of Democratic Security.[16]

It remains unclear what the exact impact of Democratic Security was throughout the whole region of Uraba. In May 2003 one of the faculty from the law department of the University of Antioquia who was advising the peace community on human rights issues stated that neither the ending of the peace process, nor the policy of demobilizing the paramilitaries had made any real difference to the number of blockades, assaults, and killings in the region, which continued to be very high, and this pattern continued to repeat itself over the years of both the first and second Uribe administrations.[17] As far as San Jose itself was concerned, one of the most shocking of these attacks occurred in February 2005, when eight peace community members, including three children, were murdered near the settlements of Mulatos and La Resbalosa. Among the adults who were murdered was one of the founders and leaders of the peace community, Luis Eduardo Guerra, who had been forced to leave San Jose in 2002 but who had returned there two years later and resumed his organizational work in the community. The Colombian army claimed that the murders had been perpetrated by the FARC. However, local people were firm in their conviction that the killings had been carried out by members of the 17th Brigade, a suspicion that was shown to have some foundation in truth when, in 2008, Colonel (previously Captain) Guillermo Gordilla confessed to the Attorney General's Office that the killings had been carried out by members of that brigade, together with paramilitaries from the *bloque* "Heroes of Tolova."

The February 2005 massacre was revealing of many things and among them was the highlighting of a new and threatening challenge to peace communities brought about by the adoption of democratic security. On this occasion President Uribe himself took the opportunity at a local "town hall" meeting to attack members of the peace community as having links with the local guerrillas and of using the community "to protect terrorist organizations."[18] While such attacks were nothing particularly new, what was new was the expression of such criticism by high ranking members of the Uribe government such that it became a systematic campaign of criticism and denigration of peace communities in general. For example, in August 2003 the head of the Colombian army, General Jorge Enrique Mora, had publicly claimed that San Jose itself was a "guerrilla concentration camp" from which citizens were forbidden to leave. In the immediate aftermath of the 2005 massacre, the Minister of Defense preceded his President in announcing on March 8 that the government would no longer tolerate demilitarized zones "without the presence of government forces."[19]

The President's March 20, 2005 remarks at Carepa also contained an important insight into one of the key results of democratic security, when he mentioned that some community leaders from San José were being "seriously signaled by people living there" as helping the FARC. Clearly, the policy of paying informants for information was having the inevitable effect of encouraging local inhabitants to accuse fellow community members of being guerrilla sympathizers, supporters or agents—and, of course, doing so secretly and perhaps profitably. In the case of San José, the Community's rupture from the Colombian state made them highly vulnerable to others who sought to become informants in exchange for financial rewards or other forms of state support, which could often take the form of land and houses from which previous owners had fled.[20] Individual members of the Community formed easy targets for profit seeking informants providing welcome information about "guerrilla support" to the ears of state security agents—and others.

The extent to which this process of informing on one another affected peace communities, as opposed to regular *municipios* and *corregimientos*, is almost impossible to gauge. It could—hopefully—be argued that the formidable internal cohesion, identity, and solidarity that many such communities seem to have built up might render them—to some extent at least—proof against such divisive practices. Nonetheless, the temptation to earn necessary cash, to pay off old scores, or even simply to protect oneself from being accused of lack of collaboration with increasingly assertive state authorizes must occasionally prove irresistible.

Another result of democratic security was an increasing reassertion of state authority which clashed with peace communities' rejection of state control and even state presence in that community.[21] Again, this conflict surfaced as a result of the February 2005 massacre and the Uribe government's response to that event. The President took this opportunity to repeat something he had asserted previously, namely that peace communities could not exclude the security forces of the state from their territory if they expected these forces to provide them with security. President Uribe stated flatly that "they cannot, as is the practice in San José de Apartadó, obstruct justice, reject government troops."[22] Given that a major danger to local peoples' security often emanated from these forces themselves, this line of reasoning was quite ironic but it was a natural conclusion of the thinking that underpinned the democratic security strategy.

The practical result of this for the community in San José was that, over the protests of the local community, President Uribe ordered troops to occupy the town and that a permanent police post should be set up in the center of San José itself, which was duly done in April 2005. The response of the peace community was unambiguous. Agreeing to sever all connection with the state, they abandoned the town, which became virtually deserted save for the security forces. The Community then set up a new settlement at some distance from their previous home, which they named San Josecito and where they continued to resist efforts to embroil them in the ongoing struggle between state and insurgents.[23] However, this whole episode symbolized the profound dilemma posed generally for peace communities seeking to withdraw from the continuing violence but confronted by a government that was determined to enlist them on one side of that struggle.

For the community of San José de Apartadó, the period after the February 2005 massacre and the reincorporation of their town into state controlled (and guerrilla attacked) territory became even more difficult. Overall, the strategy of democratic security had had the effects of isolating the rural population in the region and deepening the urban–rural split. (Observers say that local towns in the region are full of "demobilized" but identifiable paramilitaries in mufti, which makes visits to towns and markets by Peace Community members highly perilous.) People living on the margins of urban areas have become especially vulnerable to pressure from state forces to turn informer, which in turn makes them potential targets for guerrillas. Some *campesinos* have made the choice of taking sides with the state and hoping that the military and police can protect them.

Attacks on and harassments of the Peace Community continued, especially from local reformed, regrouped, and renamed paramilitaries who had officially "demobilized" but nonetheless continued their activities in association with local security forces. Throughout the country, community leaders were harassed and murdered. Others were killed and then—suitably dressed— presented as dead guerrillas to boost body counts presented as an indication of the success of the other major aspect of democratic security—counter-insurgency operations.

It remains difficult to assess how "successful" the Peace Community has been when faced with the challenges posed by the government's local implementation of democratic security and the elastic longevity of Alvaro Uribe's presidency, although local observers contend that the level of overall violence has remained roughly at the same level throughout the period 2002–9. In one of the rare, comparative, and data based studies of a number of peace communities in the Urabá region and of their success in increasing their safety and security or diminishing local violence, Dr Pedro Valenzuela of the *Universidad Javeriana* presents a mixed report of the fortunes of three of the peace communities (Valenzuela 2009). In the case of San José, there is a clear pattern of diminishing assassination and deaths between 1997 and 2009, with the exception of 2005. On the other hand, Valenzuela's data reveals little change in the overall level of such indicators as armed incursions, blockades, and general levels of harassment, mainly by military and paramilitary units. Some cases of non-lethal harassment have involved armed groups entering settlements and burning houses, barns and warehouses, seizing or killing animals, and smashing communication and electrical equipment (Valenzuela 2009, 78). The clear objective in these cases has been to intimidate the community but to avoid the opprobrium that attends actual massacre of its inhabitants. In response to the question about the success of these communities, Valenzuela concludes that, "Harassment, threats, intimidation, arbitrary detentions, blockades and pillaging become more frequent as forced displacement and murder or disappearance become less common" (Valenzuela 2009, 124).

Nonetheless, the members of the San José Peace Community have continued with their efforts to remain non-violent, neutral, and outside the continuing conflict. Contacts have been made with local indigenous communities, such as Las Playas. Small but important development projects have undertaken, including establishing a cooperative to buy and market organic chocolate and bananas. To some extent, national isolation has been alleviated by international attention—Fellowship of Reconciliation (FoR) presence, regular visits by Peace Brigades International, visits by foreign embassies and NGOs on special occasions. In 2007, the Peace Community of San José de Apartadó, together with the indigenous organization ACIN, was nominated for a Nobel Peace Prize by the American Friends Service Committee. If survival is a measure of success, then San José has clearly succeeded.

Mogotes: Departamento de Santander (North-eastern Colombia)

Like the peace community of San José de Apartadó, Mogotes was one of the pioneering peace zones in Colombia and was central to the development of REDEPAZ's efforts to create *100 Municipios de Paz* during the late 1990s and early 2000s. The impetus for the foundation of the *Asamblea Constituyente de Mogotes* (AMC) was the kidnapping in December 1997 of the Mayor by local ELN guerrillas of the Frente Efraín Pabón, which had been active in the region throughout the decade and whose activities had increasingly encroached on the life of the *municipio*. This action provided the trigger which led the local population to demand the return of the Mayor, Dorien Rodriguez, on the grounds that the community itself—and not the guerrillas—should deal with the problem of political corruption and cronyism. The Mayor was subsequently released, dismissed and, unfortunately, later assassinated by the ELN while trying to undermine the reform movement in the *municipio*. The reform movement mainly took the form of the establishment of the first popular *Asamblea Constituyente* (Constitutional Assembly) in Colombia and the creation of a large number of specialized committees to oversee development, health, education, and human rights.

Leading the reform movement in Mogotes was the local parish priest, Fr. Joakin Mayorga, encouraged by the Bishop of Socorro and San Gil, Msgr. Leonardo Gomez Serna. The former became nationally known through his development of an eight-stage model through which communities could establish self-rule and the full development of "popular sovereignty" through their own efforts.[24] This model, the initial success of Mogotes and the efforts of REDEPAZ to use the example of Mogotes to encourage other communities, had a direct influence on the establishment of a number of other peace communities—for example, Tarso and Sonsón in Antioquia and Samaniego and San Pablo in Nariño. Thus, from 1998 onwards, Mogotes became a crucial example of the opportunities offered by the local zone of peace model, helping to spread the practice of establishing local peace *experiencias* throughout the country during the Pastrana years. In October 1999 it was awarded the first National Peace Prize, and in his speech at the award ceremony President

Pastrana emphasized that Mogotes' example "shows us that peace has to be built day after day, in our own environment and according to the capacities of each of us"[25]

Unfortunately, the subsequent history of Mogotes demonstrates some of the problems of maintaining a peace community even without having to contend with the hostility of the national government and the imposition of the general "either you are with us or against us" policy of Democratic Security at the national level. Three factors played an important role in undermining the activities of the Mogotes Municipal Constituent Assembly. The first involved the radical change in the Catholic Church's attitude towards the peace community. The second, linked, factor involved the internal conflicts that developed as a result of divisions within the overall community. The third involved the resurgence of traditional, conservative forces engendered by the new popular movements represented by the AMC.

While one of the crucial factors in creating the peace community in Mogotes was the activity of Fr. Mayorga together with the support of his bishop, clearly there were powerful elements of the Church hierarchy who saw the development of a movement for popular participation as dangerous and probably left-wing.[26] The simplest strategy was to remove both Fr. Mayorga and Msgr. Gomez Serna. In 2003, in short order, both were transferred to the diocese of Maguange in Bolivar, Msgr. Gomez Serna as Bishop and Fr. Mayorke as the Director of the Social Action Office. These two supporters of the Mogotes Assembly were rapidly replaced by local clergy hostile towards the idea of grassroots participation in local decision making, who proceeded to undermine the whole popular movement. This was done with some success, at least as far as encouraging the polarization of the community into "pro-" and "anti-" Assembly factions was concerned. The replacement for Mgr Gomez Serna was the already retired Msgr. Jose de Jesus Pimiento, well known for his ultra-conservative views and named as apostolic administrator for the diocese of Socorro and San Gil. The new parish priest of Mogotes, Fr. Jorge Velandia Rodriguez, once appointed, stated publicly that the purpose of the Assembly was "laudable" but that it was "badly orientated" as far as the Church was concerned—and he proceeded to preach against the Assembly's activities and condemn those that continued to be associated with it. Inevitably, members and supporters of the Assembly were accused of being guerrillas or at least guerrilla sympathizers, a follow up of the original accusations leveled by the family of Mayor Rodriguez at those responsible for dismissing him in 1998.

In addition to this reversal of the Church's attitudes, there arose what might be seen as an inevitable power struggle with the political hierarchy within the *municipio*, between the new institutions established as part of the Assembly and the old governing institutions of the *Alcaldia*. A complementary relationship between the Assembly and the mayor and city council might have continued beyond 2002, but in that year a traditionally oriented Conservative party candidate, Norberto Tijo, was elected to the *Alcaldia* and proved as hostile to the Assembly as the incoming clergy proved the following year. To some degree, there was always likely to be some tension between the two competing power centers, but relations between the Assembly and the mayor deteriorated rapidly to the point where the latter simply ignored the Assembly and its suggestions, deciding unilaterally how funds from the central government were to be allocated and on what projects. *"Politiqueria"* had returned to Mogotes with the treasurer of the AMC talking after the mayoral elections in 2004 about the Assembly having converted itself into a parallel *Alcaldia*. From that time on, much of what occurred depended upon who was elected to the *Alcaldia* and whether the *alcalde* supported or disapproved of the Assembly and its principles of participation, popular sovereignty, and grass roots input to official decision making.

A third factor that contributed to the difficulties of the peace community in Mogotes was the fact that not everyone had been or remained committed to the original vision of the peace community's founders. Divisions and differences inevitably remained and new ones emerged over time. In July 2004 *El Tiempo* was reporting that the *municipio* was split in two and that this division had revealed itself clearly in that summer's campaign for mayor, which resulted in the election of another Conservative party candidate, Nelson Calderon. However, the internal divisions within the community were more complex that simple bilateral "polarization" or a return to the old Liberal—Conservative division. There were difficulties between the Assembly and the Association of United Artisans of Mogotes (ARUMOS) over schemes for producing articles made from *fique*, a locally grown fibre (Quinto 2004). Even within the Assembly itself, serious divisions had surfaced and in 2006 there were reports of complaints about development strategies being skewed in favor of the urban center and *veredas* in the north and center of the *municipio*, while people living in the south were being neglected (NotiLibreSur 2006).

Overall, it seems that, unlike the case of San Jose de Apartadó, it was not external pressure from the national policy of Democratic Security that began to undermine the peace community of Mogotes and its Constituent Assembly. Rather it was the internal opposition centered on the Church and the *Alcaldia*. Ana Teresa Bernal, the Director of REDEPAZ noted as early as 2004 that, since Mogotes had received the National Peace Prize in 1998, all the world had praised it, but *"nadie le dio nada"*—including the government (Quinto 2004).[27]

To date the Assembly and the peace community barely survive, its radio station continues to broadcast, and it continues to have representatives elected to the Mogotes City Council. In October 2007 a mayor sympathetic to the Assembly succeeded in getting elected but the divisions within the overall community in Mogotes had been thoroughly exploited by its opponents. An assessment written in 2009 talks of the peace community being "immobilized by fear" and the overall process as having been "destroyed." The *casa soberana* in Mogotes had not seen a full meeting of the Assembly for four years and the Executive Committee of the AMC had zero funding to continue the work, each general meeting costing over a million pesos (Nieto 2010). The AMC in Mogotes may be revived but this will probably have to await a change of local Church leaders and the end of democratic security.

Samaniego: Departamento de Nariño (South-western Colombia)

Of the four *municipios* revisited and reassessed in this chapter, Samaniego is the only one situated in the south west of the country as part of the *departamento* of Nariño which borders on the neighboring departamento of Putamayo and the international boundary with Ecuador. Samaniego is a crossroads town and commercial center, where communities from nearby municipalities such as Providencia, Sotomayo, and Linares converge. This strategic and geographic importance partly explains why many armed actors seek passage and control of the municipality. At the end of the 1990s, this entire region was a guerrilla stronghold and a center of the coca-growing and cocaine-producing industry, which involved many local communities in the most profitable form of agriculture available to local *campesinos*. In many *municipios*, including Samaniego, the political influence of local units from both FARC and ELN was unchallenged, and the guerrillas interfered in many aspects of local life, removing unpopular and corrupt officials and settling local disputes between, and even within, families.

It was as a reaction to this level of involvement that led the people in Samaniego to establish themselves originally as a local zone of peace in order to minimize the guerrilla presence within the *municipio*. In 1997, the FARC had issued a blanket threat against anyone standing in the mayoral elections throughout the country, while in Samaniego the local *frente* of the ELN kidnapped the populist, reforming candidate, Manuel Cuéllar. Cuéllar and his wife had previously taken the lead in establishing a Working Table for Peace as a planning initiative for more open and transparent governance, post-1998. In spite of the threats and the kidnapping, local people nonetheless voted the candidate into office *in absentia* as mayor and successfully demanded his release in order to carry out far-reaching reforms, which were duly put into place during his period in office. In January 1998 Samaniego formally declared itself a zone of peace.

In spite of this determined start, Samaniego's progress as a peace community was anything but smooth or certain. Ironically, while the mayor's strong and positive involvement in the early years was an undoubted benefit, the fact that the fortunes of the peace zone were highly dependent on support from municipal authorities made continuous progress dependent on that support. Samaniego traditionally had a history of bitter political conflict between traditional political forces and when other candidates less committed to the idea of a peace community and its projects were elected into office, this had a huge effect on the projects and institutions initially set up. By the end of 2002, most of the initiatives started four years previously were struggling or in abeyance.

Moreover, Samaniego's fortunes were also affected by region-wide factors set in train by decisions made at a national level. Efforts by the national government in Bogotá to eradicate drug production in the south west of the country through the implementation of "Plan Colombia," plus efforts to re-establish a state security presence throughout Putamayo, Meta and Nariño, created a situation of constant turmoil and violence in the region from 2000 onwards. This was increased after 2002 when paramilitary forces, supported by local landowners, emerged throughout the region, and—often with the help of the Colombian military—challenged the guerrilla presence there. Together with vastly increased military forces, acting as part of "Plan Patriota," a huge number of refugees and IDPs was created either fleeing the fighting or deliberately expelled from their villages. These became a transient population moving throughout the region and putting further strain on limited resources. Particularly hard hit were indigenous communities in the region. Overall, regional factors posed increasing challenges for the local population, predominantly for those peace communities confronting the effects of President Uribe's strategy of Democratic Security.

Since 2002, the number of organized groups actively pursuing violence ranged from the long-established FARC (29th front) and the ELN (*Frente Comuneros del Sur*) to the then newly established paramilitary *bloques*, some of which would later reappear as "emerging groups," such as *Aguilas Negras or Rastrojos*—the by-product of Uribe's DDR policy for right-wing insurgencies. Such groups have dramatically complicated the already troubled picture in Samaniego. The number of kidnappings, disappearances, and forced displacements has intensified as a result of the upsurge in organized crime and internal vendettas within and between groups in dispute.

Samaniego clearly illustrates what Democratic Security policy looks like in practice. Prior to 2002, the Colombian army had a minimal presence in the region. Since 2002, the army is directly battling the insurgents in the mountainous regions resulting in their weakening and further retreat to even more remote areas. In turn, the guerrillas have responded by mining the territory where civilians travel, work, and live. By 2009, Samaniego was the second most-mined municipality in the whole country. In 2008 alone, 18 mining accidents affected civilians. Landmines were causing even more families to leave the area. The former mayor of Samaniego (2004–7), Harold Montúfar Andrade, responded by creating a project entitled *Pacto Local de Paz* or Local Pact for Peace. Former mayor Montúfar worked to highlight the deterioration of human rights in the municipality and to highlight the drama behind anti-personnel mines. Montúfar was decorated in 2007 as "Mayor of the Year" given his efforts to build peace in the area. Samaniego's increased visibility even led the mayor to send a delegation to Cuba to have a dialogue with ELN on "humanitarian de-mining," a holistic approach that includes work with victims and insurgents and is accompanied by reparation, education, prevention, and identification of safe paths. Unfortunately, Samaniego's demining is only being carried out by the military.

If the main goal of Democratic Security is to increase the state's military presence, then Samaniego can be seen as a "successful" case. If the purpose of increasing military presence is to enhance security of its citizens, then Samaniego illustrates the ill-defined nature of such a goal. For example, in 2009 the military decided to use indigenous communities living in the surrounding area as their informants, in accordance to the principles of Democratic Security. The guerrillas retaliated by massacring eight indigenous leaders. Furthermore, these communities already live in the mountains where many of the anti-personal mines are located. In the words of one resident of Mogotes:

> Democratic Security is a policy that serves the war machinery while the population remains unprotected. There are a lot of groups, all of whom claim to work for enhancing "security" while criminal acts abound, impunity is rampant and criminal acts are unaccounted for.[28]

Despite the worsening security conditions for civilians in Samaniego, organized civil society and local governments alike continue to develop peacebuilding initiatives. During the administration of Mayor Montúfar Andrade, local civil society organizations launched the *Consejo Municipal de Paz* or Municipal Peace Council to integrate civilians in the municipality's affairs and to work together on peacebuilding initiatives for Samaniego. Seventeen representatives from civil society organizations (farmers, women, youth, indigenous) converged at the *Consejo to* assess and map out the conflict, identify their strengths and vulnerabilities, as well as potential peacebuilding strategies. The citizenry's need to find avenues for understanding and addressing the conflict, as attested by the *Consejo*. This would respond directly to the increased military presence since 2007, which was perceived as a precursor for an even greater wave of violence. While the military surrounds the area, citizens in Samaniego feel that they are trapped amid a web of paramilitary-related crimes, extortion, and common criminality—all tainted by a very precarious economic situation.

Economically, Democratic Security is conceived as being best implemented by offering monetary incentives to the poor. The economic assistance packages devised by the Colombian state to increase educational attendance and increase literacy rates are perceived at best as a "band aid"—temporary cures rather than long term systemic changes. At worst, citizens feel that policies such as *Familias en Acción* (Action Families); or *Adulto Mayor* (Senior Citizens) are simply the public-relations arm of the Uribe administration. The policy of *soldado campesino,* or farmer soldier, also operates in Samaniego. Poor farmers accept the government aid, less out of conviction and more because of fear and poverty, thus increasing their chances of becoming military targets of the guerillas.

It is common knowledge—both in Colombia and abroad—that, overall, the two Uribe administrations have successfully weakened the left-wing insurgencies. Thus, the country seems to have succeeded in producing lower levels of violence at the national level. This is held to be one of the positive results of policies such as Democratic Security. It is only when focusing on local and regional processes—such as those in Samaniego, which has the third greatest rate of IDPs in Nariño, and is the second municipality in Colombia with the highest number of active landmines—that questions about the costs of military intervention begin to be raised, and raised insistently. The local security situation continues to rapidly worsen and degrade. On December 22, 2009 civilians rallied from the mountains to the urban center to protest against their homes becoming a battlefield between the military and the insurgents. The local populace claimed that armed actors constantly violate civilian rights by stealing food, quartering in their homes, and even firing from civilian houses.

However, it is the methods of violence employed in the towns by armed actors that is concerning civilians the most. Insurgents are using explosives as a basic strategy, setting bombs in schools and on roads, and even sending a female suicide bomber to a police station.[29] Given that they experience two to three explosions each day, citizens in Samaniego are feeling more insecure than ever before. What many civil society voices from Samaniego articulate about the future is a desire to work seriously towards the transformation of the existing a culture of war to one of stable peace, together with the conviction that peace is intimately connected with social justice and with real poverty alleviation policies.

Tarso: Departamento de Antioquia (Central Colombia)

Of the *municipios* surveyed in our original study, Tarso appeared somewhat atypical for a variety of reasons. The community formed a "Constituent Municipal Assembly" in 2000, although proposals for such a move had been made a year earlier. However, it did not appear as though this move was in response to serious local violence or a desire to become neutral in an ongoing struggle between local guerrillas and the security forces. There had been a strong ELN presence in the area up to 1997 but this had declined markedly when paramilitary forces moved into that region of Antioquia and became the dominant armed actor there, although the guerrillas were believed to continue to periodically use the *municipio* as a transit corridor. By 2000, however, the area was not in contention and seemed reasonably quiet and free from major violence.

As we noted in previous studies, the main driving forces behind the community's decision to establish a Constituent Assembly were political and economic, with the perceived danger of the *municipio* being politically downgraded to the status of *corregimiento* together with the need for economic development—a need shared by many other peace communities but not with such prominence (Rojas 2007). This meant that, when the Uribe strategy of democratic security was put into effect after 2002, Tarso presented a different range of problems and conflicts to government (and "pro-government") agencies, and a different environment within which the local community had to face the challenge of coping with demands for conformity, commitment, and cooperation with security forces.

Democratic Security is a centralized policy initiative. Therefore, any autonomous, bottom-up, and decentralized citizen-led initiatives clashed with the "spirit" of the strategy. Stigmatization and lack of recognition of the "Constituent Municipal Assembly" by central government authorities is one of the main issues, as emphasized by one member of the Assembly.[30] Colombia's 1991 Constitution clearly stated the fundamental rights of citizens to be engaged and participate in public decisions in the form of constituent assemblies. Nonetheless, it is important to note that this Assembly is neither a judicial entity nor does it endorse any particular political party. Tarso's Assembly started in 1999 with a series of awareness raising campaigns carried out with various community sectors; including farmers, students, and unions. After fifteen months of community-trainings led by Tarso leaders and accompanied by REDEPAZ, 150 delegates were selected to be part of the Constituent Municipal Assembly. In addition, Church leaders, municipal council members, members of armed forces were included as participants.

The Assembly had as one goal the production of *Pactos de Comportamiento Electoral Transparente* – Pacts for Transparent Behavior in Election Processes. These pacts outline the government agenda for the municipality, which is then submitted to the new mayor for his/her consideration. The "Constituent Municipal Assembly" works on creating Tarso's Development Plan. Moreover, the Assembly also examines and recommends initiatives to increase the community's participation in budget design.

One of the purposes of this chapter was to observe and reflect upon the effects of President Uribe's Democratic Security policy in several municipalities since its implementation in 2002. Similarly, the question of the outcomes of Tarso's Consitutent Assembly is also a valid one since it has been functioning for nearly a decade. The results of Tarso's Assembly can be divided into two categories; factual and attitudinal changes. By factual changes we mean that the Assembly facilitated a process of streamlining Tarso's finances. Rather than being simply "in the black," the Assembly facilitated a process that led Tarso to produce surpluses which could be invested in programs such as the purchase of 600 affordable housing units; a water-treatment plant, which provides potable water to 95 percent of the population; programs for developing farms and the construction of a new hospital and a new sports stadium.[31]

These positive and practical results further contribute to attitudinal changes among Tarso's inhabitants. Earlier we mentioned how Tarso was dealing with rampant corruption, which threatened to downgraded Tarso from a *municipio* to a *corregimiento* (hamlet). Since the Constituent Assembly began in 2000, perceptions of the community about existing corruption have changed dramatically. According to one council member of Tarso's Assembly, local public institutions have gained credibility among the population. The notion that public institutions exist to serve the community (and not simply to fill a few pockets) has gained momentum. Renewed faith in public institutions and public declarations not to cooperate with any armed actor, are indications that Tarso may be developing the beginnings of a "culture of peace."

Tarso is currently a relatively peaceful area. It is still a corridor but guerrilla presence is not a constant. In fact, many former members of the AUC currently reside in Tarso and some of them are even active in the Assembly. It is interesting to note that Tarso's efforts to combat corruption, or what Assembly members refer to as *ejercicio de transparencia* have had positive repercussions in decreasing levels of violence. Armed actors who pass through, or operate near Tarso, respect the community.

Finally, Tarso allows us to examine the interactions between local government and national policies. Tarso's Assembly operates independently from Antioquia's (state) or national policies—in this case, Democratic Security. As mentioned earlier, this policy is perceived as highly centralized (the budget decisions come straight from Bogotá) and little input is required at the regional and local levels. Furthermore, members of the Assembly disagree with the widely asserted argument that in Colombia there is no armed conflict but just criminal activities.[32] Democratic Security is viewed as a purely military intervention that ignores social and economic investment in local areas. Tarso's accomplishments have neither been sufficiently recognized by the government of Antioquia nor by the national government. Tarso is an example of a bottom-up experience of civil society engagement in local governance issues. Its accomplishments demonstrate the important role of communities in changing perceptions about corruption. In fact, Tarso is identified as a municipality where citizens are engaged and watchful, threatening the status quo of traditional political parties. If Tarso's Assembly firmly establishes transparency in local politics, will it threaten the status quo for those that flourished under corruption—as happened in Mogotes? This question remains to be answered.

Conclusion

At the time of writing, it is difficult to make a thorough assessment of the overall impact of President Alvaro Uribe's strategy of Democratic Security—a strategy which seems likely to be continued by his successor and former Minister of Defense, Juan Manuel Santos. It is clearly the case that the strategy has proved popular among the most urban dwellers of Colombia, especially in most large cities where the level of violence has diminished and a degree of tranquility achieved; except in the *barrios* that surround cities such as Bogotá, Medellin, or Cali. Roads are open and travel between urban areas is less perilous. It is also clear that the increased numbers of soldiers, armed police and technical equipment (especially US-supplied helicopters), together with an aggressive counter insurgency strategy, has inflicted major blows on the guerrillas, and driven them back into the remoter and more inaccessible regions of Colombia. It may be that part of this success is due to the increased use of paid informers and *campesino* soldiers in locally contested areas.

However, the associated policy of disarming and demobilizing the para-militaries and offering—for some paramilitary leaders—amnesty in exchange for acknowledgement of responsibility for wrongdoing and restitution of land and property acquired illegally—can hardly be presented as an unambiguous triumph. Too many of the paras have simply "reintegrated" by joining newly formed groups of toughs—"Black Eagles" and the like—or continuing their previous behavior under other auspices and for other employers. Barrancabermeja in Magdalena Medio, for example, remains a notorious "paramilitary town." The scandals of "Para-Gate" have revealed the extent to which paramilitary influence has penetrated the national political system and corrupted it. Locally, and in rural areas close to many local peace communities, the problems for communities such as San Jose de Apartadó (or Sonson in Antioquia) that are posed by paramilitary threats and violence does not seem to have diminished much, save in the sense that ex-paras now generally avoid the publicity resulting from the extremes of mass murder and massacre.

Even if we discount the possibility that the guerrillas of the FARC and—to a lesser degree—the ELN have simply retreated into remote, safe areas to regroup and reorganize and, though damaged, are not fatally and finally destroyed, there remains the question of the damage caused to civilians in rural as opposed to urban communities by Democratic Security. The insertion of military and police posts into rural communities may, indeed, increase the level of security enjoyed by local inhabitants. On the other hand, equally—as in the case of San Jose de Apartadó—it may increase the number of potential targets for the guerrillas to attack, and will clearly call into question the perceived neutrality of peace communities. The experience of Samaniego also suggests that efforts by the military to wrest control from local guerrilla fronts has turned regions into major battlefields, with peace zones and indigenous communities caught in the middle of and suffering from assaults by both military and guerrilla forces.

The experiences of San Jose de Apartadó during the Uribe years also suggests that the solidarity of peace communities and their declared principles of neutrality and avoidance of contact with state agencies stands in direct opposition to efforts to recruit *campesino* soldiers and local informants This may insulate peace communities from being recruited into the "democratic," state supportive aspects of democratic security. However, the resumption of fierce local political rivalries in both Samaniego and Mogotes suggests that opportunities for state agencies—military, security, and civilian—to use local divisions to obtain information—both accurate and inaccurate—about rival factions, their leaders and alleged links with or sympathy for the guerrillas, may not have diminished in peace communities whose unity and solidarity are less than complete.

It may be that it is this solidarity and refusal to abandon fundamental neutrality (or to adapt to any demands imposed on local communities by Democratic Security) that explains the vehemence of attacks on this particular peace community by state officials, from President Uribe downwards. The people of San Jose would not tolerate the establishment of a police station within, or an army camp close by their community. They would rather move the community. They would not provide informants for the state—or the guerrillas—and they would not become *campesino* soldiers and make themselves targets for the

FARC. In this they may be typical of other peace communities and atypical of other rural communities that had not adopted this local, peacebuilding strategy as a basis for their continued survival, before Uribe. The problem for the peace communities during the Uribe presidencies may have been that the underlying philosophy of local peacebuilding simply and drastically ran wholly counter to the national level policy of the government, and to its underlying philosophy. The latter may have had much success and generated much support in the cities and in many urban areas. It may have increased security and diminished death and overt violence in many rural communities. However, for peace communities in rural areas it seems to have confronted those living in such communities with a stark challenge, which demanded that they abandon—or at least modify—their own values, their own strategy and their own achievements. At least in San Jose, the community seems to have refused.

Notes

1 We are most grateful to Julia Nelson from American University, who spent six months between August and December 2008 accompanying members of the peace community of San Jose de Apartadó with the Fellowship of Reconciliation team and who shared her reflections and recollections of this time with us.
2 REDEPAZ, *Red Nacional para la Paz y contra la Guerra* (National Network for Peace and Against War), was founded in November 1993 and has played a central role in maintaining links between local, regional and national peace institutions within Colombia. It has undertaken a wide variety of organizational, educational, research and political tasks, among them the development and presentation in 1996 of a draft "peace statute" to promote the regulation of Article 22 of the 1991 Constitution which states that peace is both a right and a duty for Colombians.
3 The connections that carried these ideas of local peace communities from the Philippines to Colombia tended to be local Catholic priests and academics who had observed the initiatives taken by local people, tired of being fought over by guerrillas and security forces in places such as Luzon or Mindanao, and who had then come to Colombia and found similar problems of local peacebuilding.
4 By 2004 the Colombian government was claiming that the military had increased the number of troops available for combat by 60 percent and that it had many more helicopters—including attack helicopters—helping to increase mobility and striking power—presumably courtesy of the United States.
5 The fact that, in many regions of the country, the main threats to individual and institutional security emanated from the state security forces themselves—or from their paramilitary allies or surrogates—made this a questionable strategy from the outset.

6 Embassy of Colombia, Washington, DC. Defense and Security Briefing. Online at: http://www.colombiamb.org/opencms/opencms/defense.

7 Alvaro Uribe had enthusiastically embraced a similar strategy—known as CONVIVIR—while he was Governor of Antioquia, at a time when the Samper government was implementing a policy of arming local "neighborhood watch" groups to provide security for local communities and intelligence to security forces. In very many cases, CONVIVIR units simply recruited local paramilitaries as well as victims of guerrilla attacks and became out of control, local toughs, similar to the mercenary forces set up under Law 48 of 1968 by local elites—which was subsequently declared illegal in 1989 by the Colombian Constitutional Court. In a similar manner, the Court gradually placed restrictions on CONVIVIR units' rights to carry arms and to "gather intelligence," so that by 1998 many units had refused to hand back their arms and phased themselves out of existence or simply joined paramilitary groups such as Carlos Castaño's ACCU which continued to operate during this period.

8 President Uribe introduced a one-time tax increase for Colombian corporations and members of the country's elite that was said to have raised over US $650 million and was to be spent on 6,000 elite soldiers, 10,000 new police officers, 150,000 peasant soldiers, and over 100,000 local "informants" to provide intelligence to authorities.

9 Describing the complex and fraught process of demobilizing the AUC over the period 2003–7 would require a separate study in itself. Major criticisms of the process include claims (1) that many of those demobilized were never actual fighting members of the AUC—or members at all, but merely recruited to boost overall numbers and—individually—to obtain proffered benefits; (2) that many of the hard-core, rank-and-file paramilitaries simply reorganized themselves into neo-para organizations such as the notorious "Black Eagles" or took up new roles in commercial (aka "private") security firms or as local "support soldiers"; and (3) that paramilitary leaders, responsible for the most appalling crimes against the civilian population, were not merely being given the opportunity to evade any real responsibility and punishment for their activities, but were being allowed to keep many of their ill-gotten gains in a final denial of justice to their victims. For an analysis of the whole "demobilization" process see Human Rights Watch (2005, 2010)

10 In a letter sent to Amnesty International as early as October 2002, President Uribe flatly denied any right for citizens not to be drawn into the conflict. "Nobody can be neutral in the state's fight against criminality" (Amnesty International 2002, 11).

11 See in this connection Mitchell and Nan (eds), *Peace Review* 9 (2), 1997 Special edition on "Local Zones of Peace", and Hancock and Mitchell (2004, 2007).

12 The San Jose peace "community" is actually made up of over 30 separate communities—villages (*corregimientos*), hamlets and small, rather isolated settlements (*veredas*)—spread over a wide area which makes it difficult for the institutions of the community to coordinate responses to incursions, and easy for the local armed combatants to harass and otherwise interfere with community activities. This dispersed nature of the community and the presence of guerrilla units in the surrounding mountainous areas also makes it easy for accusations of collaboration to be leveled and believed.

13 The region of "Uraba" consists of western Cordoba, the northern "neck" of Antioquia and north-western Choco. It contains "the banana belt," largely created in the 1950s by the United Fruit Company, and has been in important transit zone for drugs going out of the country and arms coming in, as well as being—at various times—a safe refuge for guerrillas of the FARC and the old EPL, at least until the incursion of the paramilitaries of the ACCU in the late 1980s–early 1990s. Conflicts over land use and ownership, unionization, the drug trade and local political control have made the Uraba region one of the most unstable and violent in Colombia.

14 One of the models from which ideas for local peace communities arose was provided by indigenous communities that attempted to preserve their culture and way of life by avoiding contact as much as possible with modernizing state influence.

15 Governor Uribe's "neutral zones" were more accurately called "CONVIVIR communities" and were directly under the control the Governor's departmental security forces, as well as the AUC. Members of such communities were required—among other things—to become informers for these forces in return for protection and security.

16 Local estimates of killings at the end of 2008 amounted to around 180 deaths in total, 20 of which were attributed to the guerrillas and the remainder to paramilitaries or the state security forces.

17 From a talk given at the First Congregational Church in Washington, DC, by Professor Elkin de Jesus Ramirez Jaramillo, May 4, 2003.

18 From remarks made by President Uribe at a public meeting held in the neighboring town of Carepa on March 20, 2005.

19 "La Fuerza Publica Ingresaria a los Denominades Territorios de Paz Annuncio el Gobierno." *El Tiempo* [Bogota] March 9, 2005.

20 Following the 2005 massacre, the local community in San Jose took a decision to sever all connections with the Colombian state, which involved avoiding all state services, even including education. (San Jose has its own schools up to fifth and sixth grades, after which local children have to go to state middle and high schools. Hence few are educated beyond this level.) The declaration stated that the community would not reopen communication with state agencies until it provided justice for the past atrocities that had been committed by the paramilitaries and the military, and agreed to respect the principles of peaceful neutrality adopted by the Community.

21 Underlying all these verbal assaults on the Peace Community as a "guerrilla stronghold" was another important aspect of the philosophy connected with Democratic Security, namely the government's dislike of the existence of areas within the country where, practically, there was no state control but also where the local people even denied the state's right to be present. The Community's claim to neutrality and autonomy and its complete rupture from the state following the 2005 massacre provided a direct challenge to the state's basis of authority, which was seen as a far more dangerous aspect of the situation that even a notional guerrilla presence in San Jose.

22 Oquiendo, Catalina. "Fuerzas Armadas." *El Tiempo*, March 21, 2005.

23 An alternative name was "La Hollandia" because a Dutch gift of funds was used to purchase the land for the settlement.

24 Fr. Mayorga's model, by which local communities can reclaim their sovereignty, involves eight necessary steps: (1) mobilization of local inhabitants to raise awareness and potential; (2) communication to focus attention on human rights as a basis for action; (3) analysis of the nature and sources of local problems; (4) creation of initiatives or a plan to deal with the problems so identified; (5) organization of a popular municipal assembly; (6) activation through communal actions under the direction of the assembly; (7) consolidation via activities intended to normalize and routinize the new processes and to cement them in place; and (8) expansion, whereby the community established links with potential allies and supporters both internally and externally in the region, the nation and internationally.

25 An English translation of President Pastrana's congratulatory message to the Mogotes AMC on the occasion of the National Peace Prize award ceremony can be found in an editorial from the *Observatorio de los Derechos Humanos en Colombia*, available online at: http://www.derechoshumanos.gov.co/Observatorio/Publicaciones/documents/2010/boletines/04_boletin_15/edit15i.htm.

26 It should always be recalled that Colombia was the country that was central to the creation of liberation theology.

27 A rough translation is that no one had given them anything.

28 "Marina" phone conversation from Mogotes, March 25, 2009.

29 Information from an e-mail sent by "Marina" from Mogotes on February 21, 2010.

30 "Carlos" phone conversation, March 31, 2009.

31 "Carlos" phone conversation, March 31, 2009.

32 A similar argument was made by Margaret Thatcher's administration with respect to the Northern Ireland Troubles.

Works cited

Amnesty International. 2002. *Colombia: Security at what cost? The Government's failure to confront the human rights crisis*. Amnesty International: London & New York.

Colombia, Government of. 2003. *Democratic Security and Defense Policy*, edited by Presidency of the Republic and Ministry of Defense. Bogotá: Provided by the Colombian Embassy in Washington DC.

Hancock, Landon E., and C. R. Mitchell, eds. 2004. *The Construction of Sanctuary: Local Zones of Peace Amid Protracted Conflict*. Arlington, VA: Institute for Conflict Analysis and Resolution.

— eds. 2007. *Zones of Peace*. Bloomfield, CT: Kumarian Press.

Human Rights Watch. 2005. *Smoke and Mirrors: Colombia's Demobilization of Paramilitary Groups*. New York: Human Rights Watch.

— 2010. *Paramilitaries' Heirs: The New Face of Violence in Colombia*. New York: Human Rights Watch.

Mason, Ann. 2003. "Colombia's Democratic Security Agenda: Public Order in the Security Tripod." *Security Dialogue* 34 (4): 391–409.

Nieto, Patricia. 2010. "Los Soberanos." In *Crónicas. Premio Nacional de Paz.* Bogotá, Colombia: Friedrch Ebert Stiftung en Colombia – Fescol.

NotiLibreSur. 2006. *No Todos Mogotes (Santander del sur) esta conforme con la asamblea Constituyente (Not All Mogotes (Santander South) adhered to the Constituent Assembly).* Colombia Indy Media 2006). Available from http://colombia.indymedia.org/news/2006/10/49956.php.

Quinto, Felix Leonardo. 2004. "Constituyente Divide en Mogotes." *El Tiempo*, July 13.

Rojas, Catalina. 2007. "Islands in the Stream." In *Zones of peace*, edited by L. E. Hancock and C. R. Mitchell. Bloomfield, CT: Kumarian Press.

Valenzuela, Pedro. 2009. "Neutrality in internal armed conflicts: experiences at the grassroots level in Colombia." Originally presented as the author's thesis (doctoral), Uppsala University, Uppsala, Sweden.

4

Colombia: From grassroots to elites – how some local peacebuilding initiatives became national in spite of themselves

Mery Rodriguez

Introduction

Colombia is one of the oldest armed conflicts in the world. For more than 60 years, war has taken over many of its rural areas and, in recent years, its urban areas as well. Hand in hand with war comes "peace" and, with the dire conditions under which many Colombians live, peace at the grassroots has become—practically—the only means for surviving or fulfilling basic human needs. Hence, all of the local peacebuilding initiatives in Colombia can be regarded as having taken place during ongoing conflicts—during the period described by Hancock and Iyer as the "continuing violence" stage (Hancock and Iyer 2007, 30). It is clear that, for almost as long as the conflict has been active, peace initiatives have existed, and among them there are many "zones" of peace. Mitchell and Nan (1997) have defined zones of peace as places where attempts are made to establish rules or norms which limit the destructive effects of violent conflict within a particular area or during a particular time period or with regard to a particular category of people.[1] However, because of the ever-changing conditions of countries at war or in post-agreement situations, drawing conclusions that allow for the systematic understanding of zones of peace has been a difficult, if not impossible, task. Colombia has not escaped from this reality.

Given the difficulty of this task, this chapter is based on approaching peacebuilding from the grassroots in a broader fashion—as a variety of "local peacebuilding initiatives" (LPBI). By doing so, I have been able to note a shift in the practices of peacebuilding in different regions of Colombia. What initially started as a need to understand zones of peace has grown into a need to understand the wide range of LPBI efforts.

Even though Colombia has been affected by armed conflict for the last 60 years, it was not until the 1990s that a strong "discourse of peace" started to gain public and national attention. As civil society at the national level started to become organized and to actively participate in building peace for Colombia, regional and local initiatives also began, especially in the rural areas where "La Violencia" had been most severe.[2] These regional and local initiatives started to gain public attention in the late 1990s when rural violence dramatically increased as a result of the presence of a new organized armed actor: the paramilitary association AUC (*Autodefensas Unidas de Colombia* or United Self-defense of Colombia).

The attention gained by LPBIs also brought the subject to the national political level and they became part of political campaigns and governmental policies. With attention also came international presence and funding. "Local and regional" peacebuilding initiatives became a national public subject, making them more vulnerable in the midst of the war.

Tracing what has happened to some of these initiatives from the early 1990s to the present has been very difficult. I initially thought that many initiatives had disappeared or become governmental tools until I did personal research and fieldwork in Colombia from 2004 to 2007, which led me to realize that the communities still exist. In fact, some of them had been growing strongly, but under different names. Communities have reinvented themselves in amazing ways and initially it seems that their changes had been responding mainly to two factors: political changes (new government, new rules) and available funding.

Based on these observations, this chapter attempts to start a discussion about the risks faced by the LPBIs that have become a focus of attention, and in some cases of policy, at the national level. During the two presidential terms of Alvaro Uribe Velez two specific types of Local Peacebuilding Initiatives became part of the discourse and decision making at the national level: the *Development and Peace Programs* and the *Laboratories of Peace*. Specifically, the chapter explores three of the most representative LPBIs in the country—those in the Magdalena Medio, Oriente Antioqueño and Montes de Maria regions—in order to draw conclusions about the "nationalization" of LPBIs.

Peace and Development programs

The programs for Development and Peace in Colombia are systems of coordination arising from local civil society initiatives. They are pluralistic, inclusive, autonomous, and made up of organizations that share a common interest of building a country in peace through social and community participation at the local and regional level. They seek human development that is integral, sustainable, equalitarian, and in solidarity. Their work is based on three main principles:

1   Respect for life and the dignity of human beings in harmony with nature. This assumes the recognition of life above everything—that life should take place in dignity. The state has the legitimate monopoly in the use of force as long as it is based in the absolute recognition of human rights and citizens' rights.

2   Equity and solidarity. The recognition that all human beings are equal in rights and they should be equal in opportunity. Practicing solidarity, understood as the recognition of "the other" as "my" equal, specially the weak, the vulnerable, the excluded, and the poor.

3   Participatory democracy. The recognition that democracy is the best social practice to guarantee development and peace. Promoting and strengthening direct participation practices at the local level and installing capacity in local levels that would complement and give better meaning to representative democracy.

By 2009 there were 23 regional programs for Development and Peace, which are part of the Prodepaz Network, an umbrella organization created in 2002 with the idea of cooperation and mutual learning from the different regional programs. The idea of "Red Prodepaz" is to be a point for encounter, lessons learnt, mentoring, and promoting regional initiatives, while recognizing that each region is a universe unto itself, but that by having a network, such programs would have a bigger and better possibility of lobbying and being part of the formulation of public policies. Prodepaz's program members finance the network. It is currently the liaison between Acción Social (see below) and the regional programs, helping to facilitate access to governmental aid and programs within the framework of public policy on peace and development. The programs are constituted by both public and private institutions. Prodepaz is very keen on acknowledging the power of the Church in gaining the trust necessary to work in the community and the need for including academic and research institutions that allow each regional process, as well as the whole network, to learn more from their evaluations.

The first development and peace program in the Magdalena Medio was created in 1996. The three regional cases covered by this chapter are all Development and Peace programs that belong to the Prodepaz network.

Laboratories of Peace

The document on the European Commission's strategy for Colombia defines "Peace Laboratories" as being the main tool of its technical and financial cooperation (European Commission 2007, 27). The "Laboratory" concept promoted by the Commission arose from the existence in Colombia of broad movements for citizen participation in a campaign for peace. In some regions of the country these managed to transform themselves into social laboratories which explored (with the instruments that characterize the rule of law) paths of dialogue and peaceful coexistence, peaceful mechanisms of resistance, and the protection of the civilian population in the face of the armed conflict. With these initiatives, an attempt was made to deactivate the causes that set off the conflict and to encourage sustainable socio-economic development.

The two main objectives of the Laboratories of Peace are:

1   to construct "Zones of Peaceful Coexistence" among their inhabitants, through the strengthening of local institutions and support for the civilian agents that promote peace;

2   to encourage economic and social development, including, as far as possible, the promotion of alternative development (European Commission 2007, 28).

The objectives involve a social process of participation and the strengthening of local and regional institutions which, in the midst of conflict, seek to create political, cultural, social, and economic transformations that lead towards a lasting peace and better conditions of life for all inhabitants.

There are three Laboratories of Peace in Colombia. The first one started in the Middle Magdalena Region in 2002. The second one was approved in 2003 but officially only started in 2005 and covered three regions: Macizo Colombiano, Oriente Antioqueño, and Norte de Santander. The third was approved in 2006 and officially began working in 2007, covering two regions: Montes de Maria and Meta.

The objective the European Union has been, with cooperation through the Laboratories of Peace, to have projects that become an expression of participatory social processes, where lasting peace is based on the practice of human rights and strengthening social bonds through citizen participation. The hope of the European Union is to help Colombia have an opportunity for peace based on the idea of integral social development.

As the two types of LPBIs concerning this chapter have been described, there follows a description of the three regions forming the focus of this study, together with their Development and Peace and Laboratory of Peace programs.

Magdalena Medio

The Magdalena Medio region is located in the north-east of Colombia and contains 27 municipalities. Even though it is not formally an administrative region, it is defined by the proximity of these municipalities to the middle portion of the Magdalena river.[3] It has municipalities within the departments of Bolivar, Cesar, Santander, and Antioquia. Its area covers 30,000 square kilometers and by 2006 it had approximately 800,000 inhabitants.[4] The Magdalena Medio is incredibly rich in natural resources; it has gold, emeralds, tropical woods and substantial oil deposits (Katz Garcia 2004, 30). The country's main refinery—managed by ECOPETROL[5]—is located in the city of Barrancabermeja (hereafter Barranca), which is also the largest urban center and port in the region.

The region has a very high level of income generation—Barranca alone has a yearly budget of 125 billion pesos (roughly US $57 million). However, the level of poverty and inequality is quite high and by the early twenty-first century the number of people in the region living in poverty had risen to 70 percent (as compared to 45 percent in the rest of Colombia). Historically, there has been a high concentration of land and capital in a few hands, which is considered to be the main reason for the region's social unrest and armed conflict (Bergquistet al. 1992, 80). What at the beginning of the twentieth century was considered a frontier territory to be colonized by adventurous Colombians became a safe haven for persecuted Liberal leaders during La Violencia in the 1950s. However, the region has never had a strong state presence, with almost no social programs or basic services (Rudqvist and Van Sluys 2005, 15).

Because of the staggering absence of the state and the clear understanding of their risky conditions, the *campesinos* of the region have a long history of strong social mobilization. Peasants have demanded decent living conditions and access to land (traditionally controlled by large landowners) while oil industry workers have organized and demanded better pay, services, and—most importantly—the right to safety and security (CDPMM-OPI 2006, 59).[6]

Development and Peace program

In 1995 a development labeled the "Regional Process for Peace" began in Magdalena Medio. At the time the region was suffering from high levels of civil unrest and violence, prompting the formation of a group by members of the Catholic Church,[7] ECOPETROL, the workers' union (USO), the Center for Popular Education (CINEP), and others, in order to start thinking about what they should do as a region to make peace—and with whom they should make it. The underlying question for this group was "How to plow the fields with oil?" or how to use the profits and advantages of local oil industry to benefit peasants and farmers?

During several meetings the group worked around two main questions: why does such a resource-rich region have so much poverty and why is there so much violence in a society with such a deep love of life and rich cultural diversity? In order to address these questions, the group concluded that it would be necessary to ascertain the reality of living conditions in the region, leading to a first-stage research process labeled "diagnosis." This diagnosis was carried out in 1996 by the group and was based on the two paradoxes outlined above. The process was carried out in open spaces, collecting everyone's ideas and opinions. Through these workshops, people believed to be "natural enemies," because they occupied opposite ends of the ideological spectrum, sat down and started talking, and sharing.

After the diagnosis, there followed a second phase, called "the beginning" which took place from 1996 through 1998. During this phase the group promoted the creation of a nucleus of inhabitants (*nucleos de pobladores*) throughout the territory. The basic work that took place at that time was teaching people a participatory action methodology and promoting ways for people to identify their own solutions to the problems that they faced. On the administrative side, the regional process was formalized with an official program being founded, given a legal identity and developing an organizational structure. Since its inception a Jesuit priest, Fr. Francisco de Roux, has directed the "Program for Development and Peace of the Magdalena Medio (or PDPMM)." Their work is based on the three principles mentioned above: 1) respect for life and dignity; 2) equality and solidarity; and 3) participative democracy.

In 1998 the World Bank approved a loan to the program, thanks to a new initiative called the "Learning Innovation Loan" (LIL). The money given by the Bank provided the means to carry out proposals developed by individuals and communities during the "beginning" stage. While this process took place, the PDPMM saw the need to establish initiatives to address life inequality through sustainable economic and infrastructure projects and began to actively seek external funding. They found support from the government of Japan, which helped to fund some infrastructure projects, and facilitated encounters between officials of the EU and the PDPMM's director (DNP and PDPMM 2005). After an evaluation process, the World Bank approved a second loan (LIL II) to support already established projects and the PDPMM also obtained further EU funding for a "Laboratory of Peace" program.

During the last 20 years, PDPMM has become increasingly credible in the region. It is a trusted organization used by local people at the municipal and hamlet level to learn and validate their own processes. As one of the interviewees who works with the Program said, "the process started without money. During the time with no money people got organized to think about the problem and find solutions, so when the money arrived people were solid enough to carry the projects through."[8]

One of the strengths of the PDPMM is that it has had time to undertake the necessary social process and to make mistakes. They have achieved a certain level of maturity and they have a working methodology, consolidated and functioning within the associates and beneficiaries of the program. This maturity has allowed the PDPMM to become "the big brother" of other PDPs in the country and has helped the regional initiatives in Colombia become stronger and become recognized, not only nationally but internationally.

The first Laboratory of Peace

In 2002 the PDPMM became the first "Laboratory of Peace" in Colombia. The laboratory was conceived after several rounds of dialogues and negotiations between the PDPMM and the EU. Basically, the Peace and Development

Program showed the EU what they were doing and why it was worth participating in these projects. The EU's policy in Colombia was to support the country in fostering an environment that allowed a negotiated solution to the armed conflict, to help create conditions to address the deep rooted causes of the conflict and to give humanitarian assistance to the victims. Therefore the PDPMM structure and modus operandi were concurrent with the EU objectives (Rudqvist and Van Sluys 2005, 18). Many say that this was also the EU's way of creating a counterbalance to the warlike support offered by the US-supported Plan Colombia and Plan Patriota.[9]

The project's objective was and is to establish in the Magdalena Medio region a Laboratory of Peace through the defense of the basic human rights of all kinds of people, supporting their sustainable human development, contributing to peace dialogues and demonstrating different models of conflict resolution that could be applicable to other regions in the country.

The Laboratory is financed by the European Union, giving €34.8 million, and the Colombian government (using a World Bank loan), giving €7.4 million. The Laboratory's execution and management is carried out through Acción Social in Bogotá and the Program for Development and Peace in the Magdalena Medio (PDPMM), based in Barranca.

The Laboratory is implemented within a total of 29 municipalities belonging to the Departments of Bolivar, Cesar, Santander and Antioquia. The first phase (2002–5) was focused on building the conditions that allowed the strengthening of an organized civil society and democratic institutions to acquire a bigger capacity to influence and be part of a peace process through reorganizing social institutions and reorienting the course of economic activities. The first phase was implemented through four main components:

1 Peace Culture and Integral Rights;

2 Productive Activities and Alternative Development;

3 Social Infrastructure (education, health, water and waste);

4 Institutional strengthening of the State and Civil Society.

During the second phase (2005–9) the project continued some activities from the first phase, but intensified support for the resolution of the conflict, regional consensus and the peace process. A mid-term evaluation done at the end of 2004, helped to define the three main strategic "lines" for this second phase, including 1) strengthening peace, consensus and human rights; 2) social and cultural processes and governability, and; 3) productive and environmental processes oriented towards equity and sustainable development.

Strengthening peace, consensus and human rights articulates the social and institutional dynamics necessary for civil coexistence and respect for human rights. The main project of this "line" is support of "Humanitarian Spaces," which are eight municipalities constituted as Zones of Peace. Their territories are located in the outermost rural areas and the communities have been victimized and attacked by all the legal and illegal armed actors. The first Humanitarian Space was Micoahumando, followed by Tiquisio, Landazuri and Bajo Peñon. As the villagers from these areas are prisoners in their own territories (stranded by armed actors and having to endure food and general access blockades), the project wanted to make them visible so that their community process is recognized and they are seen as human beings. The idea was also to prevent displacement by helping people to live in dignity and not by being blocked in.

Social and cultural processes for democratic governability speak to the need for a cultural orientation towards life, institutional development and democracy and seeks to address what has been perceived as a culture of violence and death inculcated by nearly 40 years of civil conflict. In this "line" the work is mainly done with women, youth, and through alternative media. This line of work also seeks to help people regain trust in their institutions.

Productive and environmental processes oriented towards equity and sustainable development is a "line" that seeks to mobilize the region to create a peace economy that includes peasant farms and small industry. The idea of creating sustainable peasant farms speaks to the need for "food security" by giving each family 10 hectares on average for food cultivation or cash farming. The line also encourages the formation of associations and cooperatives for small-scale farming or industrial activity, focusing on human security and quality of life rather than on capital formation and acquisition. As one interviewee noted:

> By having these successful programs we take away people from the armed actors, the coca farming, etc. . . give them the opportunity to discover there is a way of having a good life from legal means respecting everyone . . . no coca because even though there is profit on it is in spite of the well-being of others.[10]

The Laboratory allows the design of a methodology that makes sense within the region, without taking away the idea of the global but reinforcing the identity of the region through peasants' education, basic skills training, working on sustainable development in harmony with the environment; developing areas of work for cross cutting themes like gender. It is a methodology that allows people to answer the questions that brought the PDPMM into being in the first place: the paradoxes of wealth, violence, and life.

The biggest added value of the second phase of the Laboratory is the broad participation of all actors in the definition of the local development plans, strengthening of local organizations, and the inclusion of as many actors as possible in the communities' decision making processes. The social fabric is being reconstructed and the benefits of working with networks have become evident for the communities.

Oriente Antioqueño

The Eastern Antioquia region contains 23 municipalities that occupy an area of approximately 7,021 square kilometers. It involves around 11 percent of the Antioquia Department's territory. There are 523,000 inhabitants, with 55 percent living in urban areas and 45 percent in rural areas. The area is rich in natural resources specially water, this being the region where 35 percent of the country's electricity is produced. It has a rainforest, a small mountain chain and a combination of low and high lands ideal for coffee and sugar cane production.[11] Oriente Antioqueño is very close to Medellin (the second largest and most developed city in the country).

Development and Peace program

The Program Development for Peace—PRODEPAZ—was founded in 1999, thanks to an initiative from the archdioceses of Sonsón and Rionegro; Interconexión Eléctrica S.A.-ISA; ISAGEN; the PROANTIOQUIA Foundation; the Life, Justice and Peace Corporation; the dioceses of Barrancabermeja; and the Center for Popular Education (CINEP). PRODEPAZ promotes community organization and empowerment for its members, so that they can become political and social actors, generating changes that improve their quality of life and their environment. This is a process of sustainable human development that marks all its institutional actions, since PRODEPAZ conceives of itself as promoting the development of human beings in their abilities, opportunities, and freedoms, in addition to economic growth and sustainable ecosystems.

The central objective of action for PRODEPAZ is any community that lives, builds its own history, organizes, participates, plans and intervenes in the territory of which it is part. PRODEPAZ interacts with the regional community, based on their needs and initiatives, while respecting their culture and values, fostering knowledge from a dialogue of learning, integrated processes and projects that become sustainable over time.

As its mission, PRODEPAZ participates in the process of integration and territorial development through the joint efforts of institutions, the strengthening of democratic governance and community empowerment, building conditions for peaceful coexistence and a good life.

Since its establishment in 1999, PRODEPAZ has initiated a process of coordination with organizations and projects with a presence in 23 municipalities in Eastern Antioquia and the five towns in the sub-region of Porce. In addition to its activities as a regional coordinator, PRODEPAZ is involved in three lines of institutional projects, including some actions that are already managed by the communities themselves, and others that are in the process of consolidation.

The second Laboratory of Peace

At the request of the government of Colombia, the second "Laboratory of Peace" was identified and established through the Peace and Development Program in Eastern Antioquia. At the end of 2003, US $33 million was approved by the European Union to assist with actions in 23 municipalities in the region. Colombia contributed US $8.4 million from a World Bank credit.

The general objective of this laboratory was to build, in a collective manner, the conditions for a durable peace and peaceful coexistence, based on a life of dignity and opportunity for all inhabitants of 23 municipalities of the eastern region of the Department of Antioquia. The specific objectives were:

- to establish and consolidate sustainable spaces and processes that reduce the level of conflict and violence and the vulnerability of the population in Eastern Antioquia;

- to create a Culture of Peace based on the strengthening of peace dialogue capacities and a respect for Human Rights (DIH and Life in Dignity);

- to encourage sustainable socio-economic development that improves the living conditions of the target populations in harmony with the environment.

This second Laboratory for Peace was negotiated and approved in 2003. However, it did not start carrying out its pilot projects until mid-2005. Changes in the Colombian government through the creation of Acción Social, plus a new set of regulations and issues of contracting from the European Union, delayed the process. The open call to everyone for possible projects started in 2005 and, in mid-2006, the Laboratory started implementing more than 300 projects, under the watchful eye of Acción Social and PRODEPAZ.

Montes de Maria

Montes de Maria is a natural region located in the central part of the Departments of Bolivar and Sucre, in the Caribbean region of Colombia. The Montes de Maria region contains 15 municipalities, seven in the Department of Bolivar (Carmen de Bolivar, Marialabaja, San Juan Nepomuceno, San Jacinto, Cordova, the Guamo, and Zambrano) and eight in the Department of Sucre (Ewes, Dealer, Colossus, Morroa, the Palm Hearts, San Onofre, San Antonio de Palmito, and Tolúviejo). The municipalities of Corozal and Sincelejo, are also considered an area of influence on the region of Montes de Maria, as they are the closest and biggest urban areas, involving small cities. This region has around 420,000 inhabitants and covers around 6,500 square kilometers.

The region is mainly populated by what has been called "the historical poor," meaning peasants who have lived there since the 1930s and 1940s but have not had any ownership of land. The majority of the people are of African descent and there are some indigenous communities, such as the Zenues. The land has been traditionally owned by few rich farmers, who do not live in the area and in many cases did not even use the land. The peasants either worked for them or took over the unused soil. The ANUC[12] was born in this region. As is the case in so many other areas of Colombia, this region had little to no state presence, either for governance or for the provision of services.

An important factor to take into account in the region is that President Uribe's government declared it a "Rehabilitation and Consolidation" zone. Within the "Democratic Security" policy of President Uribe, these were zones which were part of the pilot program for his Plan Patriota, the military offensive that declared "total war" against the illegal armed actors and promised to "restore" government control of the territory.

Development and Peace program

The Foundation Program for Development and Peace of the Montes de Maria (FPDPMMa) was born out of a specific interest of civil society, the state and the Program of United Nations for Development (PNUD) to promote peace and development in the region. The process started in 1997 when a number of mayors from the region met in the municipality of Carmen de Bolivar and decided to ask then-President Samper for direct intervention in the region, given the situation of extreme violence there. This event made way for the writing in 1999 of an "Integral Development Plan for Montes de Maria." The document came about as the result of working tables and teamwork all over the region. Even though the Plan did not become part of the national interest, the relevant governors adopted it and it became the basis for the "Human Development Plan of Montes de Maria." In 2001, different organizations identified the need to create a Program for Development and Peace following the steps of the Magdalena Medio experience. The PNUD Caribbean regional office pushed the actors to take firm steps and the PDP started working. However, it was not until the production of the document, Promontes, that the FPDPMMa officially started up under the leadership of the dioceses of Sincelejo and Magangué, the Archdioceses of Cartagena, and the Mennonite Church (Justapaz) all of which constituted its charter members. The FPDPMMa headquarters are located in the city of Sincelejo in the Department of Sucre, on the North coast of Colombia.

In 2003, with the signing of the "Pact for Governability" in the municipality of Morroa (Sucre) by the two governors, 15 municipality mayors, and representatives of the Network for Social Solidarity, PNUD and the University of Cartagena, a true network was constituted. This Pact and the leadership assumed from the FPDPMMa marks the start of a stage for the dynamic and collective construction of a future based on recovering and reconstructing the Montes de Maria territory.

The FPDPMMa mission is to articulate and to lead, in an efficient and effective way, efforts, initiatives and projects to raise the quality of life of the people in the Montes de Maria area by working for human, integral and sustainable development within a lasting peace. Its main objective was to generate a participatory dynamic of social, economic, political and cultural order, by means of joint work of civil society with state, local, national and international institutions to bring development and peace to the Montes de Maria region.

The third Laboratory of Peace

The Third Laboratory for Peace is the result of the lessons learned from previous Laboratory experiences. The aim is to consolidate the local Peace and Development initiatives in conflict zones, to build a strategic sector, and to ensure better integration and coordination, so that international cooperation is more in line with the national context. Its general objective is to build a durable peace and peaceful coexistence through collective action by creating the conditions for (1) legal economic opportunities and (2) greater public security for all inhabitants.

Its specific objectives are to:

1 contribute to the construction of a transparent and effective rule of law system by establishing peace and development initiatives at the local level;

2 reduce the level of illicit crop production, conflict and violence and increase reconciliation;

3 continue to support regional Peace and Development Programs that have had an impact on violence, conflict and exclusion;

4 extend support to other peace initiatives that focus on vulnerable groups, such as women, youth and ethnic groups;

5 support the formulations of a public policy on Peace and Development that takes into account the lessons learned from the two previous components as well as the first and second Laboratories of Peace.

Having reviewed the three regions the main question becomes: how do they relate to the national level? The answer is found in the national public policy adopted by Alvaro Uribe Velez during his two presidential terms 2002–6 and 2006–10.

Uribe policies towards PDPs and Laboratories of Peace

The Colombian National Development Plan (NDP) is the guideline used by any Colombian government to implement its political platform and to set the course which Colombia will take to meet the presidential mandate. Former President Uribe's National Development Plan called "Towards a Communitarian State" lays out the path to arrive at such a goal. A "communitarian" state should be a participatory state that involves all citizens in achieving social success. It is a state that manages the public resources with austerity and efficiency. It is a decentralized state, which privileges regional autonomy with transparency, political responsibility and community participation. A communitarian state does not tolerate corruption and does not coexist with violence of any kind.

It would promote conditions in which everybody is an owner, responsible for property. It would promote public investment for the creation of productive jobs and it will work hard for the elimination of bureaucracy and "politicking."

Peace and development strategies are integrated into the Democratic Security chapter of the NDP. Line four of the objectives proposes the strengthening of the regions as central for democratic security, especially the regions affected by the conflict. The strategic actions are the same that the regional PDPs developed in communities going through their "Diagnosis" phases (DNP 2002, 74). The 2002 and 2006 NDPs also state that one of the strategies to promote the government's regional goals is to support the existing Programs for Development and Peace and the Laboratories of Peace. It should, however, be noted that this section of the document always talks about the promotion and care of "citizens" rights but it never refers to "human" rights (DNP 2002, 2006).

Democratic security and international cooperation

In two separate documents, the government developed the "Democratic Security and Defense Policy," approved in July 2003, and the "Strategy for International Cooperation of the Colombian Government," written in February 2005.

The Democratic Security policy is the cornerstone of Uribe's long-term plan to establish state control over the entire national territory (Colombia 2003, 4). It calls for better coordination of security entities in order to fight terrorism (both insurgents and paramilitaries) and crime, counter illegal drugs, better protect border areas and fight corruption. The main idea behind the policy is to "reinforce and guarantee the rule of law in all our national territory." It is worth noting that this particular document does not include the Peace and Development Plans, as the original plan did.

The Strategy for International Cooperation policy establishes the way for the creation and approval of the government agency, Acción Social, which became the articulating axis between the nation, the PDPs and any project coming from international cooperation. It also creates the way for the government's program called "Peace and Development," which was to be executed by the PDPs and was directed to ensure access and use of services for internally displaced people.

Two things are worth mentioning regarding the first Uribe administration. One is that the "democratic security" policy was considered a success, and gave Uribe high popularity numbers specially in the urban areas, even though it is seldom recognized that such "success" was built upon former President Pastrana's previous policies. The second concerns a memorandum produced in June 2005, in which Uribe's government forbids the use of the word "conflict" in any official document produced in Colombia. Because the PDPs had to report and work with Acción Social, and they produced the official reports, the PDP had to spend time in figuring out ways of explaining the dynamics of the conflict by using different concepts and definitions instead of the words "armed conflict."

From the beginning of his mandate, Uribe showed his "rule of law" attitude that translated into his public policies. By including the articulation of the work with regional PDPs and Laboratories of Peace within the ambit of "democratic security," President Uribe demonstrated that even though he would "tolerate" the programs, he would not allow anybody to change the basic course he had laid out for the country. The country, through Acción Social, now has access to all the reports and work done at the PDPs and the Laboratories of Peace throughout the country. Acción Social became a powerful actor in the regions, as it could stop a local process anytime it wanted simply by "getting lost" in policies and rules.

In June 2005, when Uribe declared that there was no "conflict" in Colombia and that the illegal armed actors were terrorists or criminals who should be prosecuted, the entire dynamic of the work in the regions changed. This declaration raised questions for peace and development organizations as how to work to better the conditions in which the victims of an ongoing conflict found themselves, while denying its existence in official reports. How to justify the need for projects based on the effects of war, when the government forbade the use of the terms "conflict" or "civil war"? Or how to discuss the actions of the National Army when the government forbade its inclusion within the categories of "Armed Actors" or "Actors in Conflict"?

That same year, Uribe publicly declared that "Humanitarian Zones," "Peace Territories," and "Constitutional Assemblies" were ambiguous terms and practices, and that if they tried to take away the right of the state to control and secure national territory, it was because these places were "friends" of the terrorists. Uribe also declared that the NGOs, networks, and people working for the survival of these institutions, or working for human rights, were also "terrorist supporters" and, as such, would be investigated and treated as such.

During the first Uribe administration and thanks to the democratic security policy, programs such as the PDPs and Laboratories for Peace were constantly monitored and became well known by the President. Local initiatives like the "Humanitarian Spaces" in the Magdalena Medio region were in grave danger.

One of the main lines of strategic action for the PDPs and the Laboratories was the Human Rights component. Uribe's public position about human rights workers has brought a new threat to the people working with and for the PDPs and Laboratories. After such public declarations, the programs saw an increase of threats against them or their work. The threats came from regrouped paramilitary bands who believed they were fulfilling the President's commands.

Basically, the peace and development policies of Uribe, as stated in his NDP, are in contradiction with the policies towards the end of his first term. Yet somehow, he has been fairly successful in co-opting the regional peace and development processes.

Acción Social: Governmental cooperation

The presidential agency for social action and international cooperation, Acción Social, is an agency created by the Colombian government with the objective of channeling national and international resources to carry out the social programs of the Office of the President. It takes care of vulnerable and at risk populations affected by poverty, drug trafficking and violence. This agency combines what in the past were the tasks of the Social Solidarity Network (RSS)[13] and the Colombian Agency for International Cooperation (ACCI).[14] The agency is subscribed to the Fund for the Investment in Peace (FIP)[15] which finances the social component of Plan Colombia with programs such as Families in Action, Youth in Action, Forest Guard Families, social infra-structure, productive projects and others. Acción Social takes care of victims of violence, the network for food security and the national system to give complete support to the displaced population. It also coordinates and promotes national and international; technical and financial non-refundable cooperation that the country gives or receives. The agency officially started work in 2005.

The agency is bound to fulfill the social objectives of the President as they are described in the National Development Plan. There are two main offices within the agency, one for social programs and one for international cooperation. The Programs for Peace and Development and Laboratories of Peace are connected to the first office mentioned above. In March of 2004 a governmental decree approved the Peace and Development programs to articulate the policies to take better care of the displaced population and to create a strategy to support the Regional Development and Peace Programs as well as the Laboratories of Peace. From 2005 onward, Acción Social was in charge of fulfilling the program's objectives financed by a US $30 million loan from the World Bank.

At this point it should be clear how and why, owing to President Uribe's strategy outlined in the two National Development Plans, the local peacebuilding initiatives in the three regions—Magdalena Medio, Oriente Antioqueño and Montes de Maria—have become connected to and immersed in the bureaucracy of national institutions through Acción Social's mandate for managing funding directed to the Development and Peace and Laboratories of Peace programs. The next section briefly presents the "Smití Case," which shows how, as a result of such connections, national institutions can co-opt the ongoing, local peace-building processes and the successes achieved by local initiatives.

From paper to practice: The Smití Case

Smití is a municipality within the Magdalena Medio region that is part of the Peace and Development Program of the Magdalena Medio. Smití was heavily affected by armed violence, first in the 1970s and 1980s with the ELN and FARC fighting to get access to the territory; and in the 1990s between FARC and the AUC for similar reasons. Once the AUC consolidated its power within the territory, there was massive internal displacement of the municipality's inhabitants, which involved losing their lands at the hands of the victimizers.

The PDPMM started a process of strengthening the community, a strategy that included a return of the IDPs. One of the big challenges for this process was to find ways to ensure that the returning victims and inhabitants would have access to work and the means to have a life of dignity. One of the strategies to achieve those objectives was to find land to start productive projects. The only land available was that belonging to the National Reparation Fund (*Fondo de Rearacion de Victimas*) which possessed it as part of the land returned by demobilized former AUC combatants who, in the past, had violently taken the same land away from local peasants. The PDPMM asked Acción Social to help devise a legal way to help the peasants use the land, even if it was not being officially returned to them.

In February 2011, a court ruled that victims and inhabitants of the municipality of Smití (where Acción Social was allowed to organize a trust with the PDPMM) had the right to utilize land under the CORPOAGROSUR (*Centro Provisional de Gestión Agroempresarial del Sur*) cooperative project. The decision was made after PDPMM requested that Acción Social relinquish control of the cooperative, which was delivered to the Fondo de Reparación de Víctimas by the AUC's Bloque Central Bolívar. Although this petition was previously formulated, Acción Social was unable to support the court action due to its role as cooperative administrator. As a result, an alternative was sought through Law 1151 (2007) and article 8 of Law 975 (2005), allowing the temporary return of possessions in cases of collective and individual reparation. Article 8 of the said law defines reparation as related to "restitution, indemnity, rehabilitation, satisfaction, and procedural guarantees" and as "that related to the efforts of returning a victim to his or his prior situation before the execution of the crime." Law 1151 (2007) referenced the bill's project, which was later approved as the National Development Plan 2006–10, which focused on promoting reconciliation, creating a global strategy via collaboration with relevant actors, and designing a peace and development model. Moreover, Congress passed a motion to maintain humanitarian support and to continue negotiation efforts in the armed conflict as relevant aspects of the project. These types of decision first allow resources in the fund to be distributed to various social programs, preventing a waste of resources and their utilization by irrelevant third parties; and, second, generate additional capital to sustain the fund. Understanding the importance in avoiding the depreciation of possessions, the judge authorized the signing of the contract between Acción Social and PDPMM, under the condition that those to benefit from the said agreement would be victims of the armed conflict. Additionally, the judge gave freedom to both parties to define term limits (Iievano 2011).

Acción Social was instrumental in finding the appropriate legal figure to enable the PDPMM and the peasants of Smití to start using the land and obtain some income—and some dignity—while something was done about the formal title. However, Acción Social has taken a position in which they present themselves as the generators of the ideas and telling the country how they put together a fine solution to the Smití problem. In several venues, Acción Social has portrayed and marketed itself as the genesis of the ideas and the main reason for the successful return of peasants to Smití. In most cases, the PDPMM and the local organizations are not even mentioned or recognized as the ones who organized a successful return.

Final thoughts and conclusion

Between the mid-1990s and the mid-2000s, as the "zones of peace" in Magdalena Medio, Oriente Antioqueño and Montes de Maria transitioned, some to Development and Peace Programs and others to Laboratories of Peace, many of the original objectives, processes and achievements were appropriated by non-local actors, taking away their successes from the locals. This seems to add another possible relationship between the national and the local levels to the list outlined by Mitchell in his Introduction—one in which institutions at the national level co-opt and, to some degree, corrupt the aims and activities of local peacebuilders. This process seems different from one which simply supports or even sponsors local peacebuilding efforts.

Within the new political realities at the national level, the national government has decreased the internal capacities of the Local Peace Building Initiatives by including new institutions to manage funding and to control local aims, themes and processes; this becomes evident when reading the reports required by Acción Social. The planning, execution and reporting of projects have to be carried out within the "Logical Framework" methodology designed and required by the World Bank. As a consequence, the LPBIs have adapted their processes to a framework that is removed from the reality of local peasants who are simply trying to achieve food security. The principle of "Do No Harm," of respecting the realities of local communities and of building upon the processes and institutions already built by them has not been respected. This co-optation has had dire consequences, especially for regions where there is a strong presence of minorities of indigenous and Afro-Colombian populations.

As the three LPBIs in this study have become more visible to the entire country, there has also been a larger presence of national NGOs and mass media. In many cases, information has been compartmentalized, creating stereotypes about the range, scope and political realm of the programs.

This visibility has also brought wider interest by funding agencies and foreign governments, who offer to finance specific projects focusing on their own agendas. Local organizations become competitors among themselves to gain access to the aforementioned resources, creating breaches in a social fabric that was just becoming strong and sustainable. As funding agencies begin allocating money to some organizations but not to others, some level of disparity increases and those who were natural partners and friends in the past become adversaries.

Finally, by including the Development and Peace Programs and the Laboratories of Peace in the National Development Plan, the government has influenced and changed the course of the local initiatives, in many cases to their detriment. With Juan Manuel Santos as the new President, Colombia seems to be witnessing a shift in public policy that could become beneficial for some LPBIs. However, this remains to be evaluated as it is too early in the presidential period to have enough information for reliable analysis.

My intention is not to say that everything becomes negative when local peacebuilding initiatives become part of the national agenda. In fact the visibility can help with the security of community leaders. Funding is always badly needed and it would be foolish to deny that many people get a livelihood out of the projects. However it is important to mention that until the bottom-up approach is properly involved and used, and the full participation and history of the LPBIs is fully recognized, they are at risk of becoming a reference in a textbook, and an example of how to "go national," in spite of themselves.

Notes

1 Also see Mitchell (2007).

2 *La Violencia* is the term given to Colombia's civil war, which started in the late 1940s. The length and extent of the civil conflict are in much dispute, with some indicating that La Violencia was only ten years and others contend that outbreaks of violence in the 1990s or the current conflict are little more than the continuation of La Violencia.

3 The Magdalena river is the largest body of water in the country and was the main way of transportation of people and goods for the first half of the twentieth century. Its use has decreased as the armed struggle in rural areas makes it dangerous to travel and most goods were either despoiled or robbed.

4 This data is derived from research by *Observatorio de Paz Integral* in Barrancabermeja.

5 *Empresa Colombiana de Petroleos*—Colombian Enterprise for Petroleum.

6 During field research, one of the most compelling images I saw from a balcony serves to illustrate the point about the poverty and inequality in the region. The city of Barranca is divided between ECOPETROL (the refinery) and the rest of the town. The refinery covers approximately 20 percent of the total city. This area is fenced and you need to have either a special permit or an ID card to access it. It has its own airport, housing, entertainment center—including the town's only movie theater—shopping mall, and other facilities. Outside the fence, there are houses made out of a variety of different materials. In many cases, the outskirts do not have water, sewage systems, public transportation or electricity. I saw a town divided in two, and what lies within and outside the fence best symbolizes the reality of the Magdalena Medio.

7 Like other communities in Latin America, the Church serves as a fundamental actor in achieving social justice in the local community. Dioceses and archdioceses that work for the betterment of local people through pastoral social activity are highly trusted by members of that community and, like in the Philippines, often become central pillars of zones of peace movements.

8 Interview conducted in Barrancabermeja with author. All interviewees were granted anonymity.

9 Plan Colombia was a US $1.3 billion grant designed primarily to assist the Colombian military with anti-narcotics efforts. Plan Patriota was Colombian President Uribe's initiative to send almost 17,000 troops to southern Colombia to combat left-wing guerilla movements (see Rojas 2007).

10 See note 8.

11 Information drawn from the Regional Autonomous Corporation Rionegro—Nare (CORNARE) website at www.cornare.gov.co.

12 *Asociacion Nacional de Usuarios Campesinos* (National Association of Peasant Workers).

13 *Red de Solidaridad Social.*

14 *Agencia Colombiana para la Cooperación Internacional.*

15 *Fondo de Inversión para la Paz.*

Works cited

Bergquist, Charles W., Ricardo Peñaranda, and Gonzalo Sánchez G, eds. 1992. *Violence in Colombia: the contemporary crisis in historical perspective.* Wilmington, DE: SR Books.

CDPMM-OPI. 2006. *Estudios Técnicos de Investigación para el Fortalecimiento del Observatorio de Paz Integral.* Laboratorio de Paz del Magdalena Medio.

Colombia, Government of. 2003. *Democratic security and defense policy,* edited by Presidency of the Republic and Ministry of Defense. Bogotá: Provided by the Colombian Embassy in Washington DC.

DNP. 2002. *Plan Nacional de Desarrollo: hacia un Estado Comunitario,* edited by D. n. d. Planeación. Bogotá: DNP.

— 2006. *Plan Nacional de Desarrollo: Estado Comunitario: desarrollo para todos,* edited by D. n. d. Planeación. Bogotá: DNP.

DNP, and PDPMM. 2005. *Cifras de Violencia 2002–2005 Magdalena Medio Magdalena Medio:* Departamento Nacional de Planeación Programma de Desarrollo y Paz Magdalena Medio.

European Commission. 2007. *Colombia: country strategy paper 2007–2013 E/2007/484.* Brussells: European Commission.

Hancock, Landon E., and Pushpa Iyer. 2007. "The nature, structure and variety of 'peace zones'." In *Zones of peace,* edited by L. E. Hancock and C. R. Mitchell. Bloomfield, CT: Kumarian Press.

Iievano, Gabriel. 2011. "Judge approves that victims from Smití benefit from goods delivered to the Reparations Fund" [News Report]. Comisión Nacional de Reparación y Reconciliación, February 28, 2011 [cited August 22, 2011]. Available from http://www.cnrr.org.co/contenido/09i/spip.php?article777.

Katz Garcia, Mauricio. 2004. "A regional peace experience: the Magdalena Medio Peace and Development Programme." *Accord: Alternatives to War: Colombia's Peace Processes* (14): 30–3.

Mitchell, Christopher R. 2007. "The Theory and Practice of Sanctuary: from Asylia to Local Zones of Peace." In *Zones of peace*, edited by L. E. Hancock and C. R. Mitchell. Bloomfield, CT: Kumarian Press.

Mitchell, Christopher, and Susan Allen Nan. 1997. "Local peace zones as institutionalized conflict." *Peace Review* 9 (2): 159.

Rojas, Catalina. 2007. "Islands in the Stream." In *Zones of peace*, edited by L. E. Hancock and C. R. Mitchell. Bloomfield, CT: Kumarian Press.

Rudqvist, Anders, and Fred Van Sluys. 2005. *Informe Final de Evaluacion de Medio Término Laboratorio de Paz del Magdalena Medio*. Brussells: European Consultants Organisation.

5

South Africa's infrastructure for peace[1]

Andries Odendaal

Introduction

Peace agreements rarely put an immediate stop to violence. Of this fact, South Africa is as good a demonstration as any. There are multiple reasons for this state of affairs. One of the reasons, though, that is not receiving sufficient attention, is the role of local (i.e., sub-national) dynamics in the production of violence. In this respect, South Africa's National Peace Accord is of interest because it included provisions for an elaborate "infrastructure" to facilitate the implementation of the peace accord at the local level. This design was a tacit admission that an elite pact was in itself insufficient to make peace. There was need for a conscious link between national peacemaking and local peacebuilding. The chapter offers a description and interpretation of South Africa's experience with its infrastructure for peace.

Furthermore, the discussion below highlights local peacebuilding in the context of the ongoing, high-level negotiations for peace. Hancock and Iyer (2007, 29–31) have made the distinction between stages in a protracted, intra-state conflict in which local peacebuilding initiatives take place: (1) local peacebuilding while violent combat continues; (2) local peacebuilding while negotiations are taking place or in implementation of nationally agreed peace objectives; and (3) local peacebuilding as an aspect of long-term national peacebuilding. The discussion in this chapter is a description of the second category.

The momentum of violence

Between 1985 and 1990 more than 6,000 people died in South Africa because of political violence (Gastrow 1995). This meant more than a 1,000 deaths per year—the yardstick that is commonly used to determine when a state is in civil war.

The conflict was long in the making. In 1652 the Dutch East India Company decided to establish a base at what is today Cape Town to supply fresh water and food to its scurvy-ridden ships en route to the East in pursuit of the lucrative spice trade. It was the beginning of European settlement, a process that gathered steam as Europe increasingly exported its surplus populations to its colonies across the world. The discovery of extraordinarily rich diamond and goldfields in the late nineteenth century invited many more. The dispossession of the land and rights of the indigenous populations took place with the familiar moral self-assuredness and sense of exceptional entitlement of the colonial age. When the decolonization drive gathered momentum in the aftermath of the Second World War, the white population, which had in the meantime developed a strong sense of indigenousness, faced the prospect of being subjected to black majority rule. The policy of apartheid was the result: the segregation of the country into several ethnic-based indigenous states in order to allow the white population to maintain self-rule in the area designated "white"—which just happened to include 83 percent of the land and its most lucrative natural resources. The African National Congress was established in 1912 as a vehicle of black resistance. Initially a very moderate voice representing black aspirations, it decided in the 1960s to embark on the road of an "armed struggle." The armed conflict never really gathered momentum beyond a number of sabotage acts. Much more effective were the increasing international isolation of South Africa and the imposition of economic and other sanctions on the country.

Internally a number of developments made significant contributions to the impasse of the 1980s. On the one hand, black internal resistance escalated. A student uprising on June 16, 1976 in Soweto (which at the time led to more than 500 deaths) became a catalyst for a movement of civil disobedience and "ungovernability" that had built a seemingly unstoppable momentum towards the end of the 1980s. Most of the governance structures in the urban black areas had collapsed by then; most of the universities and schools in black areas were spaces of intense resistance to government rule; while the production of factories and mines was increasingly disrupted by the politicization of black trade unions. On the other hand, due to a combination of external pressures and internal soul-searching, the bankruptcy of the ideology and policies of the ruling National Party became increasingly clear not only to the opponents of apartheid, but also to an important section of the ruling party and its supporters.

In short, at the start of the decade in 1990 the government of South Africa had lost its legitimacy to govern in the eyes of the majority of citizens, and also much of its capacity. The consequence was a spiral of violence—perpetrated by security forces on activists and civilians; by the armed wings of the liberation movements on security and (increasingly) civilian targets; by communities on government institutions; and by community activists on those that they had perceived to be "sell-outs" or traitors.

On February 2, 1990, President FW de Klerk made a dramatic announcement to parliament that the liberation movements would be unbanned and that negotiations for a "New South Africa" would commence. This announcement and the subsequent freeing from prison of Nelson Mandela and other political prisoners signified the end of an era and, in principle, removed the reason for violence. However, during the period September 1990 to August 1991, 2,649 persons died in political violence—roughly double the figure of the previous year.

In September 1991 all the major political actors agreed to a National Peace Accord that had the specific objective to stem the violence. The National Peace Accord (NPA) was not an agreement with political substance. The negotiation of a new constitution was taking place in a parallel process. It was essentially a code of conduct binding all actors to pursue the political process in a non-violent manner. Its major objective, therefore, was to stem the violence. However, in the year following the signing of the peace accord 3,404 people died of political violence; and 3,567 the next year (Gastrow 1995, 28). Democratic elections in April 1994 and the formation of a new, inclusive government did not stop the violence either, particularly not in the troubled KwaZulu-Natal province. By April 1994 (the month of elections) the monthly death toll was 452. It dropped dramatically to 106 for the remainder of the year (which still translated into more than a 1,000 deaths per year). By December 1996 the toll came down to a "respectable" 42 per month. At this stage the KwaZulu-Natal province accounted for 84 percent of the violence (against 67 percent before the elections) (SA History Online 2010).

Rather than bringing an end to violence, therefore, the opening of the political space in general and the signing of a peace accord in particular led to a spike in violence that only subsided to some extent two years into the new political dispensation. There are probably multiple reasons for this state of affairs, but in South Africa's case two factors stand out: the nature of the negotiation process; and the complex relationship between the national political process and local conflict systems. I do not, in this chapter, pay much attention to the first factor apart from mentioning that, as Sisk (1995) has graphically demonstrated, incidents of violence in South Africa followed the ebb and flow of the negotiation process. At every point where the process was in crisis or when critical decisions had to be made, violence spiked. Such violence is normally an expression of the collective anxiety regarding making peace with the adversary. It expresses the lack of trust in the other party or in the process of negotiations; or at times the lack of agreement within a party that the deal should be made (Darby 2001; Höglund 2004). Violence may of course also be used to further political advantage by weakening the position of the adversary. Such violence may do damage to the negotiation process, primarily because of the way it destroys trust, but it may also inadvertently strengthen the process because of the urgency it adds to finding a lasting solution (Höglund 2004). In South Africa's case, various groups bent on "spoiling" the peace were involved, including sections of the security forces, which masterminded and stimulated violence. In short, the fact that negotiations for the political future of the country were continuing at the same time as the National Peace Accord tried to stem the violence, meant that the Peace Accord was always going to be only relatively successful in reaching its objectives.

My objective with this chapter is to focus on the second factor—the interconnectedness of national and local conflict systems. Rather than leading to stability, the opening up of political space often creates additional channels through which violence can be instigated or organized (Höglund 2008). Such violence is of a more opportunistic nature and is, by its nature, more local than national. There are two sides to this phenomenon. On the one hand post-agreement violence is a continuation of the national struggle, but at the local level. Darby (2001) has in this respect referred to the "replacement of political violence by confrontational violence"—face-to-face violence as communities and individuals pursue the unfinished business of the war at personal and community level. On the other hand existing local conflict systems continue to exploit the opportunity for violence in the fluid context of transitional politics—in pursuit of local agendas. These two aspects interact. The political infuses the local; the local expresses itself politically. The experience with South Africa's peace process provided ample illustration of this phenomenon.

Local agency in matters of violence and peace

Peace agreements are normally elite pacts. At the local level the acceptance of such elite pacts is not inevitable and does not happen automatically. In fact, political elites often suffer from the same bias as academic scholars who hold the view that matters of violence and peace are solely determined by the elite. In reality, though, "the loci of agency spawned by civil war are inherently multiple" (Kalyvas 2006, 365). Local communities and actors are more than mere victims of violence. They do indeed catch the (TV) eye as recipients of humanitarian aid and inhabitants of refugee camps; however, they have agency and contribute to the patterns of violence—and peace.

In South Africa in the early 1990s, violence was spinning out of control in spite of the fact that the leadership of all those political groupings that mattered had committed themselves to peace. At the local level the calls by national leaders were not heeded. Even the iconic Nelson Mandela, leader of the African National Congress, was unable to convince all his followers all the time that they should not resort to violence; neither did President de Klerk's professed commitment to peace deter sections of his security forces from stoking and committing violence.

The areas around Johannesburg and the KwaZulu-Natal province of South Africa were particularly prone to violence because of the conflict between the ANC and the Inkatha Freedom Party. The latter was at heart a Zulu nationalist party. It had at times entered into uncomfortable alliances with reactionary white forces, but it would be a mistake to dismiss its members as apartheid stooges. Of the latter there were quite a few—black leaders who were co-opted into collaboration with the apartheid project. IFP members, however, under the leadership of Mangosuthu Buthelezi, had a mind of their own and exasperated both the white government and the ANC. They fought for a federalist system, effectively to allow them substantial control of the KwaZulu-Natal province; and stood for a free market economy. Both positions irked the ANC deeply, who were at heart socialist and centrist. What irritated most, however, was their unwillingness to subject themselves to the leadership of the dominant liberation movement and their willingness to collaborate with spoiler groups within the security forces of the government. The resulting violence between the ANC and Inkatha was vicious and deeply threatening to the country's stability.

The National Peace Accord of September 1991 was not the first attempt to deal with the problem of escalating violence. In January 1991 the ANC and IFP entered into bilateral peace negotiations and concluded a peace agreement to stop the violence. Thousands of copies of the accord in English and Zulu were distributed and flyers announced "Leaders make peace." On the day after the agreement six people were hacked to death in KwaZulu-Natal and another 27 killed in the Johannesburg area due to ANC–IFP strife (Sisk 1995, 123). The peace agreement was stillborn. Some people on the ground were clearly not interested in what the leaders had done.

Though ANC–IFP violence dominated the landscape, it was not the only expression of violence. Across the country, including in provinces like the Western Cape and Eastern Cape where the IFP had a very weak presence, violence escalated in the early 1990s, though not nearly at the same scale (Gastrow 1995; Collin Marks 2000; Odendaal and Spies 1997). The violence between white and black took place mostly in the interaction between security forces and community activists. The police in particular were called in to control or disperse protest actions, events that often turned violent. There was a high level of social restiveness in the country. Protest marches, sit-ins, consumer boycotts, and other forms of socio-political discontent flourished in the new political space that the transitional period opened up, with the option of violence ever present. The triggers for these events were, in most cases, local. There were exceptions when the initiative for protest action came from the national level, such as in April 1993 when Chris Hani, the highly popular leader of the South African Communist Party, was assassinated; or when, following the Boipatong massacre in June 1992, the ANC suspended negotiations and called for "rolling mass action." The bulk of protest action that led to confrontations between local communities and the security forces, though, was triggered by local dynamics: the decisions or behavior of local municipalities or businesses; local issues that acquired political significance; local personality clashes; local competition for economic advantage (such as between taxi associations or in cattle raids); and local intra-party struggles for power. However, with some exceptions, whites were largely protected from the violence because the police safeguarded their areas.

The escalation of violence post-1990 was baffling to most observers. In an illuminating essay, Du Toit (1993) attempted an explanation. He pointed to the commitment to the idea of a modernizing state that the black elite shared with white society. The master narrative of the black resistance movement since the beginning of the twentieth century had been to end the exclusion of blacks from the modern state—not its abolition and a return to pre-colonial arrangements. This shared commitment made the dramatic breakthrough to the politics of negotiation possible. The escalations of violence at the local level, however, were "anomalous developments for which the master narrative hardly allowed" (Du Toit 1993, 28). He pointed to two possible explanations. First, the master narrative of the resistance movement did not necessarily "fully inform all the critical confrontations or many local struggles that developed on the ground." These local struggles often generated their own historical self-understandings and dynamics and created their own micro-narratives and concrete symbolisms (Du Toit 1993, 29). Second, the violence reflected the sense of exclusion of marginalized groups who anticipated that the modern state would not—for them—fulfill its promises.

This understanding points to the limitations of the master narrative of the elite and its inability to satisfy all the needs and expectations of disparate groups. It also points to the reality of local agency. Kalyvas (2006) has, in a groundbreaking work, demonstrated the role of local agency in the production of civil war violence. He has also deconstructed some of the assumed hegemonic powers of elites and argued for a better understanding of the alliance between local and national actors. "Alliance entails an interaction between supralocal and local actors, whereby the former supply the latter with external muscle, thus allowing them to win decisive local advantage; in exchange, supralocal actors recruit and motivate supporters at the local level" (Kalyvas 2006, 365). A civil war context therefore creates new opportunities to pursue local conflicts; it introduces the option of violence. Other studies on the experience of local communities in violent contexts confirmed the reality of local agency in matters of violence and peace (Hancock and Mitchell 2007; Stover and Weinstein 2004; van der Merwe 2001). Berkeley (2001, 151), in a journalistic description of his experiences in KwaZulu-Natal, described the situation as a "mosaic of discrete miniwars"—a striking description of the extent to which local dynamics determined the patterns of violence.

It was not only the production of violence that was localized. Peace too, was in some cases locally produced. Possibly the best example in this respect was the achievement of the Mpumalanga community in KwaZulu-Natal. Mpumalanga was embroiled in intense violence between 1986 and 1990 and was known as "Little Beirut." Over 2,000 lives were lost. Because of an entirely local driven peace process in 1990 they resolved to end the violence. They succeeded in maintaining that peace while, all around them, the fires kept burning for six more years (ACCORD 2009). It was an extraordinary achievement, especially as it took place before the NPA was signed.

In summary, much of the violence in the post-1990 era took place in the interaction between national and local conditions. The national leadership clearly struggled to assert their authority, while local dynamics contributed to unique and at times baffling expressions of discontent. No one, however, suggested that a complete disconnection existed between local and national levels. Disparate as they were, the local conflicts were essentially political. They expressed local discontent with an overarching political condition that was unacceptable, albeit in manners that were not sanctioned by the elite.

Sisk (1995, 123) has referred to the relative ease with which political elites mobilize their constituencies to demonstrate their power in society, but they are unable to demobilize them when the moment of peace arrives. He concluded that "In many ways, the National Peace Accord is a pact to acknowledge that very problem." The National Peace Accord, therefore, had to address the problem of local conflict dynamics out of control.

The National Peace Accord

By 1991 the deepening spiral of violence raised deep concerns, not only because of its spread and its increasingly brutal nature, but because of the perception that the violence was impacting negatively on the prospects of a negotiated settlement. President de Klerk was the first to try and organize a peace conference to deal with the problem of violence, but it was rejected by the ANC, who then proceeded to organize its own peace conference. The political opponents were clearly not ready to cede initiative in this important matter to the other.

Civil society saved the day, in particular the churches and organized business. They brought the leadership of political parties together and, through the facilitation of Archbishop Desmond Tutu and John Hall, representing the churches and organized business respectively, a National Peace Accord (NPA) was negotiated (Gastrow 1995).[2] It was signed at a public ceremony on September 14, 1991. Most political parties who had representation in the national parliament or the parliaments of the so-called homelands (quasi-independent ethnic states), including the IFP, signed. It was also signed by the ANC as the main liberation movement and by government on behalf of the security forces. Though some smaller political actors on the left and right of the political spectrum refused to sign, all major players committed themselves to the NPA.

The NPA included codes of conduct for political actors and the security forces, particularly the police. The NPA furthermore created a commission of inquiry into the prevention of public violence and intimidation (the so-called Goldstone Commission, named after Judge Richard Goldstone who was its chairperson). Chapters 7 through 9 of the NPA provided for the peace infrastructure: a national peace committee consisting of all signatories; regional peace committees in eleven regions of the country; local peace committees in all violence-affected areas; and, very importantly, a National Peace Secretariat under multi-party control to establish, coordinate and administer the regional and local peace committees. It also stipulated monitoring and enforcement procedures such as "Justices of the Peace" and an agreement on the use of arbitration in case of a dispute between signatories regarding a transgression of the NPA.

It has to be said at the outset that the national peace committee was largely ineffectual. It met only twice and was just not a factor in the further unfolding of the peace process. Also, no Justice of the Peace—empowered with legal authority to enforce compliance to the NPA—was ever appointed (more on this below); and arbitration was never used to deal with any of the many transgressions of the Accord. The impact of the NPA was confined to the work of the Goldstone Commission and the regional and local peace committees (under coordination of the National Peace Secretariat). These latter structures deserve our further attention.

The peace infrastructure

The National Peace Secretariat divided the country in eleven regions and facilitated the establishment of regional peace committees (RPCs) in these regions. The RPCs consisted of regional representatives of all signatories with a presence in that region, as well as other relevant civil society formations operating at regional level such as religious organizations, trade unions, business and industry, traditional authorities, and so on. The police and military also had to be represented, as well as relevant government ministries such as those tasked with the administration of black townships.

The RPCs coordinated the establishment of local peace committees (LPCs) in towns and villages in the region, particularly those towns that had experienced violence. The composition of LPCs followed that of the RPCs, but it is important to emphasize that the focus was on inclusivity (Collin Marks 2000; Odendaal and Spies 1997). Civil society organizations that wanted to be on an LPC had been welcomed.

Once the regional peace committees were established it was soon realized, though, that the task of establishing local peace committees would not be a simple one. It was not going to be sufficient to fax instructions for the formation of a LPC through to relevant local authorities. The resistance to peace was too strong in some locations. Regional peace committees, with support of the National Peace Secretariat, therefore took the decision to employ full-time staff to facilitate the establishment of local peace committees and to provide ongoing support to them (Gastrow 1995; Collin Marks 2000).

As a consequence, the establishment of each LPC was a facilitated process, a mini-peacemaking exercise aimed at securing the consent and active support of all local actors. The National Peace Accord guaranteed the legitimacy of such processes, whereas RPC staff provided the facilitation services. Where local communities had refused to form a LPC, the refusal was respected by regional peace committees; and rather than coercing the community to form a LPC (which would have been meaningless), efforts were strengthened to facilitate mini-peace processes within those communities. The refusal to form a LPC was seen as an indicator that much more preparatory work was needed within that community and that the local drivers of conflict had to be addressed. Most of the "pre-LPC" work was done by RPC staff and local peacebuilders, that is, individuals at the local level who enjoyed broad-based respect, and who had the aptitude and commitment to achieve peace.

Modus operandi of the LPCs

LPCs were inclusive bodies, composed of community representatives that were still deeply divided among themselves. The "peace" between members of the LPC was, at the best of times, fragile and extremely tentative.

The first and critically important task of a LPC was to select its chairperson. Given the composition of the LPC, this was no easy task. The selection had to rest on consensus, implying that the chairperson would be someone enjoying trust across political and racial divides. In some cases the LPC chose the option of two co-chairpersons, one black, the other white, when they failed to find one suitable individual. These LPC leaders came from civil society, especially the religious sector. The chairpersons, as supported by RPC staff, became the primary interveners in potentially violent situations and facilitators of negotiations.

The LPCs performed three functions (Carmichael 2010; Collin Marks 2000; Odendaal and Spies 1997). First, they prevented acts of sporadic violence associated with protest actions. By virtue of its composition, the LPC had access to all the major political and social networks in the community. LPCs, therefore, were early warning mechanisms that were aware of emerging situations with the potential for violence. The LPC, mostly in the person of its chairperson or specifically mandated members of the LPC, would facilitate discussions between the relevant actors (many of whom were in fact represented on the LPC). Such discussions focused on strengthening consensus on the need to avoid violence and to design jointly the most appropriate process to deal with the crisis. This included agreement on matters such as the route to be followed (in case of marches), proper monitoring, and the specific responsibilities of all actors, including the police. LPC-appointed monitors had, on various occasions, defused potentially violent stand-offs that developed in the course of such events. The fact that they had a mandate from the community via the LPC to prevent violence, lent substantial authority to their interventions.

Second, LPCs mediated in local disputes that had violence potential. These disputes were varied. LPCs had mediated in disputes between local resident organizations (called "civics") and municipalities; between the police and local communities; between local political groupings; between factions in intra-party conflicts; and even in such unpolitical matters as disputes between soccer clubs or religious groups. The outcomes of such mediations were always going to be preliminary and tentative, given that most "solutions" depended on national negotiations to succeed and the arrival of the new dispensation. But, when successful, they crafted short-term agreements on a way forward, thus defusing potential violence. In the process they achieved another objective by introducing the "politics of negotiation" at the local level.

Third, LPCs contributed to an emerging social cohesion. The LPCs were in most places the first platform that enabled all sections of a local community to engage in dialogue and joint problem solving. The decision to form a LPC was the first step a local community took on the long road of reconciliation or social reconstruction. If only for this reason, it was so important that local communities were offered the opportunity to make that decision by themselves, thus claiming ownership of it. In the case study of the Alexandra LPC, Carmichael (2010) described some of the struggle to get all actors on board the LPC. The formation of an LPC was indeed an act of reconciliation in itself and one that did not take place easily or flippantly. She also mentioned the extraordinary efforts by the LPC to communicate peace in various ways to the different sections of the community. The LPCs were vital centers of communication. It meant that they dealt with the very destructive force of rumors by being a mechanism to check and distribute information. But it also meant that they actively spread information to communities about the content of the NPA and all measures taken to promote it. All these matters combined—taking the first step towards reconciliation; the dialogue and efforts at joint problem-solving; the sharing and spreading of information; the active promotion of peace; and success in jointly defusing potentially violent stand-offs—laid the foundation for an emerging social cohesion.

Impact assessment

The NPA did not impress everyone. Du Toit expressed some of the reigning skepticism thus:

> . . . [the NPA] represented a not altogether concerted attempt, at once tentative and somewhat desperate, of some political and civil leaders to regain some measure of control over the proliferating incidents of political

> violence at the local and grassroots levels. The subsequent history of the Peace Accord has not been a major success story; more often than not the Peace Accord structures have failed to function effectively and to prevent or contain violent conflicts at local levels. (du Toit 1993, 10)

His skepticism was justified, of course, by the trend of escalating violence. The NPA was clearly not delivering very well on its key objective—to stop violence. Yet, such an unqualified dismissal of the NPA and its infrastructure is not correct. In numerous cases LPCs had been able to prevent violence—at a time when nothing else was really proving effective.

A number of studies have made an assessment of the impact of LPCs (Ball 1998; Gastrow 1995; International Alert 1993; Collin Marks 2000; Nathan 1993; Odendaal and Spies 1997; Shaw 1993; Sisk 1994). By way of summary, the following has been observed.

First, LPCs had different success rates in different parts of the country. The Western Cape, for example, was more successful than KwaZulu-Natal probably because the Inkatha Freedom Party had a weak presence in the Western Cape. But even within the same region the performance of LPCs would vary. The reliance on local agency is a double-edged sword. It encourages local ownership of the peace process, but also gives local actors the space to block the peace process, at times for rather opportunistic reasons. By its nature, therefore, a process that relies on local agency is bound to have varied results. Furthermore, the success (or failure) of a specific LPC depended on a variety of factors: the quality of support received from the Peace Secretariat and the Regional Peace Committee; the presence in a community of people with the aptitude and commitment to fulfill peacemaker and facilitation roles; and the nature of specific configurations of local issues, personalities, and histories.

Second, it is extremely difficult to quantify the extent of violence prevention because we simply lack sufficient data. Success in violence prevention is an extraordinary difficult matter to assess. There are three questions that have to be answered: first, could the non-occurrence of violence be attributed to other preventive factors; second, would, in the absence of an intervention, violence have been inevitable; and third, was the intervention sufficient to explain the avoidance of conflict (Ramsbotham et al. 2005, 111). However, the observers are unanimous in their view that LPCs had indeed contributed towards containing the spiral of violence—in spite of the fact that the number of violent deaths had increased during the lifetime of the LPCs. The minutes of RPC meetings and the National Peace Secretariat contained regular reports of successful LPC interventions. *The Star*, a leading Johannesburg daily, initially expressed skepticism regarding the NPA. On September 15, 1992, however, it wrote: "Without an accord it would be easy for South Africa to be sucked up into a vortex of violence" (Gastrow 1995, 79). In other words, violence had escalated, but the general consensus is that the escalation would have been far worse if it were not for the peace committees. LPCs therefore helped to restrain the escalation of violence, but were unable to stop it.

Third, the impact of LPCs on establishing social cohesion is as difficult to assess given the absence of quantitative data. Even so their contribution towards introducing dialogue and negotiations to local communities as a primary conflict management approach was important. The fact that LPCs symbolized a community's willingness to consider peace; and galvanized local agency in the pursuit of peace, contributed to the overall legitimacy of the peace process. On the negative side, LPCs were powerless in the face of acts of deliberate violence or when political will was lacking. Local bodies that operated on the basis of facilitation and mediation were powerless in the face of deliberate, planned violence. They were equally powerless, as in KwaZulu-Natal, when some local political leaders were clearly not committed to peace.

Ball has provided possibly the most apt summary assessment:

Viewed as a whole, the peace committees had a mixed record, and a definite assessment of their 'success' or 'failure' is impossible. Peace committees were unable to stop violence completely but often limited its occurrence. They were unable to end impunity on the part of the security forces, but they were able to help equalizing the balance of power between those in power and ordinary citizens and to strengthen accountability. Their ability to address the underlying causes of conflict was circumscribed, but even in the most violence-ridden areas peace committee staff were able to mediate conflict and create a safe space within which problems could be discussed. And though unable to transform the 'struggle mentality', they were able to help South Africans take their first steps toward understanding the value of negotiations and how to engage in them constructively. (Ball 1998, 23)

The LPCs of South Africa, therefore, were not perfect. However, in a context where nothing else—neither political leadership nor coercive security measures—was effective in stopping the violence, LPCs provided communities with the option to work at their own peace. Many LPCs achieved surprising results. Moreover, it gave local communities the sense that they were participating in the national quest for peace, rather than being passive bystanders. Nathan (1993) used the metaphor of "imperfect bridges" to describe LPCs: when the bridge has been swept away by a torrent and makeshift bridges have to be crafted to reach the other side, the question is not whether the bridges are perfect, but whether they enable the most rudimentary traffic between the two sides.

Concluding comments

The South African experience has, directly or indirectly, influenced a growing trend towards the establishment of "infrastructures for peace" in post-agreement contexts (see Odendaal forthcoming). In light of the enduring relevance of this experience the following observations may be useful:

First, "top-down" and "bottom-up" peacebuilding are at times seen as two opposing strategies that, by implication, require that a choice should be made between them. Particularly when looking at practical peacebuilding interventions, the two approaches are quite visible: high-level interventions that treat civil war and post-agreement peacebuilding solely as an elite affair; and local peacebuilding projects that seek to facilitate change without engaging the political power-structures or the larger political dilemma in any meaningful way. Much progress has been made, though, in understanding the complementary nature of national and local peacebuilding (Lederach 1997; Ramsbotham et al. 2005, 215–30). The South African experience demonstrated the necessity *for* a peacebuilding strategy that understood the interaction between the local and the national; and that responded by optimizing collaboration and interaction between these levels. What is particularly important, though, is that local peacebuilding should engage national issues as they manifest at the local level. In other words, local conflict systems should be engaged by understanding the manner in which the national has become local. The national conflict should be seen through the perceptions, experiences and expectations of local actors. Resilient local conflict systems cannot be dealt with through the imposition of national agreements and top-down assumptions.

Second, South Africa's LPCs operated in a context where authority was deeply contested. Even the formulators of the NPA did not fully appreciate the depth of distrust that existed. Hence they made the assumption that breaches of the NPA should be dealt with through arbitration or through deploying "Justices of the Peace." The latter would apply the law in cases where, at the local level, the NPA had been breached and intimidation or violence had occurred. None of these provisions was ever implemented purely because it was impossible and would have been counterproductive. An approach that assumed that legal authority existed was doomed. The law itself was viewed by the liberation movement as an instrument of oppression. The option of coercive or legalistic strategies to deal with violence did not really exist. The very appearance of the police on a scene was often the catalyst for violence as the police were seen as "the enemy" par excellence. The justice system was similarly seen as an oppressive tool. After all, Nelson Mandela and many others were imprisoned by courts of law. LPCs were successful in defusing or preventing violence to the extent that they relied on a methodology of confidence and consensus-building, dialogue, negotiation and mediation. LPCs therefore relied on a "soft" methodology in a harsh context. They were often criticized for not having teeth to deal with transgressions of the NPA. In reality, being toothless was their major strength.

Third, a particular advantage of the sole reliance on the methodology of consensus-building was that the methodology was consistent with the ideals of peace. The fact that threats of violence were dealt with by strengthening relationships, promoting dialogue, and facilitating consensus, meant that peace was not enforced, but indeed built.

Fourth, the quality of support provided by the Peace Secretariat and the Regional Peace Committees was a critical aspect of the success that was achieved. They had appointed full-time staff to facilitate the establishment of LPCs and to support their functioning. The technical support provided by staff, which included a degree of facilitation and mediation skills, was essential. Especially in those places where resilient local conflict systems existed, it was impossible for local actors to break the impasse all on their own. External intervention by expert facilitators was necessary, as was the linkage that they provided with higher political resources. Having said this, the level of technical skill of full-time staff was, in terms of today's standards, rather rudimentary. Even though a number of local and international NGOs provided training to the LPCs and full-time staff, not all fieldworkers had been exposed to training and some of them had to operate solely on the basis of their own aptitude and the rudimentary guidelines provided by the Peace Secretariat. If other countries were to follow this specific model, greater care should be taken to ensure quality technical support.

Lastly, a major part of the relative success of LPCs was its encouragement of collaboration between three sectors of society: political parties, civil society, and local government (including the police). In this configuration local peacebuilders played a central role. The chairpersons and those mandated by the LPC to intervene in disputes were individuals who, by virtue of their broad acceptability and their aptitude, were able to occupy the middle ground in a community. They came, almost without exception, from civil society, often from the religious sector. The LPCs provided a significant mandate to these natural peacebuilders in their midst to intervene in disputes, and facilitate or mediate outcomes that prevented violence and strengthened collaborative processes.

Notes

1 The chapter is a modified version of a case study developed for a forthcoming publication of the US Institute of Peace, titled "Structures for Building Peace at the Local Level."

2 The complete text of the National Peace Accord can be found in Gastrow (1995).

Works cited

ACCORD. 2009. *ACCORD re-presents APA to Mpumalanga community* [Web Page]. African Centre for the Constructive Resolution of Disputes 2009 [cited February 12, 2010]. Available from http://www.accord.org.za/news/31-africa-peace-award/412-accord-re-presents-apa-to-mpumalanga-community.html.

Ball, Nicole. 1998. "Managing Conflict: Lessons From the South African Peace Communities." In *USAID Evaluation Special Study Report No. 78*. Arlington, VA: US Agency for International Development, Center for Development Information and Evaluation.

Berkeley, Bill. 2001. *The graves are not yet full: race, tribe, and power in the heart of Africa*. New York: Basic Books.

Carmichael, Elizabeth. 2010. *Communicating peace through the National Peace Accord, South Africa 1991–1994*. Sydney: IPRA Conflict Resolution and Peace Building Commission.

Collin Marks, Susan. 2000. *Watching the wind: conflict resolution during South Africa's transition to democracy*. Washington, DC: United States Institute of Peace Press.

Darby, John. 2001. *The effects of violence on peace processes*. Washington, DC: United States Institute of Peace Press.

Du Toit, André. 1993. "Understanding South African Political Violence: A New Problematic?" In *UNRISD Discussion Paper 43*. Geneva: United Nations Research Institute for Social Development.

Gastrow, Peter. 1995. *Bargaining for peace: South Africa and the National Peace Accord*. Washington, DC: United States Institute of Peace.

Hancock, Landon E., and Pushpa Iyer. 2007. "The nature, structure and variety of 'peace zones'." In *Zones of peace*, edited by L. E. Hancock and C. R. Mitchell. Bloomfield, CT: Kumarian Press.

Hancock, Landon E., and C. R. Mitchell, eds. 2007. *Zones of peace*. Bloomfield, CT: Kumarian Press.

Höglund, Kristine. 2004. "Violence in the Midst of Peace Negotiations." Ph.D., Department of Peace and Conflict Research, Uppsala University, Uppsala, Sweden.

— 2008. "Violence in war-to-democracy transitions." In *From war to democracy: dilemmas of peacebuilding*, edited by A. Jarstad and T. D. Sisk. Cambridge: Cambridge University Press.

International Alert. 1993. *Mission to Evaluate the National Peace Accord and Its Peace Structures Report*. London.

Kalyvas, Stathis N. 2006. *The logic of violence in civil war, Cambridge studies in comparative politics*. Cambridge, New York: Cambridge University Press.

Lederach, John P. 1997. *Building peace: sustainable reconciliation in divided societies*. Washington, DC: United States Institute for Peace.

Nathan, Laurie. 1993. "An imperfect bridge: crossing to democracy on the Peace Accord." *Track Two* 2 (2): 1–5.

Odendaal, Andries. Forthcoming. *Structures for Building Peace at the Local Level*. Washington DC, United States Institute of Peace.

Odendaal, Andries, and Chris Spies. 1997. "'You Have Opened the Wound, But Not Healed It': The Local Peace Committees of the Western Cape, South Africa." *Peace & Conflict* 3 (3): 261.

Ramsbotham, Oliver, Tom Woodhouse, and Hugh Miall. 2005. *Contemporary conflict resolution: the prevention, management and transformation of deadly conflicts*. Edited by T. Woodhouse and H. Miall. 2nd edn. Cambridge, UK, Malden, MA: Polity.

SA History Online. 2010. *A crime against humanity. Analysing the repression of the Apartheid State*. [Web Page] 2010 [cited October 27, 2010]. Available from http://www.sahistory.org.za/pages/library-resources/online%20books/crime-humanity/menu.htm#postelect.

Shaw, Mark. 1993. *Crying peace where there is none? The functioning and future of local peace committees of the National Peace Accord*. Johannesburg: Centre for Policy Studies.

Sisk, Timothy D. 1994. "South Africa's National Peace Accord." *Peace & Change* 19 (1): 50–71.

— 1995. *Democratization in South Africa: the elusive social contract*. Princeton, NJ: Princeton University Press.

Stover, Eric, and Harvey M. Weinstein. 2004. *My neighbor, my enemy: justice and community in the aftermath of mass atrocity*. Cambridge, UK, New York: Cambridge University Press.

van der Merwe, Hugo. 2001. "Reconciliation and justice in South Africa. Lessons from the TRC's community interventions." In *Reconciliation, justice, and coexistence: theory & practice*, edited by M. Abu-Nimer. Lanham, MD: Lexington Books.

6

Belfast's interfaces, zones of conflict or zones of peace

Landon E. Hancock

Introduction: Belfast's interfaces

Belfast has been, almost since its earliest days, a city divided between Catholics and Protestants. Unofficial divisions of both place and activity have separated the two traditions in everything from residential housing and leisure activities to workplaces. However, with the onset of the Troubles in the late 1960s this unofficial division hardened through the use of violence directed by each community towards the other, resulting in the disappearance of mixed areas and the creation of "temporary" physical barriers between many Catholic and Protestant neighborhoods (Boal 1996, 154). The fact that many of these barriers, euphemistically known as "peacelines," remain in existence—with more having been built—in the years following the signing of the Good Friday Agreement is a testament to both continued tensions between the communities and the difficulties of making peace at the grassroots levels (CRC 2008; Jarman 2005b). These areas of division, known as interface zones, remain sources of tension and sporadic violence, which have an impact both locally and across the province as events there affect the larger society.

The problem of violence at Belfast's interfaces often rears its head during the highly emotional marching season each summer. Now that some of the traditional "troublesome" parades, such as the one in Drumcree, have been rerouted or negotiated, many of the remaining centers of parade violence take place in north and east Belfast along interfaces between Protestant and Catholic neighborhoods. An additional source of conflict along Belfast's interfaces has been the increase in what is known as "recreational rioting" by youth disaffected from the peace process by their continued social and economic deprivation (Jarman and O'Halloran 2001).

In addition to the violence endemic to interface zones, data show that residents of these zones are afflicted by poverty, joblessness and other social ills at rates far higher than that of the rest of Belfast's, or Northern Ireland's, population (Shirlow and Murtagh 2006, 65–6). Higher levels of social and economic deprivation are thus combined with higher incidences of chronic violence, often driving away potential business opportunities and turning Belfast's interface zones into literal dumping grounds for the poor, less educated and dispossessed.

Many community relations improvement programs have been instituted by both local and official sources, with differing levels of success (Jarman 1999). However, the main issue at hand is the fact that most or all of these programs, regardless of their source, have failed to remedy either the outbreaks of violence—some success has been made in mitigation—or to address the social ills that give rise to the violence (Jarman 2004). Reports from local community groups continue to chastise funding agencies and NGOs for overemphasizing programs that concentrate on cultural traditions and relationship-building over economic and social development for communities living on the interface (Hall 2007).

This chapter seeks to achieve two goals. The first is to compare grassroots efforts at conflict mitigation and community development with the top-down efforts of governmental agencies, NGOs and funding agencies such as the Community Relations Council (CRC), the Atlantic Council and others in an attempt to determine points of friction between these efforts and those of local community activists. The second effort is to examine the work done by the Suffolk Lenadoon Interface Group (SLIG) in south west Belfast to determine the extent to which their model of combining community relations with community development compares to normally understood definitions of zones of peace. In doing so, this preliminary investigation relies largely upon documentary evidence, reports and narratives from published meetings.

While this study is largely exploratory, I posit that endeavors undertaken by grassroots organizations that most resemble efforts by zones of peace in other areas of study will likely show more concrete results than those whose aims are far narrower. Additionally, while I expect to find frictions between most grassroots organizations and those organizations that come from outside of the affected area, I believe that grassroots organizations that most resemble zones of peace may have more success in garnering funding and directing resources in their own areas than those who rely upon narrow achievements.

The zones of peace model:
Broad community change

While zones of peace have a number of differing definitions, ranging from historical sanctuaries to weapons exclusion zones (cf. Hancock 2010) for the purposes of our comparative analysis this chapter focuses on the model of a local zone of peace constructed either during or following a conflict and encompassing a geographic region or communal locality. Temporally, one can examine zones of peace as taking place either before a peace process, as part of the implementation of a peace agreement or following a peace agreement as part of post-conflict peacebuilding efforts (Hancock and Iyer 2007, 30).

The first of these three types of local ZoPs typically represents conflict mitigation efforts during ongoing conflicts. Examples primarily include ZoPs in Colombia and the Philippines, but also can be represented by the failed UN safe havens in Bosnia during the early 1990s and the Butterfly Peace Garden focused on trauma relief for Sri Lanka's children during that conflict (Avruch and Jose 2007; Hancock and Iyer 2007; Rojas 2007). The second main type of local ZoP typically takes place during the implementation of peace agreements and focuses on providing safe spaces for disarmament, demobilization and reintegration; allowing for the cantonment of former fighting forces during the DDR process. Cantonment zones have been widely used in conflicts ranging from Aceh to Angola and El Salvador with varying degrees of success (Iyer and Mitchell 2007; Knight and Özerdem 2004). The third, and likely most relevant, type of local ZoP is one dedicated to post-conflict peacebuilding and development. At the time of this analysis the only confirmed example of such a zone is El Salvador's Local Zone of Peace; a grouping of 146 communities located in Usulatan province along the southern coast of the country (Chupp 2003; Hancock 2007).

The conditions that tend to lead to successful ZoPs in terms of local effectiveness and, at times, longevity are often associated with some of the functional aspects of ZoPs. First and foremost among these is grassroots ownership and control over the ZoP's agenda. Without fail, those ZoPs that are under control of the central government or other outside agency tend to be either short-term affairs—such as DDR zones and aid corridors—or they tend to disappear due to conflicts between locals and central officials.

The second condition tends to be, particularly for grassroots and longer-term zones, the expansion of initial goals from conflict mitigation to addressing structural sources of conflict and deprivation. Local ZoPs in Colombia, the Philippines and, in particular, the LZP in El Salvador, engage in a diverse range of activities from conflict monitoring and mitigation to education and training, business incubation and development and local governance issues (Mitchell and Hancock 2007, 193). As covered elsewhere, the LZPs successes have enabled it to expand beyond its initial 86 communities, address natural disasters effectively and to successfully field candidates in local and regional election (Hancock 2007).

Rebuilding Belfast: Community relations vs community development

As I have described above, and as others have done elsewhere (cf. Boal 1996, 2002; CRC 2008; Jarman 2002, 2004; Shirlow 2003; Shirlow and Murtagh 2006), Belfast's interfaces are both the result and the cause of violence and attendant material deprivations faced by their surrounding communities, ranging from poverty, poor educational and economic opportunities and, for Catholic/Nationalist communities, a lack of housing among other problems.

The interfaces were created, and continue to come into existence, in order to provide physical security for the inhabitants on both sides of the divide. During the early years of the Troubles, these regions developed out of the rapid population shifts driven largely by communal and paramilitary violence. As detailed by some members of the Suffolk and Lenadoon communities in south Belfast, the creation of interface communities often involved collusion between paramilitary forces, like the IRA, and British military forces:

> In 2003, when secret government papers were released from 1973, we heard on the news that not only had the British government stage-managed the evacuation of the Protestant families but they actually handed over a cash sum of money to the Republican movement, to help them resettle the Catholic families in the houses Protestant families were being put out of! So that was all a big shock to us. And not only that, but I also found out that the two soldiers who were sent to guard our house were actually breaking our windows as well, to try and encourage my husband and I to get out! (Hall 2007, 7)

So, like local ZoPs, the creation of interfaces is intrinsically linked to violence. Jarman defines an interface as "the conjunction or intersection" of territories that are contested or claimed by the parties to the conflict. He goes on to note that "violence, the threat of violence or the fear of violence" is at the heart of the interface concept, transforming "otherwise peaceful locations and boundary areas into interfaces" (Jarman 2004, 6). While we should note that there are few, if any, instances of established interfaces or peacelines being dismantled, a number of new interfaces have been built in areas that were previously considered stable. There are a number of possible reasons for this transformation of stable areas into new interfaces, including demographic changes, gentrification, redevelopment of brownfield sites, polarization of shared space, and the displacement of violence from one interface to others as a result of increased police and CCTV presence (Jarman 2004). The Belfast Interface Project's 2005 mapping project identified 12 interface areas out of over 40 in the city and its suburbs which had been either constructed or strengthened since the 1998 signing of the Good Friday Agreement (Jarman 2005a).

One particularly problematic source of interface violence has been an increase in rioting by young people, who engage in what is known as "recreational rioting." As described by community workers in Ainsworth, these conflicts are not necessarily the product of sectarian conflict but are "an outlet for the boredom and alienation felt by those young people" (Hall 2008, 6). Their sources of alienation are the same sources of deprivation, poverty and alienation that affect the rest of the community. Another activist described the reasons for recreational rioting as follows:

> I think much of the problem stems from social deprivation, on both sides of the peaceline. There's next to nothing for the kids in our areas to do, and that's something we're trying to rectify. If you don't give them an alternative they get sucked into the culture of drink and drugs and what we would term recreational rioting. It's boredom that makes than riot. I've even seen kids in our area riot among themselves when they couldn't get a riot across the peaceline. (Hall, Springfield Inter-Community Development Project, and Farset Community Think Tanks Project 2003, 20).

Overall, what we can see is that while violence at the interfaces themselves is a serious issue, it is intrinsically intertwined with issues of poverty and deprivation felt by the working class communities on both sides of the interface's divide. As with much of conflict and its analysis, the view we take of the causes for these types of violence will, in large part condition our primary responses to them. In Northern Ireland, as we will see below, there have been two primary responses to violence and deprivation at Belfast's interfaces.

The first response is that typically favored by the government and many in Northern Ireland's social service and NGO communities; namely to treat the majority of these problems as stemming from sectarianism. The main response to sectarian problems has been, and continues to be, a focus on improving inter-community relations between Catholics and Protestants, often with initial foci on single-identity projects designed to strengthen communities in preparation for cross-communal activities. In this view, deprivation and development are best left to UK and Northern Irish services that do not deal with sectarianism, such as Making Belfast Work and other initiatives to improve housing, education or other areas.

The second response has largely been championed by community activists, many of whom have been working locally throughout the length of the Troubles. Here the focus is on community development, improving resources, and skill and capacity-building for residents. While there are plenty of opportunities for cross-communal work here, and much does take place, the rationale for such work is alleviating and ameliorating poverty and deprivation, not necessarily improving community relations.

After examining these two responses we take a look at one group that has consciously attempted to combine both approaches in an overall plan, rather than in a one-off fashion, in order to take advantage both of inter-communal synergies as well as funding opportunities. This group, the Sufffolk Lenadoon Interface Group (SLIG) has many other features which may align with the key elements of local ZoPs outlined above. This analysis, while initial, may help to determine whether these elements have helped to make SLIG more or less successful than other initiatives, both top-down and bottom-up pursued across Belfast's interfaces.

Community relations from bottom to top and back again

One of the main issues with top-down efforts aimed at Belfast's interface zones is that they, like many of Northern Ireland's other community relations schemes, are primarily focused on improving local relationships and only to a lesser degree are focused on community development. Part of this stems from the nature of the conflict as being between two identity groups who share centuries of antagonistic memories, accentuated by narratives of violence and threat which inform each side's view of the other (Darby 1976, 1997; Nic Craith 2002; Stewart 1997). Another part stems from the work of the Community Relations Council and other organizations whose primary purpose has been to prepare both communities for the possibility of peace and to improve relationships in order to bring that peace about (Frazer and Fitzduff 1994). These efforts stem from the belief that "motivated individuals" can make a difference in addressing both relational and structural sources of conflict, primarily by improving relationships and reducing tensions through the use of person-to-person contact across the communal divide (Hancock 2008, 217). Community relations efforts are all largely based upon Allport's (1954) Contact Hypothesis, which posits that identity barriers can be broken down through the use of controlled contact, focusing on shared concerns and creating superordinate goals to bring the two groups or communities together. Within the context of Northern Ireland, the contact hypothesis model has its supporters as well as its detractors, but its guidelines are largely followed by the CRC and other major funders, whose primary goals are to improve community relations, engender reconciliation and expand the community relations model until it "infuses every sector" of society (Bloomfield 1997, 140).

Given that the CRC was tasked with managing and disbursing funds from the UK, EU and other sources, the role that community relations began to play in civil society grew exponentially following its creation in 1990 (Hancock 2008). The result of this funder focus on community relations has been the general requirement that any initiative that wished to receive CRC-controlled funds needed to ensure that its proposals contained a strong, central community relations component.

Unfortunately, throughout Belfast's interface communities, there is a deep suspicion regarding community relations work, which is perceived to focus on "feel good" activities to the detriment of meeting community needs. In a 2001 publication, the Community Bridges Team of the Community Development Centre in North Belfast brought together a number of community activists to discuss issues related to the concept and the practice of community relations in the city. Overall, the participants expressed elements of cynicism towards the concept, noting that they "preferred to focus on community development work" reflecting "a widespread belief . . . that there were other, more pressing needs in the communities . . . than . . . the state of Protestant/Catholic relationships" (Hall and Farset Community Think Tanks Project 2001, 7).

With regard to the requirement for community relations foci in their funding proposals, a number of comments indicated that they thought the focus of the government and the CRC was misplaced, with one respondent indicating that they believed that the focus on community relations was:

> . . . a deliberate attempt by civil servants in the NIO to find a way of *redefining* the conflict here. They wanted to present that conflict as basically a 'problem of community relations'. And if the problem could be defined as one between Catholics and Protestants who couldn't get on together,

then that allowed the powers-that-be, particularly the British government, to detach themselves from what the real problem was. (Hall and Farset Community Think Tanks Project 2001, 8 emphasis in original)

This speaker goes on to note that they felt that the community relations model focused responses to violence within the community, largely to save tax dollars and to use them "on the cheap" to quell disturbances, stating that, "community relations funding is manipulating people in local communities, community activists, to do the dirty work on the front line. Because it saves money on security, and overtime for RUC officers" (Hall and Farset Community Think Tanks Project 2001, 9). Furthermore, a group of activists in north Belfast were highly skeptical of the nature of community relations work, indicating that they believed many proposals add community relations elements as a form of window dressing. One activist indicated their skepticism by stating:

Do you not think that 99% of cross-community work is bluff, there is no real cross-community building in it? It's done because it's part of the criteria for whatever funding package is supporting the project, which insists that some element of cross-community be included . . . We all know that there's been a multi-pound industry built up over the years around so-called 'community relations', but with what result? . . . Does it benefit those people who live in the interfaces and have been forced to move? . . . I don't think that cross-community, as we have grown to know it, is of any great benefit in terms of the people who live on the sharp end of all this. (Hall and Farset Community Think Tanks Project 2003, 18)

Despite this skepticism, many groups do feel the need to add community relations elements to their proposals. Some do so because of the funding requirement and others who feel that the cross-communal component will bring desired results, as well as additional resources. But all recognize that the imperatives of the CRC and other funders do have an impact upon some of the form and some of the focus of their work; with those who are more negative indicating that:

Because of all the suspicions which exist at grassroots level about 'community relations', coupled with the fact that a lot of community relations funding has been spent on ludicrous things like yacht races and flower shows, I think there is a concern among community activists that we might somehow be seen as suspect too. And so we shy away from having a direct 'CR' label being attached to the work we do. (Hall and Farset Community Think Tanks Project 2001, 17)

Others at the same meeting described the value of cross-community contact:

I found that in some of the stuff we were involved with you get a more frank, open discussion with people when you actually sit down with them and listen to their personal stories. You get a better understanding of where they're coming from, and why they believe in what they do. (Hall and Farset Community Think Tanks Project 2001, 14)

Reflecting on his experience with a group of community activists from both sides of west Belfast's interfaces, Hall expressed some of their sentiments when he stated:

There is an understandable resentment within both working-class communities at the constant exhortations from government to indulge in cross-community projects, especially when there are so many other social problems desperately needing attention. Many feel the enticement that "if you go cross-community you will receive funding" is itself a form of institutionalised sectarianism. (Hall 1993, 28)

This is echoed by the sentiment that these types of initiatives are aimed only at working class people and are not evident across all elements of society, with one respondent expressing indignation that:

I don't see any urgency among the political parties to promote harmonious 'community relations' between those at the top of the political structures. Yet at grassroots level *we* are all supposed to be focusing all our energies on doing just that. Why are *they* not under the same expectations as we are? I don't see Trimble or Mallon or Adams, in return for being awarded their wage packets, being asked the type of questions we're all asked, such as: 'how many Protestants did you sit down with over the last year; how many Catholics?', or 'how effective/productive do you think your interaction has been?' (Hall and Farset Community Think Tanks Project 2001, 11 emphasis in original)

Overall, these sentiments with regards to the role of funding institutions, most especially the CRC, reflect the sentiment that even though many recognize that community relations can play an important role, its shift from the sidelines to the main focus of top-down resources, at times, places constraints on communities who might wish to address what they see as root sources of conflict; deprivation and a lack of economic opportunity. Instead, they tend to focus on "one off" events like the aforementioned yacht races, football matches or carnival events rather than developing resources for either or both communities.

Criticisms of an overabundance of focus on community relations as opposed to community development does not mean that local activists do not see the need for or value of initiatives that do improve community relations or mitigate conflict. In fact, they often note how building relationships with members of the other community can allow them to reduce tensions and address problems associated with inter-communal rioting. But they often express impatience with the idea that this type of work is the only thing that they should be doing. This is largely because they view community relations projects as necessary but not sufficient to address the sources of conflict.

While this section could continue on at great length detailing both the successes and limitations of community relations work at Belfast's interfaces, it is worth noting that, on balance, many interface communities have made some progress in limiting or mitigating interface violence. These successes, though, are often described as fragile or temporary, highlighting the feeling among activists that "feel good" activities proposed and supported by the CRC, governmental sources and other funders have a limited ability to impact the underlying conditions that lead to poverty, deprivation and, ultimately frustration and violence at Belfast's interfaces.

Community development:
Beyond good neighbors

As detailed above, many activists have felt that their primary reason for becoming involved in community work has been their desire to address problems of poverty, deprivation and other ills that often existed before the Troubles, but became worse when violence entered into the picture. While recognizing that improving community relations could help with conflict mitigation, community activists generally felt that development needs were more important than improving community relations. Michael Hall noted that he felt that there was a consensus among activists that development spoke more to grassroots needs than relations efforts, with one activist indicating that:

> I think we all agree that a lot of the problems in inner city Belfast stem from this cycle of deprivation, alienation and violence we have already talked about. And I don't believe that community relations can break

that cycle, because community relations – certainly as it is currently perceived – doesn't acknowledge the core reason behind social conflict: deprivation. It seems to think it is all about Protestants and Catholics 'not understanding' each other. But people don't always join paramilitaries or get involved in riots because the other side is Catholic or Protestant, it's because they're living within a cycle of deprivation, alienation . . . and community relations doesn't attempt to break that cycle. But *community development* does. (Hall and Farset Community Think Tanks Project 2001, 11–12 emphasis in original)

Community activists from Ainsworth agreed with this sentiment, particularly as they attempted to address community relations issues, finding that:

We needed to find jobs for our young people, we needed to work for real change in people's everyday lives. And in the process we gained more expertise in community development-type work. And these things were being brought about by our own community-based efforts – the politicians couldn't deliver this; and, anyway, their main concern was to marginalise us. (Hall 2008, 20)

However, the sentiment that community development was more important than community relations did not mean that politics took a backseat. Often the lack of impetus in a political direction could mean that some needs were not likely to be able to be met by community development projects. For instance, as one community activist noted:

. . . there are housing crises facing both communities, but they involve a 'political' dimension so nobody wants to talk about it, and that's the reality of it. Housing involves peacelines and some communities losing out, others gaining. People won't come together to try and resolve housing issues because they want them resolved to the advantage of their own community, mostly because they believe that offers them the most protection. (Hall and Farset Community Think Tanks Project 2001, 14)

Finally, it is worth noting that funding community development by itself remains a particularly hard sell to NGO and governmental funding agencies, who are most concerned about improving community relations and are far less likely to fund any project that doesn't have a CR component that was front and center. But stepping into the community relations arena also means that these local groups are often in competition with larger NGOs who also institute community relations programs. Two results of this were increasing pressure on local organizations to become more professionalized and the concomitant decrease in available jobs for local residents in these programs. As noted by Tommy Gorman, a former IRA member and community activist in the Falls area of west Befast:

> ... the evolution of community development itself, as a means of confronting social problems, has also seen an input of people who have come in partly because they can make a living out of it, and I think that has weakened its effectiveness. And the constant struggle for bites of the funding cake has also been detrimental, in that it has turned some groups against one another. (Wilson et al. 2005, 23)

Loyalist activist May Blood agreed with the dangers of professionalism, indicating that not only did it reduce the number of local people who were qualified for community relations and development positions, but the influx of outsiders led to a decrease in local ownership and local control, eventually affecting participation:

> As funding grew bigger and bigger in the 1990s organisations were forced to become more and more professional. Then it eventually came about that community development in an area was no longer being done by local people: you had a consultant who came in and told you how it should be done and then you had four or five professional people – who in some cases didn't even live in the area – who took the jobs and they in turn told you what should be done. Once again you lost that energy which comes from doing things from the bottom up. (Blood et al. 2005, 9)

It appears that while community development can be successful at times in addressing some of the sources of deprivation that have plagued both communities, both the political reality that Northern Ireland's conflict is inter-communal and the structural reality that funders are most interested in community relations schemes means that even the most successful community development programs has had only a limited impact upon the continuing drivers of inter-community violence. Thus, it appears that approaching the interface areas from either a community relations or a community development perspective does little to address problems rooted in both deprivation and in fear and mistrust of the other. Returning to the central premise of this chapter, we turn next to the efforts of two communities in south-west Belfast to address both community relations and community development issues through a systematic structure, much as the successful zones of peace studied in this volume and elsewhere have done.

Suffolk Lenadoon Interface Group: Combining relations with development

While there are a myriad of groups and initiatives working on community relations, community development (or a times both) at Belfast's interfaces, the work being done by working-class Protestants from the Suffolk housing estate in west Belfast and their Catholic counterparts in the adjoining Lenadoon estate is well worth examining both for its innovation and its high rate of success.

Like many other of Belfast's interface communities, violence had been a staple of life in Suffolk and Lenadoon for much of the Troubles. As Hall notes, there was little perception that members of both communities would be willing to come together to improve this situation and address the violence, especially given the bitterness of the conflict and the trauma that each side had experienced:

> But something drove individuals in both communities to set their personal experiences aside and to strive to work together, not though any sense of 'community-relations'-type reconciliation, but for the betterment of their two communities and with an eye to their children's future. (Hall 2007, 2)

Part of this desire seems to have stemmed from the fact that, like many zones of peace we have examined elsewhere, the people in Suffolk and Lenadoon were left to their own devices by the central government for an extended period of time.

> It being a 'no-go' area, you got no services, no bins emptied, no gas people in; the Housing Executive largely ignored you and never consulted you – indeed, they would have talked down to you . . . During the '70s and '80s people had been largely ignored. (Hall 2007, 12)

This encouraged, indeed required, local activists to organize and improve their own communities. At first, it appeared that while each community began to organize, they did so alone rather than working across the interface:

> After you had that dividing line established, and two polarised communities, your focus was on your own community then, and it was a matter of getting through your day . . . It was all about individual survival. (Hall 2007, 12)

However, as people on each side of the divide began to assess their needs and figure out how to address them with governmental authorities, they noticed that their problems were bigger than a single issue, a single concern or even a single community. That didn't mean that cross-communal action came quickly or easily, as one member of the Suffok community detailed:

> Twenty years of very gradual process preceded our current cross-community work. In the late '70s the local Methodist minister and his elders decided that they would make contact with the people in Lenadoon, though this was quite an unpopular idea in Suffolk. It began very informally; a coffee shop was started, then a thrift shop, and I ran that thrift shop for about five to six years . . . Before the minister left in 1980 he had formed Suffolk Community Services Group. (Hall 2007, 15)

After a number of secret meetings between organizers on both sides of the divide, they began to make progress towards working together:

> And the first joint thing we did was a protest about the lack of traffic lights on the Stewartstown Road – Lower Lenadoon Housing Committee and the committee of Suffolk got together on that. We asked people from both sides of the road to come out and protest, and bring their children along. And they did; I was amazed. We blocked the road for fifteen minutes, and the police came up and told us that what we were doing was illegal. And we said: 'We know, but we want lights here; it's too dangerous, and there's been a couple of kids knocked down already.' (Hall 2007, 15)

This initial success in persuading the government to put up traffic lights led to a slow process of rapprochement between organizers and between the two communities. While there were many difficulties faced by organizers, including threats and suspicions within their own communities, informal contacts were kept up, either directly or through intermediaries until both groups realized that they had more to benefit from working together than from working separately. Further successes in anticipating and heading off violence following the Drumcree IV marches in 2002 led to the formalization of contacts and the creation of the Suffolk Lenadoon Interface Group, largely as an umbrella organization for the two separate community groups.

Some of the impressive elements—and there are many in the SLIG experience—have been their desire to improve relations and development through turning their interface from a no-go area into a community development zone. One of their first projects, and the one for which they are best known, was the creation of the Stewartstown Road Regeneration Project, which was an umbrella organization for improving a row of abandoned shops and houses along the interface between Suffolk and Lenadoon. The original impetus for working across both communities was that organizers saw a need for both community relations and community development, leading to their decision to put forth what they described as the "radical initiative" of creating their own "company" to direct a project which would rehabilitate the shops, renting out the bottom floor for commercial rents and dividing the upper story into offices for community projects or other commercial endeavors. The project would be run like a company, with four directors from Lenadoon, four from Suffolk, and four independents brought in for their expertise.

> As long as the company didn't go bankrupt or get into debt, any profit would be divided into three parts. One third would be given to Lenadoon Community Forum – to fund projects or services within Lenadoon – another third would be given to Suffolk Community Forum – who would do likewise within Suffolk – while the final third would be retained by the Company to continue to develop its needs. (Hall 2007, 22–3)

There are many interesting facets to SLIG's choice of initial project, but what is important for our study is the fact that, like many ZoPs, this project sought to address a number of needs rather than just one. This development project was consciously designed as cross-communal, but was more than that. Rather than creating a project which would require support from outside clients, such as Farset's hotel and conference center, this project was designed to provide services to both communities *and* provide an attractive venue for both local and outside businesses to set up shop.

Additionally, given the cross-communal focus, the organizers needed to be careful about how the umbrella company was created and run:

> In other circumstances, setting up a company would have been straightforward. But in our case we had to unpick absolutely everything. We had to analyse *every* possible aspect of the building: its non-political use, flags and emblems, who could come into the building and who couldn't. We had to devise criteria for use, under every conceivable scenario; we had to work out our mission statement, our core value statement . . . We also had to determine how to build trust and relationships between our two communities – and even between ourselves on the interface steering group. We were six months in mediation, and none of it was simple or straightforward. (Hall 2007, 23 emphasis in original)

Similar to work done in ZoPs, the organizers from both groups needed to achieve and maintain buy-in from their respective communities. This is similar to the buy-in that ZoPs organizers need both within and without their communities, often with the same risks of ostracism or even violence run by people in Colombia or the Philippines. This need for buy-in led to a number of community meetings on each side which, while they did not lead to overwhelming support, at least did not generate enough opposition to prevent the group from moving forward. As an organizer from Suffolk put it:

> ... there were a group of key people here in Suffolk, most all of them women, who were prepared to take a risk, who were prepared to say: well, I don't know whether this'll work or not but it's worth giving it a go. But ultimately, I believe that within Suffolk we couldn't have gone ahead without the support of the community. I remember going to the public meeting down in the old community centre and the hall was packed and we were trying to persuade the people of Suffolk to go ahead with our proposal to form this joint company. And at the beginning some people were saying: 'No chance.' One guy even said to me: 'Over my dead body!' Another guy said: 'We've spent the last 25 years trying to keep that lot out of this community and you want to invite them over!' ... But when I asked for a show of hands, *every single person* in that room put their hands up to allow it to go ahead. I mean, there was one hundred percent support from people, even from doubters and those with bitter memories. (Hall 2007, 25)

Like a ZoP, the members of SLIG worked best by being as transparent as possible:

> I think some of it was around the fact that we were doing our best to be totally up front. We were aware that, in the past, people in the community had been excluded from decision-making – it had always been left to one or two individuals – and we were determined that nothing like that would happen again. (Hall 2007, 25)

Additionally, members of SLIG realized, through their own experiences with governmental officials, that grassroots ownership of the process and the rewards was absolutely necessary:

> Furthermore, over the years the people who had been making key decisions about Suffolk weren't actually from Suffolk. This was the first time that people from their own community were doing it; those in the leadership of the Forum at that stage were all from Suffolk. (Hall 2007, 25)

After the creation of SLIG and its approval by both communities, the search for funding began. Unlike many of the programs described above, this was neither just a "feel good" community relations initiative, nor was it a community development initiative that had community relations shoehorned into it in order to attract funding. Instead, "the fact that this proposed enterprise was owned by *both* communities and would help to turn part of a violence-prone, sectarian interface into a 'shared space' was surely something which would have appeal" (Hall 2007, 26). And indeed it did: SLIG was rapidly successful in obtaining monies from the International Fund for Ireland and the Belfast European Partnership Board, while the Northern Ireland Housing Executive gave them the land as an in-kind investment. As they began their funding drive:

> We were told by one of them that this was the first time in Northern Ireland that such a process had brought two communities together like this, and that this was the first community-owned company of its kind in Northern Ireland. As the funder said, we had created the 'footprint' for others to follow. (Hall 2007, 26)

SLIG's "love-fest" with many funding organizations didn't always translate into smooth sailing in their governmental dealings. One or another problem has always cropped up, though many of these have been dealt with through their continued successes in attracting clients, funding from outside sources and their ability to manage interface violence while encouraging development. SLIG members note that:

> The civil service gave us no amount of hassle, putting us through endless hoops and obstacles. They openly called our initiative a 'white elephant', questioned what was in it for Lenadoon, or Suffolk, and passed the opinion that it wouldn't be used, it would just stand idle. And, okay, such questions had to be answered, but at the same time they put deliberate obstacles in our path. (Hall 2007, 26)

Despite this, SLIG organizers and activists were able to generate impressive amounts of success, enabling them to retain the support of their communities and to garner even more funding. At times their own successes has created problems for them, especially with the Belfast Regeneration Office (BRO) who, according to SLIG members, fail to understand the nature and delicacy of interface situations:

> I remember, after we had applied for further funding to develop the project into its second phase, a representative from BRO said at a meeting: 'You've cured the interface, so why would you need more funding?' As if it was some sort of disease to be 'cured'! (Hall 2007, 27)

Additionally, because BRO was supposed to administer monies for their phase II project, SLIG found that their successes could cost them their needed revenues:

> ... to our annoyance, BRO ... are trying to tie things up in such a complicated way that we will not be able to get our hoped-for percentage of the profits. They say that if the two forums receive any of the profits, then they will reduce their own funding to the Forums accordingly. I mean, it's bureaucracy gone mad. (Hall 2007, 27)

Despite this, SLIG has continued to increase their activities and to garner funding from ever more distant sources. In 2007 they began working with Atlantic Philanthropies, who, at that time, had not decided whether to fund their phase II project, but had "decided to fund us over the summer, through Suffolk-Lenadoon Interface Group, to produce an extensive peace-building plan" (Hall 2007, 28).

A project which brings SLIG and the Suffolk Lenadoon interface full-circle to what we see as a zone of peace; which is a locality or community that uses grassroots peacebuilding and development as a method of both ameliorating the effects of violence and addressing their sources in social deprivation and political marginalization. Like working in a ZoP, SLIG's peacebuilding initiative "involved the most intensive consultation" ever done in either community with the purpose of seeing:

> ... how we could promote contact between the two communities, even for groups like the band, asking them: how do you see yourself linking into peace-building, into shared space, shared resources ... And everybody was saying: 'Yes, I think that's the way we must go forward.' Every group, from the Protestant Boys Flute Band to the pensioners said: 'This is a brilliant idea; we'd love to be involved in it.' (Hall 2007, 28)

After the massive amount of planning and consultation the outlook for the interface and for SLIG efforts continues to look good, though none of the members of either group will state definitively that violence is a thing of the past:

> The interface still has its tensions. But that is something we might never ever change. I think there'll be something along every interface ... We always say that no matter how successful this gets you could never sit back and say: well, we can relax now, we don't need to worry any more, because the interface is going to be an issue with people here for a long time to come. (Hall 2007, 31)

Despite this pessimism, representatives of SLIG realize that they have created something unique among initiatives in Northern Ireland and want to share their story widely:

> Hopefully what we have created as a result of our patient work over the years is a model for other groups to follow. We get loads of people coming here from different parts of Belfast, and further afield; this initiative is now recognised by people all over the place as a role model of reconciliation and good practice – even though 'reconciliation' as such was never our priority; our priority was simply to improve the wellbeing of our two communities. (Hall 2007, 33)

Talking tensions and successes: An evaluation

This initial look at community work and development work at Belfast's interfaces, and particularly at the Suffolk-Lenadoon interface, has several important lessons for both our understanding of the Northern Irish conflict and for our wider understanding of zones of peace as methods of peacebuilding and development. Overall, we can see that while a great deal of good work has taken place at a number of Belfast's interfaces, the initiatives which only focus on improving community relations or on increasing community development cannot be said to have been as successful as the all-inclusive approach that SLIG has taken to address both community relations and community development. Like the zones of peace we have examined elsewhere, the impetus for these two communities to work together was not initially some sort of "beautiful vision of peace" but was rather a realistic attempt to address what they saw as their local problems. And in this case what they understood as their shared problems with each other as members of opposing communities.

As with ZoPs, initial assessments of problems facing both communities, such as the lack of a traffic lights and dilapidated buildings, led to the realization that both peacebuilding and development needed to be carried out if the quality of life for local inhabitants was to improve and if the conditions which led to interface violence were to be addressed. This pattern is similar to that of El Salvador's LZP, where the goals of economic development were impeded by gang violence (Chupp 2003; Hancock 2007) but differs from ZoPs found in ongoing conflicts, like those in Colombia or the Philippines (Avruch and Jose 2007; Rojas 2007), where the initial goal was to mitigate violence, with community development being seen as a necessary component for achieving that goal.

Additionally, we have seen through this analysis, that like many of the successful ZoPs we have studied, one of the continuing needs for members of SLIG has been to keep their communities informed of initiatives, progress being made, benefits and difficulties. As one member of the group indicated:

> What we have done is to have built relationships among ourselves and, of course, we have erected this building as a product of that relationship. But we now have to bring the rest of the community more fully on board. And that is an ongoing process; there's always new issues, there's always new things which arise. (Hall 2007, 32)

And like the most successful ZoPs that we have studied, both in the first volume and this one, a key element in SLIG's success has been the continued reinforcement of grassroots ownership, as a member from Lenadoon put it:

> I think what contributed most to our success was that it was from ground level up. This wasn't a government initiative, this was two communities saying: look, we have tolerated a lot here over the years, and it's in both our interests to do something about it. (Hall 2007, 33)

Finally, in examining the premise of this volume, this study finds that although all of Belfast's interface initiatives and community groups have, on occasion, difficulty in dealing with governmental directed initiatives or the goals of funding agencies like the CRC, the fact that SLIG has been able to harness community development within the mantle of peacebuilding and improving community relations means that they, to a larger extent, have been able to both minimize the adverse effects of governmental oversight and extend the reach of their fundraising beyond the local community. This, in effect, gives them more power to chart their own course, much as the self-reliance and economy of scale allowed the Local Zone of Peace in El Salvador to chart their own course during successive right-wing governments in that country.

Works cited

Allport, Gordon W. 1954. *The nature of prejudice*. Reading, MA: Addison-Wesley.

Avruch, Kevin, and Roberto S. Jose. 2007. "Peace Zones in the Philippines." In *Zones of peace*, edited by L. E. Hancock and C. R. Mitchell. Bloomfield, CT: Kumarian Press.

Blood, May, Joe Camplisson, Michael Hall, and Farset Community Think Tanks Project. 2005. *Grassroots leadership. 1, recollections*. Island pamphlets. Newtownabbey, Co. Antrim: Island Publications.

Bloomfield, David. 1997. *Peacemaking strategies in Northern Ireland: building complementarity in conflict management theory*. New York: St. Martin's Press.

Boal, F. W. 1996. "Integration and Division: Sharing and Segregating in Belfast." *Planning Practice & Research* 11 (2): 151–8.

— 2002. "Belfast: Walls Within." *Political Geography* 21 (5): 687.

Chupp, Mark. 2003. "Creating a culture of peace in postwar El Salvador." In *Positive approaches in peacebuilding: a resource for innovators*, edited by C. Sampson, M. Abu-Nimer and C. Liebler. Washington, DC: Pact Publications.

CRC. 2008. *Towards sustainable security: interface barriers and the legacy of segregation in belfast*. Belfast: Community Relations Council.

Darby, John. 1976. *Conflict in Northern Ireland: the development of a polarised community*. Dublin: Gill and MacMillan.

— 1997. *Scorpions in a bottle: conflicting cultures in Northern Ireland*. London: Minority Rights Group.

Frazer, Hugh, and Mari Fitzduff. 1994. *Improving community relations: a paper prepared for the Standing Advisory Commission on Human Rights*. 3rd edn (orig. 1986). Belfast: Community Relations Council.

Hall, Michael. 1993. *Life on the interface: report of a conference held on 8.10.92 and attended by community groups from the Shankill, Falls and Springfield Roads in Belfast*. Newtownabbey, Co. Antrim: Island.

— 2007. *Building bridges at the grassroots: the experience of the Suffolk-Lenadoon Interface Group*. Island pamphlets, 81. Newtownabbey, Co. Antrim: Island Publications.

— 2008. *Self-help at the grassroots: how communities responded to the Northern Ireland troubles*. Belfast: Island/Farset Community Think Tanks Project.

Hall, Michael, and Farset Community Think Tanks Project. 2001. *Community relations: an elusive concept: an exploration by community activists from north Belfast*. Island pamphlets. Newtownabbey, Co. Antrim: Island Publications.

— 2003. *Beginning a debate: an exploration by Ardoyne Community activists*. Island pamphlets. Newtownabbey, Co. Antrim: Island Publications.

Hall, Michael, Springfield Inter-Community Development Project, and Farset Community Think Tanks Project. 2003. *'It's good to talk': the experiences of the Springfield mobile phone network*. Island pamphlets. Newtownabbey, Co Antrim: Island Publications.

Hancock, Landon E. 2007. El Salvador's post-conflict peace zone. In *Zones of peace*, edited by L. E. Hancock and C. R. Mitchell. Bloomfield, CT: Kumarian Press.

— 2008. "The Northern Irish Peace Process: From Top to Bottom." *International Studies Review* 10 (2): 203–38.

— 2010. "Zones of Peace." In *The Oxford international encyclopedia of peace*, edited by N. Young and Oxford University Press. Oxford: Oxford University Press.

Hancock, Landon E., and Pushpa Iyer. 2007. "The nature, structure and variety of 'peace zones'." In *Zones of peace*, edited by L. E. Hancock and C. R. Mitchell. Bloomfield, CT: Kumarian Press.

Iyer, Pushpa, and Christopher R. Mitchell. 2007. "The Collapse of Peace Zones in Aceh." In *Zones of peace*, edited by L. E. Hancock and C. R. Mitchell. Bloomfield, CT: Kumarian Press.

Jarman, Neil. 1999. *Drawing back from the edge: community initiated responses to public order problems in North Belfast*. Belfast: Community Development Centre.

— 2002. *Managing disorder: responding to interface violence in North Belfast*. Belfast: Office of the First Minister and Deputy First Minister, Government of Northern Ireland.

— 2004. *Demography, development and disorder: changing patterns of interface areas*. Belfast: Community Relations Council.

— 2005a. *BIP interface mapping project*. 1st edn. Belfast: Institute for Conflict Research and the Belfast Interface Project.

— 2005b. "Changing Places, Moving Boundaries: the Development of New Interface Areas." *Shared Space* 1: 9–19.

Jarman, Neil, and Chris O'Halloran. 2001. "Recreational Rioting: Young People, Interface Areas and Violence." *Child Care in Practice* 7 (1): 2–16.

Knight, Mark, and Alpaslan Özerdem. 2004. "Guns, Camps and Cash: Disarmament, Demobilization and Reinsertion of Former Combatants in Transitions from War to Peace." *Journal of Peace Research* 41 (4): 499–516.

Mitchell, Christopher R., and Landon E. Hancock. 2007. "Local Zones of Peace and a Theory of Sanctuary." In *Zones of peace*, edited by L. E. Hancock and C. R. Mitchell. Bloomfield, CT: Kumarian Press.

Nic Craith, Mairéad. 2002. *Plural identities – singular narratives: the case of Northern Ireland*. New York: Berghahn Books.

Rojas, Catalina. 2007. "Islands in the Stream." In *Zones of peace*, edited by L. E. Hancock and C. R. Mitchell. Bloomfield, CT: Kumarian Press.

Shirlow, Peter. 2003. "Ethno-sectarianism and the Reproduction of Fear in Belfast." *Capital & Class* (80): 77–93.

Shirlow, Peter, and Brendan Murtagh. 2006. *Belfast: segregation, violence and the city, Contemporary Irish studies*. London, Ann Arbor: Pluto.

Stewart, Anthony Terence Q. 1997. *The narrow ground: aspects of Ulster, 1609–1969*. Belfast: Blackstaff Press.

Wilson, Desmond, Tommy Gorman, Michael Hall, and Farset Community Think Tanks Project. 2005. *Grassroots leadership. 2, recollections*. Island pamphlets. Newtownabbey, Co. Antrim: Island Publications.

7

Zones of peace in the South Caucasus: Polyphonic approaches to state-building

Irakli Zurab Kakabadze

The disintegration of the Soviet Empire and the new states

By the end of 1980s the new policy of *glasnost* announced by Soviet leader Mikhail Gorbachev proved to be the beginning of the end for the Soviet Union. The Soviet state was already in a condition where it could no longer deal with the growing expenses of the military industrial complex, economic development and sustaining the largest state police apparatus in the world. As Pleshakov (2009) writes, by the end of the 1970s even old Soviet leaders were aware of a deep economic and ideological crisis penetrating the Soviet Empire and they had started to think about reforming it. But by 1989, it became obvious that reform of the empire was an impossible task. Russian imperialism proved to be a devastating force for the Soviet state, since it had alienated many small ethnic groups and "nationalities" as they were called in the former Soviet space. The basic human need for identity was a prevailing factor during the years of disintegration of the Soviet state; a state where identity was supposed to not matter at all. Even during the last years of the empire during the late 1980s, different identity-based ethnic conflicts started up—ethnic tensions were high in Nagorno Karabakh between Armenians and Azerbaijanis and violence erupted in the Moldova-Transnistria region, as well as in places like Abkhazia and South Ossetia within Georgia. It was becoming obvious that many different ethnic and religious minority groups were being reduced to the status of what Georgio Agamben calls *Homo Sacer*, whereby a person is excluded from all civil rights, while his/her life is deemed "holy" in a negative sense (Agamben 1998). In the new configuration of the states, "identity" would be focused mostly on ethnic origins.

As the result of the breakup of the Soviet Union in 1992, it became obvious that the process of the formation of new "nation-states" on the territory of the former empire was not an easy task. On the contrary, in some cases it proved to be an almost impossible goal that created hundreds of thousands—if not millions—of internally displaced and virtually stateless people from different ethnic and religious groups. Armenians were expelled from Azerbaijan, Azerbajanis from Armenia, Georgians from Abkhazia, Ossetians from Georgia, Russians from Central Asia, and Moldovans from Transnistria. Representatives of many other groups were reduced to the status of Bare Life (Agamben 1998). Many different groups of people felt that they did not belong to the new order—or the new "nation" states—since, in their understanding, the idea of "the nation" was very much tied to the notion of ethnic identity. Thus, for many minorities, being part of Armenia, Moldova, Azerbaijan or Georgia was perceived as giving up their own ethnic identity in favor of that of the dominant ethnic group in that region.

Of course, there is much to say about the uniqueness of the each region and each historical moment when different empires have disintegrated, but the post-modern and post-Cold War disintegration of the Soviet Empire was not completely unique. In fact, the situation in the Soviet Union very much resembled the situation after World War I in Europe. Hannah Arendt, writing in 1951 in *The Origins of Totalitarianism* on the failure of the nation-state model in the period of 1918–39, noted:

> With the emergence of the minorities in Eastern and Southern Europe and with the stateless people driven into Central and Western Europe, a completely new element of disintegration was introduced into postwar Europe. De-nationalization became a powerful weapon of totalitarian politics, and the constitutional inability of European nation-states to

guarantee human rights, made it possible for the persecuting governments to impose their standard of values even upon their opponents. (Arendt 1958, 269).

Her words could well be applied to contemporary post-Soviet space and especially to the South Caucasus. The nation-state system has never worked there and is not working now.

One glance at the demographic map of Europe should be sufficient to show that the nation-state principle cannot be introduced into Eastern Europe . . . For these new states this curse bears the germs of a deadly sickness. For the nation-state cannot exist once its principle of equality before the law has broken down. Without this legal equality, which originally was destined to replace the older laws and orders of the feudal society, the nation dissolves into an anarchic mass of over- and underprivileged individuals. Laws that are not equal for all revert to rights and privileges, something contradictory to the very nature of nation-states (Arendt 1958, 270, 290).

The failure of the classical "nation-state" model is already a fact in the former Soviet space but the remedy to this dysfunctional existence has not been found yet. Events between 1992 and 2010 clearly demonstrate that the traditional system of "nation" states is not working. Most Abkhaz do not want to live in Georgia, or Georgians in Abkhazia, Armenians in Azerbaijan, Azerbaijanis in Armenia, Slavs in Moldova, Uzbeks in Kyrgyzstan, Russians in Kazakhstan, Chechens in Russia, or Poles in Belarus. According to the 1998 census there were about 181,000 Armenians in Azerbaijan out of the total population of 7,856,000 who did not want to recognize Azerbaijan as their own nation-state. Elsewhere, there were 89,000 Abkhaz and 163,000 Ossetians out of the total population of 5,109,000 who did not want to live under the Georgian flag (Gurr 2000). This problem, of course, is not unique to the South Caucasus, since identity politics has become a major source of widespread contention, especially since the end of the Cold War. Ideological struggles have given way to what Galtung (1996) describes as "ethnic-mythological" struggles, in which each nation and ethnic group has fostered the myth of being "chosen" at the expense of others, who were to be treated as goyim. In the Georgian context, the word goyim does not only signify "The Other" in terms of ethnic or religious identity, but also applies to internally displaced people, economic migrants within the country who were forced to change their residence due to violence and war. Living under a status of goyim in Georgia is a humiliating experience since these people are always reminded that they are not welcome to live in Tbilisi, Kutaisi, Batumi or most other places and that they always have to think about going back to their real home—which is Abkhazia or South Ossetia.

The South Caucasus: A history only of conflict?

Even a brief account of the history of the South Caucasus reveals the effects of the ethnic and religious divisions discussed above, and of the difficulty of imposing a twentieth-century nation-state model onto the region. Over time, Georgia, Armenia and Azerbaijan have all suffered from the impact of both feudalism and imperialism. Indeed, all Caucasian countries, north as well as south, have a long history of feudal statehood. Georgia and Armenia trace their history thousands of years, as does neighboring Azerbaijan, once known as Caucasian Albania.

Clearly, the contemporary use of force in recent years to try to create conventional nation-states in a region that has known only feudal and imperial rule has been a costly failure. In the two decades following the disintegration of the Soviet Empire, the South Caucasus has been plagued by ethnic unrest and divisions. Several developments contributed to this outcome.

The region divided

First, by the early 1990s the Russian and then Soviet Empires that had served as a facilitating tool for different ethnic groups in the Caucasus ceased to provide such a unifying force. While some of the nationalities of the Caucasus pursued aspirations toward independent and conventional nation-statehood (Georgia, Azerbaijan, or Chechnya), others chose to try to stay close to Russia (Abkhazia, South Ossetia, or Nagorno Karabakh). Armenia was in between those two extremes—it remained loyal to Russia, but as an ally that had also acquired nation-state status. In the end, the process of "modernization" of Caucasian states—in the early twentieth-century sense—became a very complicated process, which faced considerable internal resistance. Identity-based conflicts became more and more connected to the notion of a "right" of self-determination as opposed to a need for the maintenance of territorial integrity. Some former Soviet republics, even within the Russian Federation chose to move towards establishing some form of nation-state within Russia, while others decided to cling to their identity by embracing self-determination and separatism. In the end, what we have at the beginning of the second decade of the twenty-first century is the aspiration of many different groups to be recognized as independent states and a conflict of identities that does not have any way of resolving differences peacefully.

One major reason for the failure of the traditional nation-state model after the collapse of the Soviet Empire was the legacy of the Russian Empire whereby some elements of "modernization" were forced upon ethnic entities in the nineteenth and early twentieth centuries. There was no experience of voluntary nation-building in former Soviet space and, as such, the whole concept of the nation-state seemed to be imposed from outside rather than built from within (Pleshakov 2009). One result of this imposition from the top is that, throughout the region, the army is considered a very important tool in "solving" not only problems of aggression but also in dealing with problems of internal unity and disunity (Taylor 2003).

Moreover, throughout history the Caucasus has always had many different tribal and feudal groups that used one common language as a tool of communication for trading and cultural relationships—and this has often been an "imported" language. There were many different dominant languages that Caucasians have used for communicating with each other, usually the tongues of outside cultures—Greek, Persian, Arabic, Turkish, Russian. It is true that at certain points in the history of the South Caucasus, the Armenian or Georgian states were strong enough to have their languages become the dominant means of communication. But these were largely isolated times and mostly the dominant language came from outside the region. Over the last two centuries, Russian has served as a lingua franca of the Caucasus, but since the disintegration of the Soviet Empire the Russian language has lost its legitimacy as a common tool for the different nations and ethnicities. It remains a main language for certain separatist groups, but is has ceased to be a main language of discourse in Georgia, Armenia and Azerbaijan. Since the recent wars in South Ossetia, Abkhazia and Nagorno Karabakh, when separatist movements were backed by Russian forces, the Russian language became associated with trauma and renewed imperialism in different parts of the Caucasus. At the same time, English as a language of communication has become more and more important. However, there is currently no common tongue of communication between different groups in the Caucasus and this is one of the underlying reasons for the continuation of identity-based conflicts.

This is also linked to another tendency towards so called "modernization" in the South Caucasus. This area never had independent nation-states, even in the traditional sense, apart from a short period of independence between 1918 and 1921, before the South Caucasus was forcefully incorporated into the Soviet Empire. Hence, the South Caucasus was always a multi-ethnic and multi-actor entity itself and even its dominant ethnic entities such as Georgians, Armenians and Azerbaijanis fell under different feudal principalities. Pre-modern, decentralized, feudal principalities constituted the dominant political order before the Russian empire came into the Caucasus as a uniting and conquering force. So, after the disintegration of Soviet Union, the so called "modern nation-state" system of territorial division does not look very relevant to the Caucasian states. Principles based on territorial integrity and homogeneous populations make no sense in this region. However, going back to pre-modern principalities is also not the answer. This kind of structure cannot sustain itself in the twenty-first century.

The Georgian example

In 1801 Georgia was annexed by the Russian Empire of Paul I. By the mid-nineteenth century the entire territory of the South Caucasus had been incorporated into the Russian Empire. After their short term of independence as nation-states in 1918–21, the South Caucasian countries were reconquered by the Bolshevik armies of Stalin and Orjonikidze and were incorporated into the new Soviet Union. Georgia was actually reconquered by the Soviet Army in February 1921 and officially stayed under Soviet rule until 1991, when its first elected leader, Zviad K. Gamsakhurdia, declared the country's independence. After Georgia's declaration of independence, wars of secession erupted in South Ossetia (1990–2) and Abkhazia (1992–3). It is widely accepted that Russian military forces were heavily involved in fighting on the separatist side during the armed conflicts in South Ossetia and Abkhazia. With the help of the Russian military, separatist forces were able to defeat the Georgian military and to expel the entire Georgian population from many conflict areas. By 1994, there were about 300,000 internally displaced persons in Georgia resulting from those two conflicts. Attempts to mediate the crisis by both the Organization of Security and Cooperation in Europe (OSCE) and the UN did not lead to any tangible results through a long period of time from 1994 to 2003.

In November 2003, Georgia was shaken by the so called "Rose Revolution" when its then leader, Eduard A. Shevardnadze, was forced to resign by mass protests in the streets of Tbilisi. A representative of a younger generation of Georgian politicians, Mikheil Saakashvili, became the President after this revolution. He promised reforms and started to implement some changes in policy. But he has failed to formulate a peacebuilding policy towards either Abkhazia or South Ossetia. The failure to resolve the situation peacefully has resulted in renewed conflict in South Ossetia, firstly in 2004 and then again in 2008.

In the beginning of August, 2008 the world watched a bloody confrontation unfold between Georgia and Russia over South Ossetia. The conflict was sparked by a miscalculation on the part of President Saakashvili, who apparently felt emboldened by perceived US backing, despite State Department warnings not to provoke Russia. Russia responded with military aggression, and it remains an occupying force in some parts of Georgia today (Barry 2009).

The search for an alternative model for South Caucasia

There have been calls for re-establishing the old Russian Empire to control and prevent the current set of ethically based conflicts afflicting the region, but as Rubenstein (2008) has suggested in his chapter "Conflict Resolution in an Age of an Empire," an empire almost always contributes to creating conflicts in the long run and has a very limited time frame in diminishing ethnic and religious tensions. It is clear that the heritage of Russian imperialism, plus recent Russian involvement in regional conflicts, has left a very bitter taste in the mouths of many national and ethnic groups within "post-Soviet Eurasia," as it is called today by many geopolitics experts.

Instead of an imperialistic approach, I wish to examine a new polyphonic or multilateral approach that could prove to be more effective for this region in which ideas of meaningful boundaries, territorial integrity, and homogeneous populations are lacking—a horizontal cooperation without a single empire imposing its rules. The situation in South Caucasia in the beginning of this new century suggests the need for a wholly new form of international citizenship that would not be based upon exclusion of the Other (or the *goyim*) but would, rather, incorporate different groups and individuals into new post-modern unities and unions. Later in this chapter, I would like to propose a solution that is based upon a voluntary integration of nations into a new post-modern union where different nations and ethnic groups all have equal rights, as well as individual rights being respected. I call this a polyphonic approach to post-modern state building. Considering the fact that the South Caucasus have a long, if underplayed, tradition of polyphonic living, I would argue that the region is a good ground for a basic shift in international relations thinking, moving towards a real "problem solving" solution.

Among a number of contemporary scholars, Sandole (2007) has talked about the notions of "post-modern warfare" and "post-modern peace and security" in his work on the OSCE and conflict resolution. The underlying question is: how to integrate apparently conflicting notions of territorial integrity, self-determination, and security? This has been a very difficult issue for different international organizations, including the UN and OSCE, which are still trying to deal with the conflicts in the South Caucasus within a traditional framework. A new, polyphonic approach tries to deal with those questions simultaneously and tries to find solutions to those three pressing questions; at the same time trying not to take away sovereignty from existing states and empowering small ethnic minorities to have equal power in territorial questions. These tensions between national and local aspirations generate extremely difficult questions to answer in current circumstances, but nevertheless it is possible to find solutions by expanding our view beyond traditional international relations theory.

However, for the region like the South Caucasus, the issue of its continuing likely dependence upon outside "great powers" remains very important. This place can never become any kind of a region of non-violence, a peace zone, or a safe haven without a consensus among surrounding big powers and the global powers. In no small measure, "fear of foreign wrath" has been a factor in South Caucasus for centuries. However, as Mitchell mentions in his study of historical peace zones, this kind of deterrent factor was sometimes needed in order to create some form of accepted sanctuary (Mitchell 2007, 20). A territory like the South Caucasus is obviously not as big and independent as—for example—the European Union, making it difficult for local actors to be able to freely implement their own ideas. The agreement of global powers and their consensus would be very helpful in creating a sanctuary in South Caucasus.

Without changing the system of "monopoly on violence," it appears almost impossible to think about solving the problems of our post-modern world. However, here again, the concept of "a sanctuary" comes to mind. Is it ever possible to have a sanctuary protected from state sponsored violence? And if so, is it possible to spread the influence of this kind of sanctuary? Since there are a number of successful examples of peace zones or peace communities in the Philippines, in Colombia, and in Peru and Ecuador, could such a model be copied—or subject to successful diffusion as Bunce et al. (2010) suggest? It is not easy to find a recipe for the diffusion of political units based on the principles underpinning a small, non-violent sanctuary. What we are looking for is not just a small camp for IDPs or refugees, or a peace community founded within a small homogenous population, but a whole region turned into some form of non-violent and non-threatening sanctuary. This is a challenge for the twenty-first century and especially, it could be said, a challenge for regions such as the South Caucasus.

The main issue at hand is to be able to construct a sanctuary not merely for various IDPs and refugees but also for those simply but consistently seen as second-class citizens—the *goyim* or *Homini Sacer* of South Caucasus. It is obvious that in today's situation, a radically different approach is needed to establish people's security in Eastern Europe and the former USSR. Neither the Soviet approach of Russian domination nor a post-Soviet approach of unilateral NATO extension seems useful. In this kind of situation the search needs to be going on for that dimension of equal security that the Russian president proposed in 2008. Here I am proposing the polyphonic approach which would provide equal security to small and big powers in the region—as well as to ethnic minorities and to currently unrecognized states.

The polyphonic approach to peacebuilding

From recent history we have seen that the old ways of dealing with violent conflicts through the use of power—often based on a single state—has usually proved to be unsuccessful. In the new multi-polar world, "polyphony" becomes more important as an organizing concept. It is especially interesting to view this in terms of new security arrangements where bigger states will not necessarily have the competitive advantage and a dominant voice over international affairs. The realities of the post-Cold War period suggest that the old unilateral or imperialist approaches are no longer applicable (see Rubenstein 2008; Sandole 2007). It is a very difficult task to identify the way of progressing towards a peaceful multi-polar world, but it is clearly necessary to find ways to accommodate the interests of multiple Others on the international scene (cf. Derrida et al. 2008). There are many different types of actors that need to have their basic human needs for identity and security recognized and accommodated (Burton 1996). In order to create effective safe spaces or an appropriate form of sanctuary some multifaceted approach is needed, where all the voices have equal ways of expressing themselves (Mitchell and Hancock 2007). Details of security arrangements can be discussed, but respect is due to each of the involved and affected groups. As the post-Cold War experience of the 1990s and 2000s shows us, a truly multi-polar world needs multiple voices to be included in its social and political architecture.

The nature of polyphony

What I am proposing here, as an alternative method to traditional domination based on the conventional "imperial model," is a form of "polyphonic" approach. It is interesting that both Georgians and Russians have something to do with the whole notion of "polyphony" in the arts and now this principle could be applied to their conflict. In music, polyphony is a texture consisting of two or more independent melodic voices, as opposed to music with just one voice that is called monophony or music with one dominant melodic voice accompanied by chords, which is usually called homophony (Smith 2003). Georgian traditional polyphony is the most significant of all stylistic features of the national musical language that significantly defines the originality and expression of the Georgian musical tradition. Multi-voiced singing is not characteristic of Georgians only, but Georgian folk music attracts the attention of experts for its diversity of forms. Each form has extraordinary and complex harmonic or contrapuntal combination created by the interrelation of voices. Many experts say that multi-voiced singing and its choral character are the most remarkable features of Georgian musical tradition (BBC 2003).

In literature, polyphony (Russian: полифония) is a feature of narrative, which includes a diversity of points of view and voices. The concept was invented by Russian philosopher Bakhtin (1984), based on the idea of musical polyphony. One of the best known examples of polyphony can be found in Dostoevsky's prose and Bakhtin has characterized Dostoevsky's work as polyphonic. Unlike other novelists, he does not appear to aim for a single vision, going beyond simply describing situations from various angles. Dostoevsky engendered fully dramatic novels of ideas where conflicting views and characters are left to develop unevenly into an often unbearable crescendo (see, for example, *The Brothers Karamazov*). Through his descriptions, the narrator's voice merges imperceptibly into the tone of the people he is describing. *The Brothers Karamazov* has been also used by number of conflict scholars while talking about the alternative to a traditional or realpolitik approach (Galtung 1996).

Speaking in terms of conflict resolution, Bakhtin has identified the principle of satisfying human needs for identity as respect for multiple sides at the same time (cf. Burton 1996; Galtung 1996; Sandole 2007). When dealing with the participants in conflict, the need for identity can be one of the main obstacles to peace in the region, which is the major issue in many other places also affected by intra-state conflict. Multiple voices need to be heard at the same time and in their own forms of communication—that is, speaking in their own language. This is the challenge of today's world. When we see many different identities aspiring for recognition in the twenty-first century, we need to ask a question in the style of Bakhtin—is humanity able to translate the principle of polyphony into the structure of international and inter-ethnic relations? Galtung (2004) proposes a Swiss model of multilingual democracy, as an example of conflict transcendence. Indeed, Switzerland has been an early model for cohabitation of different ethnic groups with different languages in the same country. Canada has been suggested as another example of—at least—bilingual coexistence, although there are different opinions about this.[1] In the world of contemporary liberal democracies there are few instances of polyphonic intra-state structures. As a general principle, homophony is the dominant model in the Western nation-building tradition.

The remaining issue involves asking whether the "truth" that Kartvelian Georgians, Abkhaz, Ossetians, or Russians are articulating are all fundamentally different from each other. Yet, each of those voices has its truth. How to create a system that would be able to respond to each of those voices—and how to accommodate such an approach within the contemporary political system—remains to be answered by the theoreticians and practitioners in international relations and political science. Most immediately, the question arises: how can the principles of "polyphony" be applied to the South Caucasian ethno-political region? Are there any successful examples of polyphonic discourse used in the contemporary world?

Existing polyphonic models

First of all, a clear example of ethnic and national polyphony in the contemporary world is the creation of European Union. This is a very recent phenomenon and obviously it is very early to talk about definite success of this enterprise, but one thing is already obvious—that a multicultural and multilingual approach can be seen working and could be applied successfully elsewhere to post-modern state building processes. The EU, with its 23 languages, is a good example of this process.[2]

The European Parliament is elected every five years by the diverse and multi-ethnic population of Europe to represent their interests. The main job of the Parliament is to pass European laws on the basis of proposals presented by the European Commission. Parliament shares this responsibility with the Council of the European Union. Parliament and Council also share joint authority for approving the EU's €130 billion annual budget. In addition, as a legislative body, the European Parliament has the power to dismiss the European Commission.

One of the most important factors for European polyphony is that Members of the European Parliament (MEPs) do not sit in national blocks, but in Europe-wide political groups. These include parties such as the European People's Party (Christian Democrats), and there are blocs of socialists, liberals, greens and others. Between them, MEPs represent all views on European integration, from the strongly pro-federalist to the openly Eurosceptic. Here is one very good example of constructive channeling of identities (cf. Kriesberg 2007) and focusing the arena of many disputes to a different space. Like all EU institutions, the Parliament works in all the 23 official EU languages, but it is also the case that the EU shows respect for all languages and cultures of Europe, and none of these linguistic groups is considered second class.

It is also extremely important to recognize that today the common currency of the euro already unites Austria, Belgium, Cyprus, Finland, France, Germany, Greece, Ireland, Italy, Luxembourg, Malta, the Netherlands, Portugal, Slovakia, Slovenia and Spain. The eurozone is about to expand even more and represents one more example of the principle of polyphony being applied through economic and social policy. The European welfare-state model plus a common economic currency has very positively contributed to the creation of post-modern state identity, demonstrating that economic factors can be extremely important in creating international and inter-ethnic polyphonic structures.[3]

The European Union was formed after the two hugely destructives wars of the twentieth century, initially as a form of sanctuary from inter-state warfare through economic cooperation. Today it can be seen as one of the largest "peace zones" of the world. During the last 60 years, between 1950 and 2010, the EU has functioned as a sanctuary from ethnic and religious violence "within," while there has been no necessity to have borders between different countries. As a result, a birthplace of traditional nation-statehood has become the birthplace of something definitely post-modern. Instead of dominating imperialist models used by different European powers in the nineteenth and early twentieth centuries—France and Germany particularly—a collaborative approach involving partnership has become most relevant during the formation of the new union. In many ways, the European Union represents a good example of how it might be possible to transcend existing conflicts into finding collaborative solution in a Galtungian sense (cf. Galtung 2004).

Even though there is much work to be done and many serious problems to be resolved, the European Union might well be the best model to follow for the South Caucasian countries and communities currently seeking separation. Since Europe also has had a long history of different separatist struggles, the EU model appears to be the best so far in dealing with the problems posed by inter and intra-state conflicts.

Zones of peace

While it might seem overly ambitious even to envisage the current tangle of conflicting relationships in the region as a potential "Caucasian Union," such a long-term goal might not seem too far-fetched if approached gradually and in stages. The gradual establishment of local or regional peace zones in the entire area could offer a process leading towards some form of post-modern statehood, providing a sense of security and identity for all the various ethnicities in the region.

Zones of Peace have been defined in many ways, depending on their form and focus. For many years the concept was used mainly for the protection of places of worship and cultural sites. Accordingly, the Zones of Peace International Foundation (ZOPIF) defines the term as "a site with sacred, religious, historic, educational, cultural, geographical, or environmental importance; protected and preserved by its own community and officially recognized by a governmental authority." It is not merely a demilitarized or a weapons-free zone, although these can be important features of a zone, but "a sanctuary that operates within ethical principles of non-violence, is free from weapons, acts of violence, injustice and environmental degradation."[4] This definition stresses the absence of active violence which often also involves the creation of a haven which supports community-based dialogue to foster mutual understanding and inter-communal peacebuilding.[5]

The academic field of conflict resolution and peacebuilding has been introduced into the South Caucasus relatively recently, although many different Caucasian nations and ethnic groups have a very rich tradition of using indigenous "insider-partial" elements of creative and practical conflict resolution (Lederach 2003). Most of those involved village elders, relatives or institutions such as Khevisbers in the Eastern Georgian Mountains or Makhvshvs in the Western Georgian Mountains of Svaneti. In the thirteenth century, Queen Tamara introduced the idea of female political mediation by appointing Khvashag Tsokali and Kravai Jakeli to mediate a dispute with Georgia's feudal elites. But the history of proposing South Caucasus as a potential zone of peace has more recent foundations.

In June 1997, Johan Galtung, founder of Peace Research Institute of Oslo (PRIO), visited three South Caucasian countries in his tour to promote his "Transcend" method of conflict transformation and to conduct collaborative workshops with the students of Tbilisi State University, Georgia, Yerevan State University, Armenia, and Khazar University, Azerbaijan. He held a large meeting with civil society representatives at the Caucasian Institute for Peace and Democratic Development (CIPDD) in Tbilisi. It was at this round table discussion, chaired by CIPDD director Dr Ghia Nodia, that Galtung proposed creating a Peace Zone, including a new international airport in the border area between Georgia, Azerbaijan and Armenia—namely at the Red Bridge area, one of the centers for regional trade during at least the last 50 years of the twentieth century. Dr Galtung also suggested that creating a Peace Zone in the South Caucasus was the only viable alternative to the continuous state of war and ethnic conflict.

Three years later, in 2000, Ambassador John W. McDonald, Chairman and CEO of the Institute for Multi Track Diplomacy, attended a conference in Tbilisi, Georgia, organized by Georgia-America Business Development Council. At the conference, Ambassador McDonald also suggested creating a linear peace corridor or zone in Georgia, around the Baku–Tbilisi–Ceyhan pipeline as a way of protecting Western energy interests through peacebuilding and economic development (Drake 2008). Throughout the following nine years Ambassador McDonald has continued to work with different Georgian governments on the formation of Peace Zones in Abkhazia and South Ossetia. In 2003 the Vice-Speaker of the Georgian Parliament, Vakhtang Rcheulishvili, came to Washington, DC, to support the idea of peace zones in conflict regions. He met various US officials, such as Senator Tom Harkin, Congressman Dennis Kucinich, Matthew Bryza of the National Security Council, representatives of IMTD and George Mason University's Zones of Peace Group. In 2004 the new Prime Minister of Georgia, Zurab Zhvania, endorsed Ambassador McDonald's plan for peace zones in conflict regions. State Ministers Bendukidze and Khaindrava were also very much supportive of this plan. After the Rose Revolution of November 2003, when non-violent protests brought down the corrupt government of Eduard Shevardnadze, the idea of peace zones became a grassroots concept, popular with certain segments of civil society and university students in Georgia. However, President Mikheil Saakashvili chose a different path—he chose to pursue a strategy of strengthening Georgian military forces, and practically abandoned peace talks by 2006. The Russian government has also shown little interest in this approach to peacebuilding. Any proposals for establishing different forms of peace zones thus faced a major setback when the militaristic policies of Georgian, Russian and separatist governments led to the renewed violence and, in August 2008, to a full-scale war between different parties in South Ossetia. The approach still remains, however, one of the most promising means of breaking the cycle of contemporary violence in the South Caucasus.

Problem-solving through polyphonic models in South Caucasia

The South Caucasus is desperately in need of exploring new types of post-modern structures which could form the basis for building a new and peaceful Caucasia. To accommodate the demands of a new era, some form of post-modern state structure needs to be adopted by the existing Caucasian states and perhaps the European Union is the model to be followed—voluntary integration, while keeping and respecting national identities of different ethnic actors. Creating a new "Caucasian Union" following the example of EU could be one answer to the problems of reconciling unity with diversity, given that it is obvious that the "nation-state" model has not worked in the region. It is, of course, not going to be easy to do this, but for reasons of intra-national and international security some form of a common security mechanism needs to be elaborated. A final destination will also have to involve a new lingua franca, as well as new legislative procedures for the whole area of the regional peace zone. However, in the beginning, small areas in Georgia could become very much a first experiment for building peace communities in the region.

We should recall that, locally, South Caucasian peoples have lived in peace for centuries. For them, embracing the idea of the South Caucasus as a Peace Zone will be a return to their centuries-long tradition of coexistence. However, in the larger picture, this will represent a new paradigm in international relations, where the sovereign nation-state will give up traditional reliance upon armed force and will try to build its relationship with neighbors based on mutual economic, social, political and cultural gain.

The proposed plan suggests the EU as a main implementer of a "peace zone agreement" among the states of the South Caucasus. Meanwhile, the United States, Russia, Turkey and Iran could be co-signatories of a "Caucasian Peace Zone" pact that would politically guarantee peaceful coexistence to different ethnic, religious, cultural groups in the region. Georgia could start the process, since it is viewed as the center of the Caucasus and it is essential for initial peace zones to work locally in Georgia for them also to be successful in Azerbaijan and Armenia. In actual fact, in May 2009 the European Union proposed a strategic partnership with six countries of the former USSR, including the South Caucasian countries. This proposal could be a good incentive for South Caucasian countries to start a process of initial economic integration.

A proposal for a "peace zones" approach to the region can offer a win-win solution to all involved and it could be a way of tackling problems of confrontation in the region—between Russia and the USA, Azerbaijan and Armenia and between Georgia and South Ossetia and Abkhazia. Everyone could gain from it and no one would lose—except the illegal drug and arms traffickers and the different interest groups that are heavily invested in having illegitimate territories in the South Caucasus.

This is a new vision for the South Caucasus. The approach could be called "Polyphonic Coexistence" where—instead of one leading, dominant voice—there are multiplicities of voices "in charge." Polyphonic folk songs are part of the Caucasian tradition—so this multi-polar concept is not entirely alien to the region. On the contrary, it is very much ingrained in the culture of the South Caucasus. As noted above, the South Caucasus has a long tradition of peaceful coexistence of different ethnic groups but it has also a tradition of multi-voice polyphonic arts, where all the voices are singing together and not dominating each other.

However, while embracing a new vision for the South Caucasus it is very important to be realistic and to understand certain points of criticism from different viewpoints. It is extremely important to adopt a "pragmatically idealistic" stance—as opposed to simple utopian understanding of things that have never worked in practice. For this, it is very desirable to understand the critique of peace zones from the local neoconservative and realist points of view.

Debating peace zones in Georgia

There are many different points of view about the possibilities of realistically implementing any form of polyphonic approach to peacebuilding in Georgia. Different arguments are articulated by Georgian neoconservatives and realists; making it worthwhile to explore both arguments seriously.

Neoconservatives: Enforcing democratic approaches

For the last six years, neoconservatives in Georgia have argued that "modernization" of the contemporary Georgian state could not be implemented without some level of coercion by a centralized state structure. This argument has some truth to it, of course. As we have seen, Georgia—as well as other South Caucasian societies—still suffers from feudal and imperial legacies and there are relatively large portions of the community that are actively challenging the current "modern nation-state" order. Rather, they are arguing for some sort of return to a "Soviet" reality.

At the same time, enforcing a modern and liberal "state"—mostly through coercive methods—can backfire and seems unlikely to yield as durable results as culturally sensitive 'reforms' that do not completely rely on brute force. The attempt by the Saakashvili government to bring "modernity" coercively to Georgia has created a very large backlash. Thousands and sometimes even hundreds of thousands of people came into the streets to protest this coercive "modernization." Instead of looking at creative options of peaceful reform through more post-modern methods, President Saakashvili tried to enforce a "democratic and secular" order.

Georgian neoconservatives make one point that is difficult to dispute: throughout the history of the Caucasus, there was always some consensual enforcement mechanism between the Caucasian nations and even within each society and ethnic group. So some mechanism needs to be created for a joint enforcement of whatever "post-modern" order emerges in the Caucasus—an order of things that is built on consensual and inter-cultural understandings of justice and the relations between humans that South Caucasian nations often shared through their history.

A common and shared enforcement mechanism is a necessary attribute of peacebuilding and democracy building in the Southern Caucasus. This "peace and democracy enforcement," however, should be provided by a third party viewed as legitimate by all sides. For instance American participation as a third-party enforcer would be considered highly partial by many. Russian involvement was never considered impartial in the region. Neoconservatives in Georgia assert that the United States and NATO are going to be the best "peace and democracy" enforcers in the region, and particularly in Abkhazia and South Ossetia. However, currently it appears as though Abkhaz and South Ossetians are not well disposed towards NATO or American participation in any peacekeeping operations, at least during a first stage. The European Union, since it is not a military power and is considered a highly desirable partner by different separatist powers (as well as by Russia and the United States), might well be a much better able to meet the challenges at the first stage of any region-wide peacebuilding process.

We need to admit that, so far, the enforced "modernization" of the South Caucasus is not working as intended by the originators of this process. The process of building so-called "modern" nation-states on the territory of the Southern Caucasus has produced very bad results to date. A more sensitive approach to the issues of identity, security and "statehood" in the Caucasus is needed. A successful post-modern approach would have to incorporate the best elements of traditional cultures to rebuild a shared "South Caucasian Identity" and at the same time adopt an effective method of administration that would benefit all parties involved. All parties should be able to maintain as much autonomy as possible but at the same time—in order to avoid identity-based conflicts in the future—we need to have some unifying common denominators.

Even though the neoconservative policy of Georgian President Mikheil Saakashvili to force the "modernization" of Georgian society and nation-state building has not worked, we still need to find new ways of building a sustainable sense of overall community. The South Ossetian and Abkhazian regions have not accepted the model of a Georgian nation-state, and Saakashvili's policy of building a "modern nation-state" by force has failed in many ways, even inside Georgia itself.

The conclusion at this point of time must be that instead of "forced modernization and liberalization," Georgia—as well as other countries in the South Caucasus—needs to embrace a new way of "voluntary post-modernization and horizontal egalitarianism" that recognizes not just individual freedoms but also collective rights of different ethnic groups. This is definitely not an easy task, but experience with a number of failed attempts at "modernization through coercion" has shown that new approaches need to be elaborated. Finding a new model will help establish a more stable environment in the South Caucasus in which the question of how to acknowledge different identities is not always dangerous.

A further concern of Georgian neoconservatives is the relationship with Russia. Levan Ramishvili, for example, makes the valid point that Russia will not demilitarize.[6] Russia is a huge country and a former superpower and surely it will resist demilitarization. It is completely understandable that Russians would want to have a strong military and to maintain control over the Northern Caucasus. There is no doubt that after two bloody campaigns in Chechnia, Russians will not allow total demilitarization of that region, just as their leaders are not very likely to discuss demilitarizing their state. But this is a different issue. Neither a region-wide nor local peace zones in the South Caucasus involve any degree of Russian demilitarization.

Moreover, Russia has an existential fear of NATO enlargement and will oppose this in any shape or form. The Russian President, Prime Minister and Foreign Minister have all stated this number of times. For the Russians, Georgian membership in NATO remains unacceptable, but they are willing to negotiate other issues, including the status of separatist regions. So, direct involvement in regional wars was a Russian reaction to the proposal of NATO enlargement into South Caucasus. In that sense, NATO and the West can have a strong bargaining position with Russia—a regional peace zone in exchange for avoiding military confrontation in the region.

The Georgian population has already voted for NATO membership and they have welcomed the presence of NATO soldiers. In contrast, Russian soldiers are welcomed in separatist enclaves—Abkhazia and South Ossetia. A mutual compromise could be worked out: the Russians could withdraw from their occupied territories in Abkhazia and South Ossetia in exchange for NATO giving up its plans for enlargement. Instead, the EU could take control of the process as a more neutral actor and launch a peace zone process, starting with the conflict areas throughout Georgia. A peace zone project could therefore also offer a win-win solution for Russia and the West—resulting in neither the continuing Russian occupation of strategic enclaves nor a NATO military presence.

Georgian neoconservatives also make a strong point about the impossibility of neutrality for Georgia and the rest of the South Caucasus. Levan Ramishvili pointed out that Soviet Russia broke a pledge to respect Georgian neutrality in 1921, and that post-Soviet Russia will do it again.[7] In fact, this argument has more than historic relevance, since Georgia already has had a very negative experience with proclaiming neutrality as a state. In the words of Georgian neoconservatives, "neutrality is not an option for Georgia." But here I offer different view of "neutrality" for Georgia and the region. As far as "neutrality" is concerned, we are discussing a very different arrangement from traditional understandings—existing neutral countries are in many cases military powers, such as Switzerland and Sweden. Even though they refuse to enter different military alliances, they are not non-violent states that have completely abandoned force and violence. On the contrary, they are part of an old post-Westphalian model of a nation-state entity, where the state is considered to be built upon the idea of monopoly over violence.

At the state level, Costa Rica remains the only example of a post-modern peace zone; a country without a military force.[8] This conception of a "peace zone" forms part of a new, postmodern paradigm of international relations based on multiculturalism and involving a new relationship between dominant "nations" and other ethnic entities. In essence, we are talking about a disarmed, "non-violent zone" and not simply about a neutral power. Our arguments are based ultimately upon the unity of the South Caucasus region, and not simply about one state declaring neutrality. We are advocating a step-by-step process that will eventually lead to a demilitarized South Caucasus.

According to another neoconservative argument, the EU is not a military bloc, and it is naive to think that, separate from US, the EU can provide any meaningful security guarantees. In addition to that, the EU suffers from so called "enlargement fatigue." Hence, it is not realistic to think that Georgia can become even an EU candidate country in foreseeable future. Moreover, Russia will object to any arrangement that might lead to real independence for Georgia.

However, this is exactly the point here. We need the participation of US and Russia in building a new regional security system around the South Caucasus. This is not a call to disengage, but a call to engage. The process would need active US as well as Russian participation. The EU might be the best arbiter of the situation precisely because it is not a military bloc and so it would not be seen as a threat to Russian national security. The European Union united in spite of a crushing legacy of animosity between its members arising from two devastating world wars in the first half of the twentieth century. We have seen this example and this is exactly why the EU could be the best facilitator to building up the Southern Caucasus into a region-wide peace zone. The EU could act as a party that is uninvolved in the confrontation between the US and Russia. Since the Iraq War, the EU has had a position that is more acceptable to Russia and is more distanced from the US than during the Cold War. Hence, the EU could be more of a neutral third party between the US and Russia, as well as being better trusted by Abkhaz and Ossetians—as well as by Georgians.

Realists: Arguments and counter-arguments

Realist arguments about peace zones are rather different from those of neoconservatives. One of the leading realists in Georgia, Dr Kornely Kakachia, a Visiting Fellow at Harvard University in 2009, has made number of very interesting comments regarding the possibility of peace zones in Georgia, much along the lines of the realist approach favored by Henry Kissinger who has argued that "Great Powers do not commit suicide for allies" (least of all small and unimportant ones) (Pfaff 2008). Realists emphasize that the interests of big powers need to be considered carefully and also that Georgian national interests need to be followed in defining the best options for solving the problems facing the country.

It is clear that addressing realists' concerns is necessary if a start is to be made at building peace in a South Caucasian community. Considering a Kissingerian focus on "national" interests, we have to recognize that there are multiple actors on both the Georgian and the regional scene, and that all of their interests (or needs) must be satisfied. There are also large numbers of outside actors who have the capacity to influence the peace process based on their own interests and these also have to be taken into account.

First of all, Russia is openly involved in many regional conflicts and is not hiding its interests—the main one currently being not to allow Georgia to join NATO. In the process of facilitating any peace zone building process, we need to understand that Russians feel very much threatened by the NATO enlargement to the East and for them any part of the South Caucasus becoming part of a "North Atlantic space" in totally unacceptable. However, a regional peace zone arrangement could satisfy Russian interests by creating a demilitarized, violence-free international sanctuary of peace which involves no outside military alliances—nor any foreign bases.

US interests should be distinguished from the rest of the West in this case, although Great Britain has played its usual supporting role to the world's only superpower. It is true that the Obama administration in Washington has shifted a little towards reconciliation with Russia, but the main US—and British—interests in the region remain that of safeguarding an alternative energy route from the Caspian Sea. US and British companies have heavily invested in Azerbaijani and Kazakh oilfields and would like to see a safe energy corridor functioning in the South Caucasus. The United States is not primarily interested in a military presence in the region, as long as energy interests are secure and protected. A peace zone in the South Caucasus could satisfy American and British interests by keeping a safe energy corridor alive and maintaining US and British companies' share in these energy fields for the near future.

The European Union does have has its own interests in the region. One of its main goals is to have good and stable relations with both Russia and the United States and keep the South Caucasus stable. While European strategic interests also include keeping an alternative energy corridor, they would also like to maintain a good relationship with Russia to keep the existing energy route alive. Hence, Europeans fall naturally into the role of potential mediators in this complicated picture and this suggests another reason why any possible peace zone scheme should involve the EU as a sponsor and protector.

Turkey and Iran also have strong vested interests and security needs in the region. Both of those countries would like the region to be more or less independent from either Russian or American influence. Renewed Russian domination of their northern neighbors would make Turkey alarmed, and same could be said about Iran when discussing a possible American military presence there. A demilitarized and non-violent peace zone under an EU mandate could serve Iranian and Turkish security interests well and come closest to a win-win solution for all concerned.

Especially in its early stages, the process of establishing some form of region-wide peace zone in South Caucasia will need some kind of minimal enforcement agency to prevent the outbreak or escalation of violence in the region, as well as some mechanism for conflict resolution. Deterrence of violence and a means for resolving conflicts are always central requirements for any peace zone, large or small. In this case, the best regional deterrent mechanism might best involve an international multilateral system rather than one based upon regional or global "great powers." In the first stages of the development of any Caucasian peace zone, the European Union might well be accepted as the most legitimate actor available. The EU could, when necessary, provide conflict resolution facilities but also, as a last resort, enforce the peace, especially if backed up by the United States, Russia, Turkey, and other neighboring countries. Realist arguments about deterrent factors have to be taken seriously, but local multilateral agreements on the non-use of force and on demilitarization are also key to ensuring an absence of violence within a regional peace zone. Multilateral deterrent forces can also be effective in maintaining stability and security while conflict resolution mechanisms seek to remove the underlying reasons for any violence.

Up to now, we have discussed the interests of the "outsider" parties in the region. Of course, Georgians, Abkhaz, Ossetians, Armenians, and Azerbaijanis all have their own interests and needs and those have to be carefully identified and addressed. However, in today's global environment, without the prior approval of outside forces, such as the US and Russia, together with the involvement of the EU, it is likely to be impossible to reach consensus on the insider level.

Even from a realist perspective the contemporary world is moving towards different security priorities in which state actors can be less important than non-state actors. Maintaining security around the world requires more and more international cooperation on issues of nuclear non-proliferation and defending different communities from the threat of terrorism. Terror has become a primary tool of inter-ethnic and intra-state conflicts today. Conflict between states is far less common than the sudden explosions of terrorist activities in different parts of the world. For this very reason it is in the interests of all major powers to have more integration in an international peace and security system. It is extremely dangerous to have regions without proper international legal mechanisms to control arms proliferation and arms trading; particularly since those places could be used by different criminal cartels to trade in arms and nuclear material, as well as other illegal substances such as narcotics. Unfortunately, the South Caucasus has not been immune to these problems. Throughout the early 2000s there were instances when individuals detained near Gori and Batumi possessed significant amounts of uranium and other nuclear materials. The implications were that these individuals were traveling from unregulated regions to various client countries. The illegal arms trade has taken refuge in many of these "unrecognized" territories and given the difficulty of applying international economic sanctions and embargoes, arms traders have been encouraged to find safe havens in places like Abkhazia, South Ossetia and Nagorno Karabakh.

Of course, this is not just a problem for the South Caucasus, but rather it represents a global problem that must be dealt with by the whole international community in the twenty-first century. From the perspective of this aspect of international security, it is very important to have the entire South Caucasus, under the legal jurisdiction of the UN and its constituent units, collaborating on issues such as arms proliferation and the safeguarding of nuclear material. Cooperation is crucial to prevent the smuggling of nuclear materials, drugs and other arms from Russia to unrecognized territories in the region. Continuing conflict between governments and ethnic and religious groups exacerbates the risk of increasing the illegal trade in arms and drugs, whereas mutual collaboration is likely to improve the chances of successful monitoring and prevention. A regional peace zone in the South Caucasus offers an opportunity for collaboration to local parties as well as to the international community.

Building a polyphonic community in Georgia and the South Caucasus

As I have noted before, the South Caucasus has a long tradition of multi-ethnic and multi-national coexistence. In many respects, different periods of history have previously shown different types of "polyphonic" coexistence in the Caucasus. However, starting to create a region-wide peace zone as a sanctuary in the South Caucasus will not be an easy task, as there are entrenched interests in the region—as in other areas—who would oppose such an initiative. In order to address, and hopefully co-opt, some of these intransigent interests, there are a number of things that need to be addressed either before, or as, any proposed Caucasian peace zone moves forward.

The first of these is that the recognition of different ethnic groups as the equal partners of dominant national groups will be a very important part of Caucasian polyphony, since most ethnic groups consider themselves to be nations—and need to be respected as such. Their main attributes of ethnic identity need to be protected to ensure that there is no clash between the various contrasting cultures.

The second is that it would undoubtedly be most desirable to start the process of constructing peace zones in conflict areas or in border towns, such as Ergneti, Zugdidi, Sadakhlo, or Red Bridge. There have been many suggestions that the process of peace zone construction needs to start in those small places in order to address the greatest need and to, hopefully, appear less threatening to state forces and institutions.

In the second stage, the process could be expanded to cover the entire territory of Georgia, which could become the first demilitarized state in the South Caucasus. At the third stage, Abkhazia and South Ossetia could create their own demilitarized peace zone under international supervision and as part of an overall security regime, perhaps monitored by the EU and the OSCE. The fourth stage would involve expanding the model to include Armenia and Azerbaijan; starting a cautious demilitarization process in these two countries.

The fifth, and perhaps final stage, would involve starting discussions about creating conditions for moving beyond the individual nation-state in the region and towards a South Caucasian confederative or federal union. This could take the form of a demilitarized South Caucasus that would—at least in the initial stages—be under international supervision and would develop an integrated police force together with region-wide legislative and executive institutions. The entire region could use Abkhaz and Ossetian as well as Armenian, Azerbaijani, and Georgian as official languages. Recognizing multiple "official" languages and having a plurality of of accepted ethnic identities could help to deal with past problems associated with *Homo Sacer* and *goyim* in the region, given that ethnic minorities would never be willing to recognize any superior position for national majorities.[9]

Eventually, it is to be hoped that such a "South Caucasian Union" would elect its region-wide legislative body, just as does the EU. This would need to include representatives of the different communities making up the Union. A "South Caucasian Commission" could act as the executive organ of the Union. Creating a common "South Caucasian currency" would be highly desirable, while the economic basis for regional unity could be founded upon the fact that many of the existing national economics are complementary rather than competitive. Quite apart from the oil industry, tourism could be one of the most important building bridges between the different regions and constituent communities.

The balance between "local" and "national" peacemaking here is the dichotomy between the need for peaceful coexistence for the peoples of the South Caucasus and the needs of the major powers for either security or access to energy resources. I argue that a Caucasian Zone of Peace may be the best, and perhaps only, way of bridging this dichotomy of interests. This is so because the national aspirations for freedom on the part of both regional majorities and regional minorities have been held hostage, to a certain extent, to Russia's perceived security needs. By creating a demilitarized zone of peace in the region, backed by promises to preserve Russia's security and the West's access to oil, a major stumbling block to achieving peace at the local level will have been removed. In addition, a demilitarized Caucasian Zone of Peace could provide reassurances for local minorities, such as Abkhaz and Ossetians, that their identities will be preserved and valued rather than incorporated into larger "ethnic" nation-states and suppressed. So, while we see a possibly more intractable dichotomy here between local aspirations for peace and regional politics; the idea of a polyphonic zone of peace provides a method for addressing the dichotomy rather than a barrier to achieving peace.

A South Caucasian "polyphonic peace zone" could among other things, serve as an important example of how regional divisions and differences could be overcome through economic cooperation accompanied by respect for different identities. Increasingly, conflict in the twenty-first century is proving to be about equal respect for and recognition of identity groups—no matter how big or small. A post-modern, polyphonic principle of governance can be one way to provide the necessary respect for diverse identities and a way of avoiding the hostility, frictions and conflicts that inevitably arise when such identities are disrespected, ignored or repressed.

Notes

1 These differences largely stem from tensions between Francophone and Anglophone Canadians, particularly the reoccurring drives for independence, or "sovereignty" by Quebecois nationalists.

2 For more detail on the structure of the EU, see http://europa.eu/index_en.htm.

3 See McCall (1999) for a similar analysis in the EU–Northern Ireland context.

4 http://www.zopif.org

5 For more information see Hancock and Iyer (2007).

6 Comments made in an online discussion of Georgian peace zones in 2009. Available at http://www.facebook.com/note.php?note_id = 54188459878.

7 Ibid.

8 At the sub-state level, of course, there are many examples of peace zones, both successful and not. Some have been listed above, while others are analyzed throughout this volume and in Hancock and Mitchell's *Zones of Peace*.

9 One example of legal protection for differing ethnic identities, both majority and minority, is drawn from the 1998 Good Friday Agreement signed by the UK and Republic of Ireland. The preamble of the agreement specifically protects the national identity of those who wish to remain in the UK as well as those who wish to reunify with Ireland.

Works cited

Agamben, Giorgio. 1998. *Homo sacer. Sovereign power and bare life, Meridian.* Stanford, CA: Stanford University Press.

Arendt, Hannah. 1958. *The origins of totalitarianism.* 2nd enl. edn. New York: Meridian Books.

Bakhtin, Mikhail M. 1984. *Problems of Dostoevsky's poetics*. Translated by C. Emerson, *Theory and history of literature*. Minneapolis, MN: University of Minnesota Press.

Barry, Ellen. 2009. E.U. "Report to Place Blame on Both Sides in Georgia War." *New York Times*, September 28.

BBC. 2003. *Choirs of the World: Georgian polyphonic songs* [Web Page]. BBC News, Dec. 24, 2003 [cited June 29, 2011]. Available from: http://news.bbc.co.uk/2/hi/entertainment/3332111.stm.

Bunce, Valerie, Michael McFaul, and Kathryn Stoner-Weiss. 2010. *Democracy and authoritarianism in the post-communist world*. Cambridge, New York: Cambridge University Press.

Burton, John W. 1996. *Conflict resolution: its language and processes*. Lanham, MD: Scarecrow Press.

Derrida, Jacques, Mustapha Cherif, Teresa Lavender Fagan, and Giovanna Borradori. 2008. *Islam and the West: a conversation with Jacques Derrida*. Chicago, IL: The University of Chicago Press.

Drake, Nadia. 2008. *Peace plan for Georgia, developed with Cornell visiting scholar, is outlined by ex-US diplomat* [Web Page]. Cornell University 2008 [cited June 29, 2011]. Available from http://www.news.cornell.edu/stories/Sept08/GeorgiaCrisis.nd.html.

Galtung, Johan. 1996. *Peace by peaceful means: peace and conflict, development and civilization*. Oslo, London, Thousand Oaks, CA: International Peace Research Institute, Sage Publications.

— 2004. *Transcend and transform: an introduction to conflict work*. Bolder, CO: Paradigm.

Gurr, Ted Robert. 2000. *Peoples versus states: minorities at risk in the new century*. Washington, DC: United States Institute of Peace Press.

Hancock, Landon E., and Pushpa Iyer. 2007. "The nature, structure and variety of 'peace zones'." In *Zones of peace*, edited by L. E. Hancock and C. R. Mitchell. Bloomfield, CT: Kumarian Press.

Kriesberg, Louis. 2007. *Constructive conflicts: from escalation to resolution*. 3rd edn. Lanham, MD: Rowman & Littlefield Publishers.

Lederach, John Paul. 2003. *The little book of conflict transformation*. The little books of justice and peacebuilding. Intercourse, PA: Good Books.

McCall, Cathal. 1999. *Identity in Northern Ireland*. New York, London: St. Martin's Press, MacMillan Press Ltd.

Mitchell, Christopher R. 2007. "The Theory and Practice of Sanctuary: from Asylia to Local Zones of Peace." In *Zones of peace*, edited by L. E. Hancock and C. R. Mitchell. Bloomfield, CT: Kumarian Press.

Mitchell, Christopher R., and Landon E. Hancock. 2007. "Local Zones of Peace and a Theory of Sanctuary." In *Zones of peace*, edited by L. E. Hancock and C. R. Mitchell. Bloomfield, CT: Kumarian Press.

Pfaff, William. 2008. *NATO, Georgia and the Ready-Made War*. TruthDig 2008 [cited June 29, 2011]. Available from http://www.truthdig.com/report/item/20080812_nato_georgia_and_the_ready_made_war/?ln.

Pleshakov, Konstantin. 2009. *There is no freedom without bread!: 1989 and the civil war that brought down communism*. 1st edn. New York: Farrar, Straus and Giroux.

Rubenstein, Richard. 2008. "Conflict Resolution in an Age of Empire." In *Handbook of conflict analysis and resolution*, edited by D. J. D. Sandole, S. Byrne, I. Sandole-Staroste and J. Senehi. London, New York: Routledge.

Sandole, Dennis J. D. 2007. *Peace and security in the postmodern world: the OSCE and conflict resolution*. London: Routledge.

Smith, S. E. 2003. *What is Polyphonic Music?* [Web Page]. Conjecture Corporation 2003 [cited June 29, 2011]. Available from: http://www.wisegeek.com/what-is-polyphonic-music.htm.

Taylor, Brian D. 2003. *Politics and the Russian army: civil–military relations, 1689–2000*. Cambridge, New York: Cambridge University Press.

8

Between local and national peace: Complementarity or conflict?

Landon E. Hancock and Christopher Mitchell

One likes to believe that goodwill efforts towards achieving peace and an end to protracted conflicts must, by their nature, all work in the same direction—even if the journey towards peace is long and difficult. Surely grassroots efforts at spreading doctrines of nonviolence, at declaring neutrality, at establishing arenas for dialogue, at setting up safe havens, at encouraging contacts across local as well as national-level divisions, all must work to reinforce elite strategies of negotiation, compromise and peacemaking. Elite leaders must, surely, welcome local efforts to build bridges, discuss alternatives and propose ways forward to a future that does not involve continuing violence and destruction.

However, in actuality, it seems to be too often the case that elite-level peacemakers desire that local leaders and communities only act as passive spectators or supporters of their own worthy efforts; so that local initiatives do not "get in the way" of the real business of making peace—or bringing victory—to a divided and war-torn society. Obviously, this is going to create a tension between the two levels and between local people and both incumbents

Table 8.1 Insurgent-incumbent interaction

Insurgent-Incumbent Interaction	Coercion	Negotiation	Implementation
Incumbent favored grassroots behavior/ reactions	Collaboration, information, help, quiescence	Encouragement and acceptance; exclusion from process	Passive support for centrally controlled initiatives
Insurgent favored grassroots behavior and reactions	Protection: supplies, information, refuge	Reinforcement of demands for change	Protection, active support, maintaining authority, status
Alternative proactive local initiatives and projects	Neutrality; exclusion of combatants; peace efforts at local level	Transparency; input of ideas, aspirations and demands	Participation; monitoring changes to suit local needs; restoration; human rights

and insurgents; especially at times when the latter continue to seek success through coercion. These tensions can also exist during the negotiation and implementation phases of peace processes and, surprisingly, during periods of post-conflict reconstruction and peacebuilding efforts.

Oversimplifying somewhat, Table 8.1 summarizes the tensions between combatants (incumbent or insurgent) desired reactions from local people—who will hopefully remain disorganized and malleable—and organized actions that arise locally through grassroots initiatives for peace.

It will usually be the case that the tension between elite and grassroots levels is likely to be highest if violence and coercion continue at the national level while grassroots communities, organizations and individuals are trying to create some level of peace locally or even to have an impact at regional or national levels. However, these tensions hardly disappear completely. This seems so even when incumbents and insurgents at the national level are working out the detailed implementation of a negotiated peace agreement at that level and are expecting grateful cooperation from local communities that may not have been even remotely involved or concerned with the process by which the agreement was drafted and signed. Moreover, the fact that a peace agreement has been signed and implemented does not dissipate tensions between national-level elites or organizations and local level peacebuilding and development organizations. Here the tensions resemble those experienced by groups in violent conflicts, but with more of a focus on control over peacebuilding and development programs rather than on peacemaking initiatives. As implied in our introduction, these tensions can run both ways, and it is not simply the case that problems arise solely through leaders' insensitivity to the needs and aspirations of those at the grassroots. Tensions may equally arise from local ignorance of elite limitations or from suspicions regarding elite motives.

Questions of interaction

In returning to this complex theme of tensions between national elites and grassroots groups and individuals first outlined in the Introduction and discussed throughout the case studies, we made a distinction between:

- top-down influences that flowed from elite-level peacemaking processes onto grassroots communities and;

- bottom-up influences that were initiated at local levels with the intention of affecting elite-level peacemaking as well as peacebuilding at the grassroots.

Many of the case studies have taken up and comment on some aspect of this first, top-down, relationship; illustrated in Figure 8.1 below especially examining the efforts of different national-level policies on local peace communities or ZoPs, as well as the reactions of local people within such communities to national policies.

The dynamics of action–reaction show clearly that local leaders and institutions are not simply passive reactors to national-level policies, whether these originate with incumbents or insurgents; regardless of the temporal

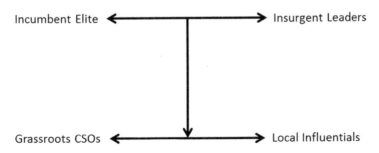

Figure 8.1 Top-down Relationships.

location of the zone—before, during or after a conflict. A common strategy, whether faced with marginal toleration, neglect or even disapproval, is for the local institutions to organize more widely, often on a regional level, and to seek support from pro-peace or development organizations nationally or even internationally. As Mery Rodriguez shows in the case of Colombia, the growth of regionally-based but internationally funded "Laboratories of Peace" has been a grassroots reaction to the Uribe government's strong disapproval and its harassment of small, local peace communities that have found it hard to survive while standing alone. Additionally, Hancock's analysis of the Suffolk Lenadoon Interface Group shows that when these two communities were ignored by local and national governments, they banded together to obtain funding from international foundations so as to further their peacebuilding and development work.

These anecdotes illustrate some of the diverse ways in which top-level peacemaking—whether through victory or negotiation—and the reactions of local leaders and communities can affect local communities and their own peacebuilding initiatives. They suggest the need for some systematic structuring of an apparently heterogeneous universe of relationships between elite peacemaking and local peacebuilding. What might be suggested about the likely impact of various types of top-down peacemaking activities— undertaken at different stages of a protracted intra-state conflict—and the possible reactions of local communities bent on launching their own peacebuilding activities? In order to analyze these tensions more fruitfully we will return to Hancock and Iyer's (2007) temporal framework, locating both top-down and bottom-up elements according to whether they take place during conflict, during peacemaking or implementation or during post-conflict reconstruction and peacebuilding periods. In doing so, we further discriminate between elite influences and grassroots responses and, where appropriate, grassroots influences on elite processes.

Tensions during conflict

Situations in which leaders are determined to prosecute an intractable conflict through continuing violence—well beyond the point where grassroots communities who have been fought over continuously have "had enough"— are usually those where elite and grassroots tensions are at their highest. Incumbents and insurgents tend to be pursuing their own strategies for "peace," resulting in armed clashes, the denying of resources to the other side and—at least—the search for a position of clear advantage over the other side; to enable the imposition of a one-sided settlement through asymmetric "negotiation." In response, local leaders have few choices. They can either engage in local initiatives to opt out of the struggle or they can opt in to an external process of calling for alternative strategies from both sides by trying to put their limited resources into a campaign for national peace. The resulting tensions are often the most complex and complicated for study, as well as being the most dangerous for members of grassroots peace communities. "Successes" on the battlefields often result in further alienation of community members, and possibly of many in the rural population. Despite the tension that renewed operations brings upon peace communities, there is some evidence from our Colombian studies that increased military actions have met with some success in weakening the power of insurgent groups; making these types of actions popular both with elites and with urban populations who may benefit from the increased stability that shifting the bulk conflict into the countryside may bring.

Top-down influences

Several of our chapters, particularly those focused on Colombia, have shown the pervasive influence that central governments can have, or attempt to have, on grassroots peace activities during times of active conflict. Examples of Colombia's two "plans" (Colombia and Patriota) can be combined with their intense focus on restricting the activities of peace communities or bringing them into the government fold. As a part of the former, we can see that the kinds of activities that define peace communities, removing armed actors and declaring neutrality, are precisely the kinds of activities that are likely to raise the ire of both insurgents and incumbents. Mitchell and Rojas outline a number of instances wherein not only do government policies declare activities of peace zones to be out of bounds, but the zones themselves are targeted by presidential rhetoric and incumbent action; including statements indicating that members of peace zones were little more than guerrilla sympathizers—or even guerrillas themselves—leading to increased threat from right-wing paramilitaries, "ex-paramilitaries" or members of the armed forces. The more concrete actions of arming peasant soldiers and paying informants did a great deal to undermine the strength and neutrality of peace zones, often increasing physical threat from guerillas as a consequence of increased state presence in those zones.

Attempts to bring peace zones into the government fold also take the form of governmental sponsorship or control over peace zone activities. Rodriguez outlines this kind of behavior—as well as the grassroots response—in the policy restrictions placed on Colombia's peace laboratories in order to "guide" or "direct" their peacebuilding behavior. We also have examples from our prior volume. In particular we note the attempt to exercise some control in the Philippines through the creation of Special Development Areas (SDAs) in several existing ZoPs, which led to the counterintuitive result of causing the collapse of more than one zone as the cohesiveness of the zone fractured over the allocation of these newly acquired resources (Avruch and Jose 2007). Finally, we note that Langdon and Rodriguez (2007), as well as Avruch and Jose, outline the manner in which incumbents may attempt to create their own zones as pseudo-grassroots initiatives designed either as a misguided attempt to further the success of locally-owned ZoPs, to compete with existing ZoPs and bring them under government control or to use the ZoPs concept in order to further government control or consolidation over weakly-controlled territories.

Grassroots leaders often have few options for responding to increased military activity or hostility by incumbent elites; either focusing on internal processes—such as the creation of peace zones—or on external processes like appealing to national campaigns or seeking international support. The first strategy can lead to unilateral and precarious declarations of neutrality, to the establishment of weapons-free areas, to the setting up of zones of peace, or to the negotiating of temporary time periods for humanitarian ceasefires; enabling activities deemed equally desirable to both adversaries to take place. Unfortunately, the strategy can also lead to local leaders, communities and peacebuilding institutions becoming identified as supporters or members of the "other side" and, hence, as legitimate targets under the doctrine of "those who are not with us are with them." Insurgents view local leaders and organizers who call for dialogue and an end to violence as naïve at best and treacherous at worst. They are undoubtedly viewed as threats to the cause, especially if they declare their communities, territories or even regions as off-limits to the struggle. Incumbents tend to view such a strategy as a course that should never be contemplated or taken up by loyal citizens. Those who question, implicitly or explicitly, the rights of a sovereign state to act where they will—regardless of current or past infractions by state security forces—are viewed as insufficiently loyal to the state and society. Tactics that involve "opting out" are frequently defined as legally treasonable and practically undermining by those in authority who remain bent upon peace through victory.

Nor is the option of supporting external peacebuilding or peace pressure activities necessarily viewed with any greater sympathy by leaders who remain focused on achieving peace through victory. The only benefit of this approach is the "possibility" that joining a larger pro-peace movement will diffuse some of the backlash that comes from a real, or perceived, lack of support for the agendas of either the insurgents or the incumbents. Unfortunately, a major drawback of pursuing this option is the lack of local control attendant in such a strategy. By suborning local peacebuilding initiatives to larger organizations or movements, localities run the risk of losing cohesion and/or the drive to improve local conditions in the face of continuing violence.

Bottom-up influences

Apart from the strategy of expanding on a geographical basis, many grassroots peace organizations in Colombia have also expanded functionally—and symbolically—by refocusing their activities beyond trying to bring about peace and onto less threatening objectives such as encouraging "development" or working towards greater "democracy" in the locus of regional decision-making (although the case of Mogotes emphasizes that such initiatives can meet with limited or mixed success). As Rodriguez points out, one of the changes that can frequently be observed in local peace communities founded in the late 1990s and early 2000s, originally based on *veradas* or *municipios*, was their later growth into "Development and Peace Programs" in many regions of Colombia. Likewise, evidence from Northern Ireland shows that many community development projects in Belfast (and throughout the province) have responded to governmental focus on community relations by shifting, in name or in deed, to addressing these concerns in order to obtain funding.

As we have seen, common reactions to "winning" strategies include declarations of neutral zones, zones of peace, weapons-free areas or calling for humanitarian ceasefires, negotiating local peace agreements or allying with national or international organizations calling for the same. At the more extreme end of responses, communities might ask for—and receive—internationals to accompany them and report on harassment or worse; or they might decide to relocate the entire community—as described by Mitchell and Rojas—in order to dissociate themselves from government forces or insurgents.

While we are currently able to explore and differentiate a great many responses of local groups to national initiatives, there is far less evidence that national elites, or national-level insurgents, respond positively to grassroots initiatives. In most cases, grassroots calls for peace are often ignored by those at the national level. Aside from a few notable exceptions, such as the Women's Movement for Peace in Liberia, calls by grassroots organizations for national-level peace talks are largely ignored by those "in charge" who often argue that, as either incumbent or insurgent elites, they already represent the "will of the people" and, thus, do not need to respond to initiatives sponsored by a few "malcontents."[1]

Relations during peacemaking

The relationship between elite policies and local peace efforts changes dramatically if peace is being genuinely pursued at the formal national level; and even more so if a national agreement has been negotiated and needs implementing. As we have noted in our prior volume, in the latter circumstances, the establishment of local peace zones, either as refuges to enable disarmament, demobilization and reinsertion (DDR) to take place or as confidence-building measures, can be part of a general peace agreement signed at the "top" level. This was the case with the Assembly Zones created in El Salvador (cf. Hancock and Iyer 2007) and the ill-fated peace zones implemented as a part of the 2002 peace agreement on Aceh between GAM and the Indonesian government (Iyer and Mitchell 2007). In contrast to the collapse of the Aceh agreement, the national level agreement worked out between the ANC and the South African government, discussed by Andries Odendaal, made deliberate arrangements for establishing peacemaking committees at the regional and local levels, which played a relatively successful role in mitigating the effects of violence carried out by local rivals.

Top-down influences

When elites pursue peacemaking through conflict mitigation and tension reduction there would appear to be more openings for complementary work between elites and grassroots organizations. The difficulty faced by incumbents, insurgents and local groups in these instances is the degree of control each constituency is going to have in the creation or functioning of any movement or institution designed to achieve mitigation or tension reduction. As is common during periods of all-out violence, insurgents, and especially, incumbents feel the need to justify their own control over peacemaking efforts—much as they claim justification for "sole" control over warmaking.

Our most promising example of interactions between the national level and local level during active peacemaking comes from Odendaal's examination of South Africa's Local Peace Councils, whose successful implementation of their—limited—mandate enabled national elites to move ahead without being derailed by escalating violence or by the sense that the country was spinning out of control. Unlike the ill-fated peace zones of the failed agreement between GAM and the government of Indonesia, Odendaal's description shows us that the LPCs were given significant autonomy to address local incidences of violence either before they broke out or afterwards in an attempt to make sure that they did not contribute to an escalatory spiral of violence. In many ways this meant that their remit was more limited than other zones instituted during peace processes—most of which have been associated with DDR functions and, thus were responsible for cantonment, disarmament and reintegration or reinsertion of combatants. But because the LPCs were designed to address violence between civilians and political factions as well as between government forces and insurgents they addressed the needs of a far larger and wider population.

In this arena we may find elements that hold the most promise, but only if we are examining cases like South Africa; where the negotiations leading to end of Apartheid rule were serious and both sides were considered to be genuinely seeking peace and accommodation. In other cases, such as Aceh in Indonesia, there was far less trust between the government and GAM, leading to a collapse of both the peace process and of the zones (Iyer and Mitchell 2007). Two elements which appear to be necessary for success here are some measure of trust either having been established or being established through the process and—depending on the nature of the zones themselves—respect for an agreed level of autonomy for the local zones.

Bottom-up influences

One tactic successfully used on occasions in the same country has been to take advantage of ongoing pre-negotiations and negotiations at the official level by "tacking on" unofficial representatives from local communities in order to discuss issues relevant to those communities; such as de-mining of local territories by insurgents—who cannot be parties to international anti-personnel mine agreements, but who might be persuaded to refrain from their use through informal agreements.[2] In other venues, not directly associated with ZoPs, civil society organizations have, at times, been able to impose themselves into the peacemaking process in order to ensure that either their issues are addressed—as in Northern Ireland—or that peace itself is pursued—as was the case in Liberia.

However, much like ZoPs in other temporal areas, bottom-up influences that have noticeable impacts at the elite level are few and far between. Most often, like academic problem-solving workshops, the impacts created by local ZoPs tend to be informal and, though at times lauded publically, are discounted as being prime movers of successful—or even failed—peace processes. While local peacebuilders can often be an integral part of preparations for elite level negotiations—helping to sort through acceptable preconditions about agendas, neutral venues, timing, acceptable representatives or mediators, and conditions for eventual meetings—once the point of substantive bargaining arrives, local influences often seem to diminish sharply, and in many cases, vanish altogether unless deliberate efforts are made to include some "civil society" inputs into the negotiations. This often results in what Adam Isacson describes as a situation of "a handful of elite politicians and businesspeople sitting across the table from a group of comandantes" (2003, 4).

There are some exceptions to this familiar strategy of "insulating" negotiators from outside pressures from their constituents, or significantly controlling the latters' influence, some of which involve the inclusion of local leaders on the elite negotiating team either as full members or as advisers or observers. Given that it is frequently the case that local leaders at least will have to accept, support and implement any agreements worked out at an elite level as part of any peacemaking package, it seems only prudent to obtain their reactions early on, as the bargaining unfolds. At the very least, the reality of likely local resistance to particular measures can be shown directly, and the constraints on leaders made more believable by a direct demonstration of those constraints.

However, quite apart from gauging how local grassroots might react to some provisions of a tentative deal, it does seem important for elite negotiators to take into account the aims and aspirations of grassroots interest, so that any elite negotiated peace agreement does not collapse through a lack of local support or through the elite's misreading of what the crucial issues might actually be. We noted Hancock's argument that local development issues were far more important than improved community relations to poor communities in interface zones in Belfast. The question is how reliable information about such grassroots preferences can make its way onto the agendas of incumbent and insurgent leaders trying to negotiate a durable end to a complex protracted conflict. One example of a process that deliberately built in the means for some regular civil society input to an elite level negotiation can be found in the talks at St. Vincent de Cayugan in Colombia between representatives of the FARC and the Pastrana government. Here, there were regular opportunities, through the existence of a "thematic committee," established separately from the two top negotiating teams and at government insistence, for taking note of representations from individual citizens and civil society institutions. Members of the public could address the committee directly at regular public hearings, or make an input electronically via conference calls, web sites or email. Resultant ideas and recommendations were supposed to be fed forward to the FARC and government negotiating teams. This method for having ordinary Colombians—individuals, NGOs, universities, churches, businesses—express their opinions, hopes and aspirations for a durable peace settlement was held to be unique in Colombian history—and unusual for very many incumbent/ insurgent negotiation processes.

Clearly, such processes involving grassroots opinions will always be time consuming and probably disrupting. The experience of the thematic subcommittee at San Vicente del Caguan was hardly encouraging in this regard. One estimate was that over 16,000 people took part in the "Public Audiences" arranged in the zona de distencion and were given all of five minutes each to present ideas, proposals and recommendations. However, there appears to have been no means whereby ideas on, for example, agrarian reform, drug policy or unemployment could be synthesized and passed on to negotiators (Isacson 2003, 20). Hence, the closed and secretive negotiating process continued in almost complete isolation from inputs from civil society, enabling both the FARC and government teams to ignore the increasingly divided and chaotic civil society movements seeking—ineffectually—to contribute to building peace. As Isacson argues in the Colombian case, a unified and purposeful grassroots movement can have a positive effect on elite level negotiations, but a divided and ambivalent civil society movement, not even organized into a temporary coalition, can have quite the opposite effect (2003, 20). What is needed is a way of offering an opportunity to prevent elite decisions being made in complete isolation, thus lessening the likelihood of the whole "deal" being undermined or rejected by large numbers of local people who feel excluded and possibly betrayed.

The formal FARC–government peace process in Colombia between 1999 and 2002 provides one example of an elite negotiation which, in effect, rejected any possibility of influence from grassroots or civil society organizations. It is, of course, also the case that grassroots actors can reject elite processes that make arrangements over their heads. Moreover, such rejection can sometimes occur even earlier—and be yet more disruptive—than at a stage when "an elite pact" has been concluded and announced. In the Introduction we raised the possibility that a situation might arise in which local violence continues even when elite negotiation processes are taking place, so that local instability threatens to wreck completely those negotiations.

Complementarity during post-conflict peacebuilding

One might imagine that because post-conflict situations are, by definition, post-conflict, meaning that much of the organized violence has ended, that grassroots organizations and elites would share the same goals of ensuring a peaceful civil society and rebuilding a war-torn economy. Well, most often they do share these goals, but unfortunately sharing grand goals does not always translate into agreement about how those goals will be reached or what level of agency will be held by actors at each level.

In our analysis we have found that the relationships between incumbent elites (and presumably insurgents who become part of any new dispensation) remain complex and that tensions over control of resources, specific goals of peacebuilding programs and responsibility for preventing or mitigating outbreaks of violence—be it political or criminal—remain. Once again, as we will see, elites tend to have far more ability to impact the grassroots than vice-versa, but, unlike our other two time periods, grassroots organizations have more avenues for "escaping" government control or for negotiating a more favorable balance between local and national control over programs or resources.

Top-down influences

Like our other temporal categories, there are many ways in which elites can have an impact on grassroots ZoPs engaged in post-conflict peacebuilding. However, given the transition from all-out violence and conflict to peaceful means of interaction, tensions between national-level elites and local ZoPs tend to play themselves out in the political and economic arenas rather than in the physical or social arenas.

Most particularly when we examine our two main cases, Northern Ireland in this volume and El Salvador from the last, we note that for the former elite influences are felt most strongly in the realm of funding and government oversight. One of the more significant findings of Hancock's analysis is the fact that SLIG was able to reduce the impact of the Northern Ireland Office (NIO) and the Community Relations Council (CRC) by seeking, and receiving, funding from major foundations such as the Atlantic Council. These successes, as well as SLIG's ability to reduce violence along its interface and to achieve significant development made it somewhat of a darling to the province-wide and national peacebuilding elites; though, as Hancock notes, tensions between the group and government official continue over SLIG's need for, and access to, government financial resources.

Likewise, prior examinations of El Salvador's Local Zone of Peace (LZP) show that that zone's parent organization *La Coordinadora* was either largely ignored by national elites—as well as local politicians—and was denied access to state economic and political resources; largely as a result of its links to leftists. In response, the LZP created their own US-based NGO, the Foundation for Self-Sufficiency in Central America, in order to solicit grants, donations and volunteers to support their efforts. The FSSCA was largely successful, providing monies and volunteers for a number of projects, including youth activities, construction projects and social services for ex-gang members (Chupp 2003; Hancock 2007).

Bottom-up influences

To date there is little indication that the successes of SLIG have prompted any major changes in the funding policies or priorities of either the NIO or the CRC in terms of favoring community relations projects over community development projects. Development continues to be a priority among Northern Irealnd's interface organizations while community relations continues to be the priority for the province-wide funding and coordinating agencies, keeping alive the tensions that exist between these two levels.

On the other hand, early indications are that the success of the LZP has generated the interest of El Salvador's recently-elected center-left president, Mauricio Funes' and his FMLN government. Although still in nascent stages the repeated successes of the LZP and *La Coordinadora* in addressing economic deprivation, gang violence, domestic violence and disaster prevention and relief have generated elite interest in spreading the LZP's organizational structure and culture of peace program throughout the country. At the time of this writing, few details are available regarding the extent to which this interest has been translated into actual policy, but if it comes to fruition, it will be the single-largest incidence of grassroots impact on national-level peacebuilding and development policies.

Complementarity outside of the temporal framework

Our analysis would be incomplete without addressing the two cases in this volume that do not directly relate to Hancock and Iyer's temporal framework, namely Warfield and Jennings' suggestion that ZoPs might be used for conflict prevention, and Kakabadze's extension of the ZoPs' concept of a region-wide zone that, in some senses, is designed to supersede elements of national sovereignty. One thing that is clear about both of these models is that each requires a higher level of complementarity than has been evident in all of the cases hitherto studied—with the exception of the LPCs in South Africa.

The question for both initiatives is the extent to which these higher levels of complementarity will be achieved, or are even achievable. It is clear that the CoPZoP requires a higher level of interaction between grassroots and elites in order to ensure that communication between the two levels remains active and that, when necessary, grassroots elites are able to call for the assistance of local elites in providing resources necessary to prevent the outbreak of violence. Conversely, communication in the other direction is also absolutely necessary as Warfield and Jennings point out that sources for violence exist a multiple levels within the Haitian–Dominican context. This means that national elites must be able, and willing, to communicate about events and incidents that are likely to raise tensions or even trigger outbreaks of violence.

This issue of complementarity is even more complicated for Kakabadze's proposal for a ZoPs-like "Caucasian Peace Zone" would require a great deal of integration among national elites; but, as it is currently envisioned, it is unclear the extent to which vertical complementarity between national governments and local communities will need to take place. Of note here is Kakabadze's use of the EU as an example of a polyphonic model that might be emulated by states in the Caucasus. As noted by McCall (1999), one of the key elements of success for the EU has been, in addition to its national-level integration, its focus on the principle of subsidiarity, wherein economic aid and political policies often concentrate at the sub-state level on regional needs and aspirations. It is this focus, according to McCall, that provides room for sub-state ethnic and national identities to coexist alongside those represented by states. If the principle of subsidiarity were coupled with the polyphonic model for a Caucasian Peace Zone, then the requirement for complementarity would extend both horizontally and vertically, perhaps making life more difficult, but also providing some opportunity for a reduction in tensions currently existing between local ethnicities and those represented by states. The difficulty with this model, much as that experienced by more traditional ZoPs, is the tension between state prerogatives and local autonomy, an issue that we will address again below.

Final thoughts on the "need" for complementarity

As becomes clear from the analyses both in this volume and in our prior volume, issues of complementarity between top-down and bottom-up peace processes continue to bedevil ZoPs' proponents. The question as to the necessity, or even desirability, for complementary action remains contentious, with some proponents arguing for complementarity (cf. Bloomfield 1997; Nan 1999) and others, particularly those in government, arguing that complementarity resembles a one-way street more than a two-way thoroughfare.

Of those arguing for an increase in complementarity, none do so more than the chapters at either end of our temporal spectrum. At the front end, Warfield and Jennings persuasively argue the necessity for complementarity when seeking to use a ZoPs model for conflict prevention (the CoPZoP). In calling for complementarity, Warfield and Jennings recognize that conflict prevention as an activity remains relatively specialized; particularly in the early-warning and rapid-response functions necessary for operational prevention. Likewise, they recognize that the eruption of violent conflict may have sources that exist at the local, national or international levels—and sometimes at more than one level—necessitating some level of cooperation and complementarity between elite and grassroots efforts.

At the other end of our temporal spectrum—and a little outside of it to be fair—Kakabadze's call for a transnational zone of peace for the South Caucasus has implications for local communities, national polities and the entire region. This conglomeration of local, national and transnational also necessitates a great deal of complementary efforts to align the interests of actors at all levels and to coordinate activities at all levels. As we mentioned above, given that Kakabadze's call has not been implemented or even formalized at this point, one principle that might prove useful is the EU's use of the principle of subsidiarity, which prefers that matters ought to be handled at the lowest level or least centralized level of competent authority. The use of subsidiarity as a principle for a Caucasian Zone of Peace opens the door for complementarity along a vertical axis between local communities and higher levels of authority; which might reduce some of the tensions currently existing between Georgians, Abkhaz and Ossetions, as well as between Armenians and Azeris over the fate of Nagorno-Karabakh.

Before trumpeting the benefits of subsidiarity, it is worth remembering that despite the fact that the EU has pumped billions of pounds into Northern Ireland as a part of its Peace I, II and III programs, these funds have hitherto been administered by the CRC; meaning that even when subsidiarity is applied, its manner of application can create as well as reduce tensions between grassroots groups and local elites.

In between these two bookends, the necessity or even desirability of complementarity becomes a shade murkier. While some could argue that ZoPs in conflict areas, such as those in Colombia and the Philippines, could have benefitted from some measure of complementarity, it is unclear just how this would have taken place. If insurgents or incumbents are bent upon victory at all costs, it is difficult to see how the pursuit of such divergent methods—even if the shared goal is the end of the conflict—could be coordinated. Lessons from Uribe's presidency as well as the failure of the Filipino SDAs warn us against categorically recommending complementarity even when both elites and grassroots organizations agree that strategies of peacemaking—as opposed to warfighting—should be pursued. This is because within an overarching goal of making peace, elites and grassroots organizations may diverge in terms of the different types of mechanisms they prefer to use—and the mid-level goals each will pursue.

The most beneficial time period for the use of complementarity appears to be during the negotiation or implementation of any peace agreement, with the caveat that care must be taken to ensure that: a) the peace being pursued is a genuine effort rather than a tactical choice; and b) complementarity is pursued as a two-way endeavor rather than a one-way street where local efforts are expected to mold themselves to national plans. Within these constraints it could be possible for both national elites and grassroots initiatives to work together to achieve the focused, and rather limited, goals typically addressed by confidence-building and peace implementation plans, ranging from Odendaal's description of conflict prevention and mitigation to typical DDR activities of cantonment, disarmament and training prior to reinsertion of former fighters.

Another area that would seem to be ripe for complementarity is the post-conflict time period. But as we have indicated above, unless complementarity is accompanied by adherence to the principle of subsidiarity, one runs the risk of clashing goals similar to that of community development and community relations organizations in Northern Ireland, with elites and funders focusing on inter-communal relationships while grassroots organizations wish to address economic deprivation and development.

Regardless of which time period one uses for examining the relationship between national level efforts and local peacebuilding efforts, it becomes clear that there are some commonalities that begin to emerge. The first of these is the extent to which local efforts could be considered to be autonomous, and legitimately so. As outlined elsewhere, the successful functioning of a peace zone requires a high level of autonomy and local ownership (Mitchell and Hancock 2007). However, as Odendaal shows us, a high level of autonomy may also be required for successful complementarity between local and national efforts and may be, as Hancock further indicates, vital for the successful creation and implementation of violence mitigation and development efforts in post-conflict societies. Therefore, much as our first volume identified grassroots ownership and autonomy as key elements contributing to the success of ZoPs in every temporal period, we are forced to admit that even though complementarity is desirable to a certain extent, it too runs the risk of undermining grassroots ownership and autonomy that were found to be valuable in most of the cases we have examined here.

A deeper understanding of the necessity or even desirability of complementary efforts aimed at conflict prevention, mitigation, resolution or post-conflict peacebuilding may be beyond the scope of the cases presented here. At best we can indicate where complementarity shows some promise and where that promise may be overshadowed by the pitfalls inherent in attempting to coordinate national-level concerns with local needs. In doing so, we hope that we can begin a conversation about the role of different levels of actors in promoting and sustaining peace in many troubled regions of the world.

Notes

1 This attitude is quite different from that expressed by local insurgent or incumbent commanders who may be more familiar with grassroots leaders or, at the very least, are more aware of the need to justify their own legitimacy vis-à-vis the local population. For more on this, see Rojas (2007) and Mitchell and Hancock (2007).

2 Such local activities on the fringes of national-level peacemaking processes have resulted in the Colombian government's reiteration of the claim that only the National Peace Commissioner and his team have any right to negotiate with the guerrillas of the ELN and FARC.

Works cited

Avruch, Kevin, and Roberto S. Jose. 2007. "Peace Zones in the Philippines." In *Zones of peace*, edited by L. E. Hancock and C. R. Mitchell. Bloomfield, CT: Kumarian Press.

Bloomfield, David. 1997. *Peacemaking strategies in Northern Ireland: building complementarity in conflict management theory.* New York: St. Martin's Press.

Chupp, Mark. 2003. "Creating a Culture of Peace in Postwar El Salvador." In *Positive approaches in peacebuilding: A resource for innovators*, edited by C. Sampson, M. Abu-Nimer and C. Liebler. Washington, DC: Pact Publications.

Hancock, Landon E. 2007. "El Salvador's Post-conflict Peace Zone." In *Zones of peace*, edited by L. E. Hancock and C. R. Mitchell. Bloomfield, CT: Kumarian Press.

Hancock, Landon E., and Pushpa Iyer. 2007. "The Nature, Structure and Variety of 'Peace Zones'." In *Zones of peace*, edited by L. E. Hancock and C. R. Mitchell. Bloomfield, CT: Kumarian Press.

Isacson, Adam. 2003. "Was Failure Avoidable: Learning from Colombia's 1998–2002 Peace Process." In *Working Paper #14*. Coral Gables, FL: Dante B. Fascell North-South Center, University of Miami.

Iyer, Pushpa, and Christopher R. Mitchell. 2007. "The Collapse of Peace Zones in Aceh." In *Zones of peace*, edited by L. E. Hancock and C. R. Mitchell. Bloomfield, CT: Kumarian Press.

Langdon, Jennifer, and Mery Rodriguez. 2007. "The Rondas Campesinas of Peru." In *Zones of peace*, edited by L. E. Hancock and C. R. Mitchell. Bloomfield, CT: Kumarian Press.

McCall, Cathal. 1999. *Identity in Northern Ireland.* New York, London: St. Martin's Press, MacMillan Press Ltd.

Mitchell, Christopher R., and Landon E. Hancock. 2007. "Local Zones of Peace and a Theory of Sanctuary." In *Zones of peace*, edited by L. E. Hancock and C. R. Mitchell. Bloomfield, CT: Kumarian Press.

Nan, Susan Allen. 1999. "Complementarity and coordination of conflict resolution efforts in the conflicts over Abkhazia, South Ossetia, and Transdniestria." Ph.D., The Institute for Conflict Analysis and Resolution, George Mason University, Fairfax, VA, USA.

Rojas, Catalina. 2007. "Islands in the Stream." In *Zones of peace*, edited by L. E. Hancock and C. R. Mitchell. Bloomfield, CT: Kumarian Press.

Index

Printed in Great Britain
by Amazon